Karl Kraus and the Discourse of Modernity

Karl Kraus and the Discourse of Modernity

✦

Ari Linden

NORTHWESTERN UNIVERSITY PRESS
EVANSTON, ILLINOIS

Northwestern University Press
www.nupress.northwestern.edu

Printed in the United States of America

10 9 8 7 6 5 4 3 2 1

Library of Congress Cataloging-in-Publication Data

Names: Linden, Ari, author.
Title: Karl Kraus and the discourse of modernity / Ari Linden.
Description: Evanston : Northwestern University Press, 2020. | Includes bibliographical references and index.
Identifiers: LCCN 2019022683 | ISBN 9780810141629 (paperback) | ISBN 9780810141636 (cloth) | ISBN 9780810141643 (ebook)
Subjects: LCSH: Kraus, Karl, 1874-1936—Criticism and interpretation. | Kraus, Karl, 1874-1936—Political and social views. | Modernism (Literature)—Austria. | Politics and literature.
Classification: LCC PT2621.R27 Z626 2020 | DDC 838.91209—dc23
LC record available at https://lccn.loc.gov/2019022683

CONTENTS

ACKNOWLEDGMENTS

I first became interested in Karl Kraus as a graduate student in the Department of German Studies at Cornell. Patrizia McBride was my adviser and has been, since then, a consistent source of guidance, encouragement, and support. She remains my *Doktormutter* to whom I am grateful for many reasons. The other members of my committee—Geoff Waite, Anette Schwarz, and Paul Fleming—provided constructive critiques of my work, all of which helped me move forward with this project. Leslie Adelson, finally, has always been a strong supporter of my work, and I think fondly of our time together at the International Walter Benjamin Congress in Frankfurt in the winter of 2013.

The close friends I made in graduate school are also colleagues with whom I have had countless conversations about Kraus, the Frankfurt School, German modernism, satire, German Jewish culture, and Weimar comedy. In particular, I want to thank Carl Gelderloos, Paul Flaig, and Katrina Nousek for reading and commenting on various papers, article drafts, and chapters of mine over the last several years. Their comments have sharpened my thinking, and I only hope that I've been able to reciprocate in kind. But it is their friendship and good humor that I treasure above all. Paul Buchholz was also a generous reader, especially of an earlier version of chapter 3. For his help with translations and his keen insights into the political implications of certain Krausian phrases, I would like to thank Gernot Waldner. There were others, too, who were supportive—emotionally and intellectually—during my time at Cornell and beyond. I sincerely look forward to future conversations with all of these fine people.

I would also like to recognize the organizers of, and participants in the various conferences, seminars, and symposia I have attended over the past several years. I owe a special thanks to Martha Helfer, Bill Donahue, and Steffen Kaupp, the organizers of the two German Jewish Studies Workshops (at Duke and Notre Dame) I attended in 2015 and 2017, where I presented earlier versions of chapters 3 and 5. My participation in the conference "Citing Violence, Inciting Critique: Karl Kraus, 1933" in 2017—organized in conjunction with the Institute for Jewish Studies at the University of Antwerp—forced me to more critically think through the relationship between Kraus and Adorno. The conversations I had with António Ribeiro and Gerald Krieghofer were particularly helpful. My summer spent back at Cornell in 2016 as a participant in the DAAD Summer Seminar on "The Collapse of the Secular Future" proved to be very useful regarding the organizational structure of this book. I am especially thankful for the advice I received then from Sven-Erik Rose, Dustin Atlas, and my colleague at the University of Kansas, Sam Brody. Concerning my overseas research, I would like to thank Astrid Wallner at the Literaturhaus Wien for assisting me in the early stages of my research on Kraus in the summer of 2010. The two weeks I spent at the Deutsche Literaturarchiv Marbach in 2015 were, furthermore, indispensable for gathering primary and secondary research material for my second chapter.

My colleagues at the University of Kansas are also owed a debt of gratitude. I would first like to acknowledge the College of Liberal Arts and Sciences for their support of my book. I am thankful for everyone affiliated with the Hall Center for the Humanities for making possible the generous, teaching-free semester I spent there as a Faculty Fellow in fall 2017, when I completed the first draft of the manuscript. My colleagues in my home department of German Studies—in particular, Andrea Meyertholen, Nina Vyatkina, and Lorie Vanchena—have not only supported my work in many ways, but have also been very accommodating in terms of giving me the time I have needed to do research. I have benefited from conversations about Adorno and Heidegger with Scott Jenkins, a philosopher and a good friend. I would like to thank Marc Greenberg, who was the chair of my department when I was hired and who has been something of a mentor to me ever since. Finally, I wish to thank the members of my writing group at the University of Kansas—Marike Janzen, Aimee Wilson, and Marie Brown—for their insightful feedback on my introduction and my second chapter.

I am, additionally, grateful for the thoughtful comments of the two anonymous readers at Northwestern University Press, who clearly read my manuscript with care. In this context, I wish to also express my gratitude to Trevor Perri for his excellent editorial support and his patience for the number of emails I sent to him over the course of our working relationship.

My parents, Nancy and Jim, have always provided me with unconditional love and support. They were sad when I left California to move to the East Coast, but happy that I pursued a Ph.D. and that I was finally able to finish this book. I owe them much more than words can express. My older brother, Seth, has been nothing but encouraging my entire life; he is the best, kindest sibling one could hope for. I would not, however, have been able to finish this book without the love and conversation of my best friend and wife, Lara. Her fierce philosophical mind has made me a better scholar and a better person. We laugh, think, and feel together. I owe her the world. I wish to dedicate this book, finally, to our daughter Rosalie, not yet a year old at the time I write these words. Her eyes are dark but bright, and her glances exude, alternately, awe and skepticism—a very Krausian way to view her ever-expanding world.

ABBREVIATIONS

When referencing Kraus's essays and poems in the text and notes, I have attempted to cite first their initial appearance in *Die Fackel* (*F*), then—when available—a republication in Kraus's *Schriften* or in another edited volume, and, finally—when available—a published English translation. In the cases of Goethe, Benjamin, and Adorno, I have cited the original German and then the English translation in both the main body and the notes. Unless otherwise indicated, all remaining translations are my own.

Works cited frequently in the text and notes are referred to using the following abbreviations:

A Kraus, Karl. *Aphorismen. Schriften, Band 8*. Frankfurt am Main: Suhrkamp, 1986.

AS 1 Timms, Edward. *Karl Kraus: Apocalyptic Satirist: Culture and Catastrophe in Habsburg Vienna*. New Haven, Conn.: Yale University Press, 1989.

AS 2 Timms, Edward. *Karl Kraus: Apocalyptic Satirist, Vol. 2: The Postwar Crisis and the Rise of the Swastika*. New Haven, Conn.: Yale University Press, 2005.

AS 4 Adorno, Theodor W. *Gesammelte Schriften, Band 4: Minima Moralia. Reflexionen aus dem beschädigten Leben*. Frankfurt am Main: Suhrkamp, 2003.

AS 6 Adorno, Theodor W. *Gesammelte Schriften, Band 6: Negative Dialektik. Jargon der Eigentlichkeit*. Frankfurt am Main: Suhrkamp, 2003.

AS 7 Adorno, Theodor W. *Gesammelte Schriften, Band 7: Ästhetische Theorie*. Frankfurt am Main: Suhrkamp, 2003.

AS 10 Adorno, Theodor W. *Gesammelte Schriften, Band 10: Kulturkritik und Gesellschaft, 2 Bände*. Frankfurt am Main: Suhrkamp, 2003.

AS 11 Adorno, Theodor W. *Gesammelte Schriften, Band 11: Noten zur Literatur*. Frankfurt am Main: Suhrkamp, 2003.

BL Kraus, Karl. *Brot und Lüge: Aufsätze 1919–1924. Schriften, Band 16*. Frankfurt am Main: Suhrkamp, 1991.

D	Kraus, Karl. *Dramen. Schriften, Band 11*. Frankfurt am Main: Suhrkamp, 1989.
DC	Goethe, Johann Wolfgang von. *Faust: Part II*. Translated by David Constantine. London: Penguin Classics, 2009.
DW	Kraus, Karl. *Dritte Walpurgisnacht. Schriften, Band 12*. Frankfurt am Main: Suhrkamp, 1989.
F	Kraus, Karl. *Die Fackel*. Available online at the Fackel Gate, Austrian Academy Corpus, http://corpus1.aac.at/fackel/.
G	Kraus, Karl. *Gedichte. Schriften, Band 9*. Frankfurt am Main: Suhrkamp, 1989.
GF	Goethe, Johann Wolfgang von. *Sämtliche Werke, Band 7: Faust*. Frankfurt am Main: Suhrkamp, 1994.
GS 1	Benjamin, Walter. *Gesammelte Schriften, Band 1*. Frankfurt am Main: Suhrkamp, 1991.
GS 2	Benjamin, Walter. *Gesammelte Schriften, Band 2*. Frankfurt am Main: Suhrkamp, 1991.
GS 4	Benjamin, Walter. *Gesammelte Schriften, Band 4*. Frankfurt am Main: Suhrkamp, 1991.
GT	Kraus, Karl. *In These Great Times*. Edited by Harry Zohn, with translations by Joseph Fabry, Max Knight, Karl F. Ross, and Harry Zohn. Chicago: University of Chicago Press, 1984.
HD	Kraus, Karl. *Hüben und Drüben: Aufsätze 1929–1936. Schriften, Band 18*. Frankfurt am Main: Suhrkamp, 1993.
JA	Adorno, Theodor W. *The Jargon of Authenticity*. Translated by Knut Tarnowski and Frederic Will. London: Routledge, 2003.
KW XIV	Kierkegaard, Søren. *Kierkegaard's Writings, XIV: Two Ages: The Age of Revolution and the Present Age: A Literary Review*. Edited by Howard V. Hong and Edna H. Hong. Princeton, N.J.: Princeton University Press, 2009.
LDM	Kraus, Karl. *The Last Days of Mankind*. Translated by Fred Bridgham and Edward Timms. New Haven, Conn.: Yale University Press, 2015.
LL	Kraus, Karl. *Literatur und Lüge. Schriften, Band 3*. Frankfurt am Main: Suhrkamp, 1987.
LTM	Kraus, Karl. *Die letzten Tage der Menschheit: Tragödie in fünf Akten mit Vorspiel und Epilog. Schriften, Band 10*. Frankfurt am Main: Suhrkamp, 1986.

MM	Adorno, Theodor W. *Minima Moralia: Reflections on a Damaged Life*. Translated by E. F. N. Jephcott. London: Verso, 2005.
ND	Adorno, Theodor W. *Negative Dialectics*. Translated by E. B. Ashton. New York: Continuum, 2003.
NL 2	Adorno, Theodor W. *Notes to Literature, Vol. 2*. Translated by Shierry Weber Nicholson. New York: Columbia University Press, 1992.
SK	Kraus, Karl. *Sittlichkeit und Kriminalität. Schriften, Band 1*. Frankfurt am Main: Suhrkamp, 1987.
SW 1	Benjamin, Walter. *Selected Writings, Vol. 1: 1913–1926*. Edited by Marcus Bullock and Michael W. Jennings. Cambridge, Mass.: Harvard University Press, 2004.
SW 2	Benjamin, Walter. *Selected Writings, Vol. 2, Part II: 1931–1934*. Edited by Michael W. Jennings, Gary Smith, and Howard Eiland. Cambridge, Mass.: Harvard University Press, 2005.
SW 4	Benjamin, Walter. *Selected Writings, Vol. 4: 1938–1940*. Edited by Howard Eiland and Michael W. Jennings. Cambridge, Mass.: Harvard University Press, 2006.
UW	Kraus, Karl. *Untergang der Welt durch schwarze Magie*. Munich: Kösel Verlag, 1960.
WG	Kraus, Karl. *Weltgericht*. Munich: Albert Langen Georg Müller Verlag, 1955.

Karl Kraus and the Discourse of Modernity

Introduction

✦

Toward a Krausian Theory of Modernity

> In addition to being the worldwide proclamation of the fatal news that had already been circulating for some time throughout Europe, to giving us entry into a world where the further we advance the less we know, and finally to welcoming the seeds of chaos that had long been lurking on the threshold of our psychical and social life, the war of 1914–1918 signified the pulverizing of experience.
>
> —Roberto Calasso, *The Forty-Nine Steps*

> THE OPTIMIST. What loss of nerve! What a sorry figure you will cut one day! Don't isolate yourself from such celebrations! The gates of the soul are thrown wide open. Memories of the day when we on the home front participated in the deeds and sufferings of the glorious fighting front, if only by reading the daily reports, will leave on the soul—
>
> THE GRUMBLER.—no scars.
>
> THE OPTIMIST. The nations will learn from this war only—
>
> THE GRUMBLER.—how to wage more wars in the future.
>
> THE OPTIMIST. The bullet has left the barrel, and mankind will—
>
> THE GRUMBLER.—feel it go in through one ear and out the other!
>
> —Karl Kraus, *The Last Days of Mankind*

The brief exchange above between the "Optimist" and the "Grumbler" of Karl Kraus's *The Last Days of Mankind* addresses the impact of World War I on the daily, lived experiences of those who were affected by it and those who contributed to its perpetuation. Toward the end of this conversation—a snapshot of the running dialogue between these two characters of Kraus's satirical drama—the Grumbler declares that the only lesson to be gleaned from this utterly hopeless war will be how to wage new wars in the future. His is an entirely cynical response to the optimism of his interlocutor, who carries on under the delusion that ultimate victory will fall on the side of the Central Powers. In the laconic finale to this repartee, the Grumbler interrupts the Optimist with the unsettling image of a bullet penetrating humanity's collective cranium, unsettling, in part, because the image is only hinted at and thus must be imagined by the reader. Playing with the stock phrase, "to go in one ear and out the other," the Grumbler thereby foregrounds the seamless continuity between what Walter Benjamin would later call "the age of information" and its attendant violence. More specifically, he implies that the effect of the metonymical bullet wound on those who read about it—those who follow the news—lasts no longer than the report on which it is printed, a report fated to be forgotten and replaced by another the following day. Meanwhile, the fragile body suffers, mortalities accrue, and the war continues. For the Grumbler, the modern subject—less the soldier on the front than the reader in the hinterland—appears incapable of experiencing violence and destruction in a way that is commensurate with the immediate and long-term effects of these phenomena on both the actual body and the body politic. Drawing attention to the relationship between violence, its representation, and its mediated experience, the Grumbler thus adumbrates a critique of the press qua medium of information. But on a broader level, he points to what we could call an ethical failure in the discursive structures of modernity; that is, in modernity's dominant modes of writing, thinking, imagining, and remembering. Divided into two parts—"Satire and Counterdiscourse" and "Dialogues"—*Karl Kraus and the Discourse of Modernity* probes the iterations, implications, and rearticulations of Kraus's critical insights into the relationship between mass media, the state, the public sphere, and the modern subject.

I invoke the "discourse" of modernity because language, in all of its forms, is, for Kraus, a social practice and thus a site where political impulses and ideologies coalesce, particularly those that remain unacknowledged by the speaker or writer. Kraus's polemics thus may begin with language—and each chapter addresses a distinct linguistic mode or practice—but they do not end there. Part 1 of this book provides, accordingly, close readings of three (primarily) literary works by Kraus: *The Last Days of Mankind* (1915–22), *Cloudcuckooland* (1923), and *The Third Walpurgis Night* (1933/52). Each of these works testifies to a moment of radical transformation or total collapse: World War I, the interwar experiments in social democracy, or the rise of fascism and National Socialism. Through a variety of techniques—ranging from quotation, to diatribe, to the employment of allegory, myth, and intertextuality—Kraus shows how the anesthetization of the modern reader or spectator to violence and destruction heavily informs the conditions of possibility for future iterations of violence. Part 2 then broadens the scope of the study by bringing the discourses invoked in part 1 in dialogue with three modern philosopher-critics: Søren Kierkegaard, Walter Benjamin, and Theodor Adorno. It argues that Kraus's concerns, though distinctive, are also deeply embedded in a trajectory of modern continental thought and critical theory writ large. By reassessing Kraus's work both on its own terms and in relation to these figures, the present study argues that Kraus ought to be considered a significant theorist of European modernity and, more specifically, of its self-destructive tendencies.

Briefly stated: Kraus—aphorist, essayist, journalist, poet, and playwright—was born in 1874 to an upper-middle-class Jewish family in the former Czechoslovakia (Jičín), at the time part of the Austro-Hungarian Empire. When Kraus was three his family moved to Vienna, capital of the empire, where he spent the majority of his life. After an unsuccessful stint as an actor, he founded the satirical journal *The Torch* (*Die Fackel*) in 1899, sealing it with the motto: "What we slay (*umbringen*)." This motto was intended as a riposte to the largest-circulating newspaper of the Habsburg Monarchy, *The New Free Press* (*Die Neue Freie Presse*), whose motto, "What we bring (*bringen*)," left Kraus cold.[1] With this minor linguistic alteration Kraus thus declared the satirical impulse of his journal, along with his complicated aversion-attraction to the entire enterprise of journalism.[2] From 1899 to 1911, he collaborated with several important (and some controversial) writers of the fin de siècle European landscape: Peter Altenberg, Richard Dehmel, Else Lasker-Schüler, August Strindberg, Franz Werfel, Georg Trakl, Frank Wedekind, Houston Stewart Chamberlain, and Oscar Wilde, among others. From 1911 onward, however, Kraus became the exclusive editor of, and sole contributor to *The Torch*—henceforth, he authored every single word that appeared in his journal. Kraus died in 1936, two years before Germany's annexation of Austria, having intuited but not experienced the horror that was to follow.

Kraus's earliest polemics were often directed against the double standard of the Austrian penal code and its unjust treatment of society's most vulnerable members (especially prostitutes and homosexuals); he also frequently satirized the pretensions and dilettantism of the Viennese literati.[3] But his bête noire throughout his life was the daily press, and what Kraus considered to be its deleterious effects on the imagination of the modern reader and thus on modern political life.[4] "How is the world ruled and led to war?" Kraus once wrote. "Diplomats lie to journalists and believe these lies when they see them in print."[5] Here, Kraus addresses not only the feedback loop informing the relationship between the press and the state, but the facility with which mendacity—fake news, albeit understood in a different sense from the way the phenomenon is usually discussed today—is taken for truth. Mendacity, for Kraus, takes on many different forms in the context of journalistic discourse. To offer one example: Kraus devoted multiple satires to the "translation" of a well-known contemporary journalist, Maximillian Harden, whose florid style (which Kraus called "Desperanto") Kraus found both impenetrable and unsuitable for his ideal of journalistic integrity.[6] Where Harden writes, for example: "The hour of fate summons forth the harmonious collected forces of German humanity (*deutscher Menschheit*)," Kraus "translates": "The hour of decision demands a unified Germany"—the phrase "German humanity" struck Kraus as particularly suspicious.[7] While this corrective gesture may appear petty, Kraus's larger point is that if journalism is charged with the chief responsibility of informing its readers about the social and political world, then the language and tone in which this world is being mediated demand a critique of their own, one that renders the medium itself visible, and, in some cases, audible. For Kraus, diction and style are not innocuous components of reportage but rather constitute the ineliminable subjective elements embedded in every report, article, or feuilleton.

It was indeed the feuilleton that Kraus identified as the most insidious of modern forms, since it infelicitously conflated journalism and literature, thereby belying the potential objectivity of the former and the imaginative quality of the latter—an issue Kraus takes up most thoroughly in his polemic against Heinrich Heine, to be discussed in chapter 5. To be sure: I am not arguing that it is incumbent upon us to accept all of Kraus's judgments; many of them were unfair, inaccurate, or merely influenced by the prejudices of his time and place. But it is part of the task of this book to highlight the implications of his method, which consistently draws our attention to the notion that the representation of the world is filtered through the whim of a writer or the private interests that their newspaper serves but often conceals—and, more significantly, that this world is, subsequently, altered according to its representation.[8] As Kraus writes in his satirical poem "Couplet of the Bootlegger, (*Schwarz-Drucker*)," "In the beginning was the press, and then appeared the world."[9] As a generator of public opinion, the press had thus, for Kraus, become as influential a force in modern society as the state itself, insofar as it functions as both a medium through which social relations express themselves and an augur of political formations yet to come.[10]

Yet precisely because Kraus's critiques of the press are inextricable from larger discourses concerning the predicaments of modernity—the subject's role within the public sphere; the relationship between language and power; and the dialectic of progress and destruction—this book, broadly stated, is interested in the question of how illiberal forces, regimes, and ways of thinking develop within, and in virtue of, a liberal framework.[11] Kraus is concerned, I argue, with the conditions of lived experience that permit undesired wars to be waged, democracies to flounder, and political extremism to take root. In *The Last Days of Mankind*, the Grumbler is seized by the realization that an entire civilization had become a willing audience to the spectacle of its own self-destruction. In *Cloudcuckooland*, Kraus explores the implications of nostalgia and amnesia as reactive forces in the life of a young republic; and in *The Third Walpurgis Night*, he seeks out a language commensurate with both the archaism and the modernity of National Socialism, a phenomenon that leaves him almost (but not quite) speechless. By offering close readings of these literary engagements with real or impending moments of catastrophe, this study reveals a Kraus who was deeply invested in the fate of the demos.

Given these concerns, the second part of the book addresses how certain strains of continental thought and critical theory are reflected and refracted in Kraus's work—and vice versa.[12] Why Kierkegaard, Benjamin, and Adorno among other philosophers and European modernists influenced by Kraus?[13] Kierkegaard's excoriations of the press, public opinion, and the relationship between anonymity and irresponsibility find profound resonances in Kraus's World War I-era writings. Benjamin's reflections on the relationship between authority and opinion render Kraus's satires of journalistic dispatches more radical than they initially appear. And central to Adorno's philosophical project is his critique of "identity-thinking," the dominant mode of cognition within modern, "bourgeois" experience. Kraus serves as a particularly fruitful interlocutor for unpacking different, and less studied, aspects of Adorno's critique. Informing all of these respective positions is, furthermore, an inveterate skepticism regarding narratives of historical progress: when Kraus writes, for example, "Progress makes purses out of human skin," he shows himself to be attuned to what Adorno and Max Horkheimer would later call the "dialectic of Enlightenment."[14] Yet I also claim that there is a latent redemptive moment in each of these thinkers, and thus what further unites them is what I would call their shared commitment to a notion of the modern subject as a potential site of resistance rather than a site of inward retreat. This ethical commitment, I contend, is what motivates Kraus to continue to write even under the bleakest of circumstances, circumstances that all but rendered writing impossible.

In light of the extreme specificity of his polemics and the singularity of his style—Kraus's occasional inscrutability has provided challenges to virtually all of his readers and translators—recent scholarship on Kraus (especially in the Anglophone world), with a few notable exceptions, has tended to treat him as more of a local phenomenon than as a central theorist of modernity. We encounter, for example, Kraus as an "apocalyptic satirist" and a promoter of a certain idea of linguistic purity (Timms 1989, 2005);[15] as an instrumental player, along with Ludwig Wittgenstein, Hugo von Hofmannsthal, and Sigmund Freud, in fin de siècle Vienna's related "crises" of language and identity (Wagner 1982; Janik and Toulmin 1996; Le Rider 1993); as a key figure in debates about antisemitism and Jewish identity in the larger context of German and European modernity (Gilman 1990; Lensing 1992/2017; Theobald 1996; Reitter 2008); as a modernist of a specifically interwar, Austrian hue (Perloff 2016); and as a legal thinker in a very technical sense (Merkel 1998).[16] These studies are all rich in analytic substance and indispensable for my own project. They offer close readings of Kraus's work, the historical and cultural context in and against which he was responding, and his role as a leading Viennese intellectual with a loyal coterie. Paul Reitter and Leo Lensing, in particular, have paid close and careful attention to Kraus's linguistic choices in their analyses of his work.[17] While building on these studies, *Karl Kraus and the Discourse of Modernity*, by contrast, focuses on less fleshed out aspects of Kraus's thought—without ignoring the specificity of his language, his satirical techniques, or his citational practices—as it emerges in his literary output and in light of critical theory. Kraus's insights into the relationship between the press, war, party politics, and the fascist mentality demand both a closer examination and a broader intellectual context within which they can be situated. This may be a book about Kraus, but it is also a book about theorizing the traumas of Europe's twentieth century.

Satire and Counterdiscourse: Part 1

While satire as such is relegated to a subtext in this study, a brief word on its theoretical import and on Kraus's variant in particular is necessary for a proper understanding of the first part of this book, given satire's function as what we could call the transgeneric disposition informing Kraus's body of work. In his recent book on the legacies of satire in postwar German literature, Daniel Bowles points out that satire has been defined over the course of its long history as a "genre, a form, a mode of writing, a technique of corrective criticism, a kind of literary parasitism, a manner of perception (*Empfindungsweise*) . . . and a negative figure of the 'inverted world,' among others."[18] To further compound its conceptual ambiguity, satire has not generally fared well in the German aesthetic tradition, especially relative to the related concepts of the comic, humor, and irony.[19] G. W. F. Hegel, for example, argues that while the satirist is a virtuous figure who has the good and the true in mind, his poetry does not achieve the level of free aesthetic expression that we find in Greek comedy; and for Hegel satire is of decidedly Roman (not Greek) provenance. The satirist, furthermore, is mired in "bitterness" and the pure negation of a finite reality, and is therefore unable to discover in his art the conciliatory moment that defines aesthetic expression worthy of the name.[20] Yet Hegel does not provide the final word on the matter.

Indeed, Georg Lukács, who continued the tradition of Hegelian aesthetics in the twentieth century, is more helpful for my purposes in his effort to redeem satire (under the mantle of realism) by politicizing its function. In his 1932 essay "On the Question of Satire," Lukács calls satire the "stepchild of bourgeois literary theory in Germany."[21] Not intending a value-neutral observation, Lukács suggests that satire's "openly combative" nature has been misunderstood by bourgeois society as distasteful, which explains why it has been generally repudiated.[22] Lukács wants to resuscitate precisely this aspect of satire, and thus his most memorable concept in this essay is his notion of the satirist's "holy hatred" (*heiliger Haß*), the revolutionary and self-authorized vitriol that informs satire's exposure of the social contradiction between pretense and actuality.[23] Viewed through this lens, satire never offends for the sake of offending. If it is to succeed aesthetically, it must dialectically seek out the absurdity or obscenity that has coalesced within the historical moment.[24]

When Kraus, for example, reproduces a Swiss advertisement for automobile tours through the battlefields of the recently ended war (see next page), he foregrounds the barbarism entailed in converting former sites of mass death and violence into profit-oriented tourist attractions—what we might today call catastrophe tourism. Kraus claims to hold in his hand a delusion-less "portrait" of humanity at this particular moment:

> After the monstrous collapse of the fiction of culture (*Kulturlüge*) and after the nations, by their actions, gave striking proof that their relationship to anything that was ever of the spirit is a most shameless trickery, perhaps good enough for the promotion of tourism (*Hebung des Fremdenverkehrs*) but never adequate to raise the moral level (*Hebung der sittlichen Niveaus*) of this mankind—after all this it has nothing left but the naked truth of its condition, so that it has almost reached the point where it is no longer capable of lying. (*F* 577, 96, 1921; *GT*, 89)

Kraus interlaces pathos with mordant irony as he suggests that the lie of culture has been betrayed by the unabashed truth of what it produced: a war of mass destruction.[25] He juxtaposes what he calls "scenes of delirium" with the comforts and luxuries provided by these promotional trips: "You receive, even if Russia starves to death, an ample breakfast as soon as you decide to take in the battlefields of 1870–71 as well; it's all one package" (*F* 577, 98; *GT* 92). Kraus may not be calling for revolution, but his disgust with, and hatred of, this total disregard for the loss of human life could be judged to be adequate to the phenomenon under critique. Lukács, to be sure, disqualifies Kraus as a legitimate inheritor of the satirical tradition because his is not a voice of the revolutionary class—Kraus was more concerned, for Lukács, with the "last days of *mankind*" than he was with the last days of capitalism. Yet the notion of "holy hatred" still offers a useful way to identify what is both distinctive and exemplary in Kraus's satire, which often functions as an affective foil to what Kraus repeatedly refers to as journalistic tone.

Kraus's own reflections on satire, humor, and laughter provide us with an equally insightful resource for evaluating his literary work.[26] These reflections do not necessarily show his satire in action, but they reveal, at the very least, the intention informing his satire. In his 1912 commemorative essay on the nineteenth-century Viennese playwright, Johann Nestroy—into whose tradition of language-oriented satire Kraus inserted himself—Kraus expresses what I take to be central to his understanding of the function of genuine satire. After spending much of the essay discussing why Nestroy has been misunderstood, and how the nuances of his "linguistic art" (*Sprachkunst*) have been overlooked by those who have unsuccessfully tried to stage him, Kraus cryptically but programmatically declares what satire is and does:

Schlachtfelder-Rundfahrten im Auto!

veranstaltet durch die Basler Nachrichten.

Reklamefahrten vom 25. Sept. bis 25. Okt. zum ermässigten Preis von Fr. 117.-

Unvergeßl. Eindrücke

Keine Paß-Formalitäten!

Anmeldung

bei uns und Ausfüllung eines Fragebogens genügt.

Als Herbstfahrt besond. zu empfehlen!

„... Eine Fahrt durch das Schlachtfeldergebiet von Verdun vermittelt dem Besucher den Inbegriff der Grauenhaftigkeit moderner Kriegführung. Es ist nicht nur für das französische Empfinden das Schlachtfeld „par excellence", auf dem sich letzten Endes der Riesenkampf zwischen Frankreich und Deutschland entschied. Wer immer diesen Abschnitt mit Fort Vaux und Fort Douaumont im Mittelpunkt gesehen hat, wird auf keinem Schlachtfeld des Westens mehr einen so tiefen Eindruck erhalten. Wenn der ganze Krieg Frankreich 1,400.000 Tote gekostet hat, so fiel fast ein Drittel von diesen in dem ein paar Quadrat-Kilometer umfassenden Sektor von Verdun, und mehr als doppelt so stark waren hier die Verluste der Deutschen. In dem kleinen Abschnitt, wo mehr als eine Million, vielleicht 1½ Millionen Menschen verbluteten, gibt es keinen Quadratzentimeter Oberfläche, der nicht von den Granaten durchwühlt wurde. Man durchfahre hernach das Gebiet der Argonnen- und Somme-Kämpfe, man durchwandere die Ruinen von Reims, man kehre zurück über St.-Mihiel und durch den Priesterwald: alles ist nur die kleinliche Wiederholung von Einzelheiten, die sich bei Verdun zu einem unerhört großartigen Gesamtbild von Grauen und Schrecken vereinigen ..."

600 km Bahnfahrt II. Klasse. Einen ganzen Tag im bequemen Personen-Auto über die Schlachtfelder, Übernachten, erstklassige Verpflegung, Wein, Kaffee, Trinkgelder, Paßformalitäten und Visum von Basel bis wieder zurück nach Basel alles inbegriffen im Preise von 117 Fr. Schweizerwährung.

Infolge sorgfältigster Organisation hat der Reisende von der Abfahrt von Basel bis zur Wiederankunft in Basel nicht mehr das Geringste auszugeben.

Die Basler Nachrichten veranstalten diese Rundfahrt, um jedem Schweizer zum Preise von **117 Franken** Gelegenheit zum Besuche der Schlachtfelder zu geben, in der Weise, dass den Teilnehmern alle Formalitäten und Reise-Schwierigkeiten abgenommen werden.

Die Teilnehmer erhalten nach Einzahlung von Fr. 117 auf Postscheckkonto V/5616 Schlachtfelderfahrten der Basler Nachrichten, Basel, ein Ticket, durch das ohne jede weitere Auslage folgendes geboten wird:

Sie fahren im Schnellzug II. Klasse abends von Basel ab.
Sie werden am Bahnhof in Metz abgeholt und im Auto ins Hotel geführt.
Sie übernachten in einem erstklassigen Hotel, Bedienung und Trinkgeld inbegriffen.
Sie erhalten am Morgen ein reichliches Frühstück.
Sie fahren in einem bequemen Personenauto in Metz ab und durch das Schlachtfeldergebiet von 1870/71 (Gravelotte).
Sie besichtigen in Etain unter erklärender Führung das hochinteressante Blockhaus (Quartier des Kronprinzen und Sitz eines grossen deutschen Hauptquartiers).
Sie fahren durch die zerstörten Dörfer ins Festungsgebiet von Vaux mit den riesigen Friedhöfen mit hunderttausenden von Gefallenen.
Sie besichtigen unter Führung die unterirdischen Kasematten des Forts Vaux.
Sie besuchen das Ossuaire (Beinhaus) von Thiaumont, wo die Überreste der nicht agnoszierten Gefallenen fortwährend eingeliefert und aufbewahrt werden.
Sie haben freien Eintritt ins Fort Douaumont.
Sie besuchen die Tranchée des Baïonettes oder des Ensevelis.
Sie fahren am Ravin de la Mort entlang, an den Carrières d'Haudromont und am Train Sauveur vorbei, am Fusse der Côte du Poivre nach Verdun.
Sie erhalten im besten Hotel von Verdun ein Mittagessen mit Wein und Kaffee, Trinkgeld inbegriffen.
Sie haben nach dem Essen Zeit zur Besichtigung des zerschossenen Verdun, der Ville-Martyre.
Sie fahren am Nachmittag zurück durch das schrecklich verwüstete Gebiet von Haudiaumont und gelangen wieder durch das Kampfgebiet von 1870/71 (Mars-la-Tour, Vionville usw.) nach Gravelotte und Metz.
Sie erhalten in Ihrem Hotel in Metz ein Diner mit Wein und Kaffee, Trinkgeld inbegriffen.
Sie werden nach dem Nachtessen im Auto zur Bahn gebracht.
Sie fahren im Nachtschnellzug II. Klasse zurück nach Basel.

Alles inbegriffen im Preise von 117 Franken bei reichlicher Verpflegung in erstklassigen Gasthäusern.

Jeder Anfragende erhält einen gedruckten Führer mit genauem Reiseprogramm und allen nötigen Anweisungen. Die Fahrten werden jeden Tag ausgeführt. Jedem Teilnehmer ist ein bequemer Platz garantiert.

Anerkennungs- u. Dankschreiben von früheren Reiseteilnehmern liegen in grosser Zahl in unserm Bureau auf.

Swiss newspaper advertising “Battlefield Roundtrips by Automobile,” reproduced in *F* 577, 97 (1921). For a translation of the original advertisement, see *GT*, 90–91.

> There's earthly laughter everywhere. Satire, however, has the answer to such laughter. For it's the art that, more than any other art, outlives itself, and this means the dead times, too. The harder the material (*Stoff*), the greater the attack. The more desperate the struggle, the stronger the art. The satiric artist stands at the end of a development that renounces art. He is its product and its hopeless antithesis. He organizes the Spirit's flight from mankind, he is the rear guard (*er ist die Rückwärtskonzentrierung*). After him, the deluge.[27]

An important distinction is made above between two types of laughter: what Kraus calls the "earthly" kind, and the laughter produced by genuine satire. Given the context of the essay—and the polemic against Heine that lurks in the background—we can characterize the earthly laughter as one of distraction, a laughter that does not challenge and indeed conforms to the norms of civility such that no new insights can arise from it. This kind of laughter entertains for the sake of entertainment; it can also be cruel for cruelty's sake. Genuine satire, by contrast, aims to interrupt precisely the soporific mode of experience Kraus suggests is in need of interruption; it laughs at the laughter of distraction and thereby produces a laughter of an altogether different order. This laughter contains a kind of pedagogic impulse insofar as it awakens its audience from its slumber and makes it more alert or sensitive to a reality otherwise obscured.[28] Such satire, Kraus furthermore suggests, always appears as if it were looking backward at an epoch mired in error, or what he calls the "dead times." This explains, for Kraus, the beleaguered condition of satire, which must, in a sense, outlive the moment that first occasioned its production lest it remain tethered to that moment and become illegible and irrelevant to posterity. Accordingly, the satirist implicitly claims that he does not necessarily describe who or what we are now, but rather hints at where we will be if we continue down a particular path—a frighteningly laughable path.

These claims are especially relevant to the present study in light of Kraus's subsequent reflections on the function of laughter and satire during World War I. Kraus once again draws attention to two distinct modes of laughter in an essay he read aloud in early 1915, "The Seriousness of the Times and the Satire of the Past." Contrary to what his readers and audience might expect, Kraus insists that the war has brought him no new insights regarding the nature of his satire. For his brand of humor does not produce "that wretched laugh whose business it is to distract us from seriousness and compassion," but is rather "one that exposes its victims to the test of whether they can bear the seriousness, the great mourning, and the grandeur that has grown overnight (*die über Nacht gewachsene Große*). Here humor is not in opposition to the war."[29] For Kraus, there is a type of laughter capable of making the horror (of war)—otherwise obscured to those who either read about it or wished to be distracted from it—paradoxically more salient. The argument from the Nestroy essay has remained the same, though the stakes are higher: satire, under this optic, does not have a palliative effect, but is meant rather to bring its audience closer to the brutal realities of the ridiculed phenomenon. The passage above culminates in Kraus's invocation of what he calls a *Blutlache*, a pun conflating the terms "pool of blood" and "bloody laughter," implying that only the laughter aware of its own impropriety—the laughter seemingly incongruous with the situation at hand—is capable of holding "its own alongside the horror."[30] For Kraus, such laughter draws our attention to the war's seriousness, sensitizes us to its violence, and thereby works against modernity's anesthetizing mechanisms. Satire is not a possible response to the war, for Kraus, but a necessary one.[31]

In *The Last Days*, Kraus renders comically obscene the panoply of participants who instigated, advertised, and profited from World War I; in *Cloudcuckooland*, he draws from ancient Greek comedy in order to allegorize the transition from a monarchy to a republic, ridiculing the obstructions that accompany this transition and threaten its success; and in *The Third Walpurgis Night*, Kraus concedes to the impotency of satire under conditions that have exceeded its exaggerations, yet nonetheless proceeds to subject Nazi rhetoric, terminology, and ideology to his acrimonious wit. In all three works, Kraus's satire—his citational, rhetorical, intertextual, and otherwise polemical strategies—constitutes a counterdiscourse that challenges the more innocuous representations of the phenomenon, condition, or event under scrutiny. Attempting to furnish his audience with a new kind of experience, Kraus's texts mimetically reproduce those aspects of war, political transformation, and National Socialism that have been either obscured or dangerously misrepresented.[32] The way that Kraus's language enters, or, as Benjamin writes, "creeps" inside the object of critique allows us to see how his satire is thus an immanent feature of both his modernism and his critique of modernity as it unfolds in his literary works.

Dialogues: Part 2

While never fully disappearing from the scope of my concerns, satire recedes more to the background in the second part of the book, which is oriented toward the broader implications of Kraus's critiques. It was Kierkegaard's reflections on the dangers of the press that explicitly drew Kraus to the philosopher, but it is also these writings that prove most fruitful in terms of reading the two figures side by side. Benjamin called the satirist the figure in whom the "cannibal was received into civilization," but, similarly, his critical reflections on language and capitalism, the age of "information," and the concept of "public opinion" achieve greater clarity when read next to, and in light of, his views on Kraus.[33] Adorno was most ambivalent about Kraus's satire, opting, rather, to cite Kraus's lyric poetry and his meditations on language in articulating crucial aspects of his own philosophy. These figures all allow us to view Kraus's work as embedded in a particular trajectory of critical theory; in turn, Kraus's work sheds new and unexpected light on all of their respective critical-philosophical projects.

My concept of dialogue—as opposed to a notion such as influence—is thus partially inspired by Benjamin's theory of translation, denuded of its more metaphysical claims. In his essay on the "Task of the Translator," Benjamin argues that the translatability of any given work entails a multidirectional process: the contact between two languages—the original and the target language—in a work of literature has a transformative effect on both texts, insofar as the language into which a work is translated is invariably altered by its contact with the source text, whose interpretation, in turn, has been destabilized in virtue of its translation.[34] Dialogue between two or more figures in this study functions in a similar fashion: the work of one author can inspire new interpretations when brought into contact with that of another, whose subsequent interpretations are necessarily affected by such contact. This process of reciprocal illumination informs the way I approach Kierkegaard's writings on the press and his notion of "leveling" (chapter 4); Benjamin's views on the relationship between public opinion and authority (chapter 4); and, finally, Adorno's trenchant critique of origin-oriented philosophies and the notion of "authenticity" (chapter 5). To this end, the second part of this book explores the ways in which Kraus's work—examined in this section more for thematic consonance and less stringently with respect to its chronological appearance—can be understood as something of a cipher in relation to these other figures.

Book Overview

Chapter 1, "Reciting War: *The Last Days of Mankind* (1915–1922)," reappraises Kraus's magnum opus, a merciless lampoon of bureaucrats, journalists, war profiteers, politicians, and poets. This five-act satirical tragedy suggests that World War I has become a second nature of sorts, indistinguishable from any reality that lies outside of its domain. Of overlooked significance is thus Kraus's insight that despite its unprecedented violence, the war was not sufficiently experienced by those in the hinterland who merely read of its atrocities. *The Last Days* therefore constitutes an effort to both rewrite and recite the war such that it could be experienced, paradoxically, for the first time. I first argue that Kraus's real and "invented" quotations of journalistic dispatches qualify as sound bites that only obtain their full significance when perceived as remnants of an epoch in the moment of its collapse. In this way, the drama reads like a work of historiography written from an imagined future. The second part of the chapter reassesses the play's temporal coordinates by focusing on the figure of the Grumbler—the play's resident satirist and its self-proclaimed author—and showing how his intended audience is posterity. Having renounced his contemporary world as a lost cause, incapable of recognizing its own criminality, the

Grumbler hopes that a future generation—*die Nachwelt*—might grasp the experience of this war more substantially than does his own epoch. If not, the Grumbler warns, it will have become evident that the war had never truly come to an end.

Chapter 2, "On Birds, Wars, and Fragile Republics: *Cloudcuckooland* (1923)," turns to Kraus's adaptation of the ancient Greek comedy *The Birds* by Aristophanes (414 B.C.E.), which Kraus composed in ostensible celebration of the democratic republic that formed in the Austria of the early postwar years. Kraus is still concerned in this play with the question of whether the war and the dissolution of the monarchy have been understood in all of their implications—his Athens looks strikingly similar to the Vienna of Austria's First Republic. The first two acts of *Cloudcuckooland* follow Aristophanes's play closely in both form and content, relating the story of two disgruntled Athenians who defect from Athens in order to build a bird-city in the sky, one bereft of the ailments inflicting their former home. The problem is, "Athens" has not truly abandoned these defectors. The third act departs radically from the source text, resembling the apocalyptic tenor of *The Last Days* in its staging of a war between the birds and the gods before hinting at the possibility of a new beginning, one resolutely free of "human" influence. *Cloudcuckooland* explores the conditions under which social and political renewal are made possible. In so doing, however, it examines the experience of nostalgia as a clouding political force. If genuine "self-determination" is to take root, the play suggests, the lingering specters of the recent past must be recognized, lest they be reincarnated in more radical or grotesque forms. With this play written in 1923, Kraus already warns of the threat of the swastika and thus the need to pay close attention to supposedly fringe movements emerging from the ashes of World War I.

Chapter 3, "'Where Illegality Becomes the Law': *Third Walpurgis Night* (1933/1952)," analyzes Kraus's most sustained engagement with the onset of National Socialism. Written in 1933 but not published in full until nearly two decades later, Kraus's essay notoriously begins by suggesting that Hitler brings "nothing" to mind, a line that issues into a three-hundred-page impassioned excoriation of Nazi discourse and the violence against Jews and communists that is being simultaneously denied and justified. Kraus goes beyond many of his contemporaries in his unsettling assertion that Nazism is both continuous with a certain form of liberal modernity, and, at the same time, a historical caesura for which no language is yet commensurate. This tension is best articulated, I argue, through the essay's complex engagement with Goethe's *Faust: The Second Part of the Tragedy* (1832), which, like Kraus's essay, stages a violent collision between the archaic and the modern world. Yet on a more formal level, it becomes clear that Goethe's words often appear where Kraus's fail—the stuff of myth takes over, in other words, when discursive language has reached the limits of signification. Goethe's drama, for Kraus, thus anticipates the experience of National Socialism through its violent and grotesque content, but it also supplements a text whose author (Kraus) claims to be literally dumbfounded by this nearly unspeakable experience. This chapter ultimately reassesses Kraus's controversial decision to endorse Austro-Fascism by reading this essay as an attempt to make Nazi terror a legible phenomenon, a terror that was, for Kraus, misrepresented and misunderstood even by the movement's most vehement critics.

Chapter 4, "'A Monstrous Nonentity': Kierkegaard, Kraus, and Benjamin," inaugurates the second part of the book on dialogues past and present, revisiting some of the core issues discussed in the first three chapters. Beginning with a broad historical-theoretical overview of the bourgeois public sphere and the role of the journalist within it, it next addresses Kraus's relationship to Kierkegaard. Kierkegaard and Kraus's shared views can be rendered, I argue, in terms of a hermeneutics of authority: they are both concerned with the conditions under which an authoritative voice can (still) emerge amidst the "chatter" of modernity and the diminution of subjective interiority. This ambivalent assessment of the public sphere is articulated in Kierkegaard's *Two Ages: The Age of Revolution and the Present Age: A Literary Review* (1846) and in Kraus's plea, several months into World War I, that a voice of authority paradoxically "step forward and be silent." His concern here as elsewhere is with how an ostensibly informed public could allow a war of such magnitude to erupt. In the final part of this chapter, I turn to Benjamin's reflections on the war, the press, language, and Kraus, which he articulates in a variety of texts written in the 1930s. These texts tease out some of the latent political implications of both Kierkegaard's and Kraus's work. Kierkegaard's insights into the experience of subjectivity in an "age of reflection" thus illuminate the philosophical foundations of Kraus's claims, and Benjamin's explicitly Marxist reflections on the press during an age of information (and an "age of sensation") radicalize Kraus's own brand of journalism.

Chapter 5, "'Origin Is the Goal': Adorno and Kraus," establishes Kraus's role as an indispensable figure for understanding some of Adorno's most significant philosophical contributions. Adorno is critical of Kraus in *Minima Moralia* (1944–45), where he argues that satire and irony are essentially conservative "mediums" that have been rendered inoperative after Auschwitz. This is because for Adorno, irony presupposes a strict opposition between truth and ideology and thus participates in a form of "identity thinking" inasmuch as it disavows the more dialectical relationship between these two categories that recent history has made salient. But Adorno's essay "Morality and Criminality" (1964) reflects a transformation in his thought: detecting in the satirist what he calls an "undomesticated mimetic impulse," Adorno includes Kraus among the anointed figures of European modernism, whose work seeks to articulate a language of nonidentity, or a language that bears the imprint of the violence and suffering of the twentieth century. This issues into a discussion of Kraus's function in Adorno's *Negative Dialectics* (1967) and its companion piece, *The Jargon of Authenticity* (1964), which I argue to be his most

Krausian endeavor. In both of these texts, Kraus frequently appears when Adorno arrives at an impasse in the philosophical regime under critique—often as an antidote to Martin Heidegger. But where Kraus makes his most substantial impact, I finally argue, is in Adorno's critique of "origins" as this principle has been manifested both philosophically and politically. Kraus's dialectical rendering of the relationship between "origin" and "goal" helps us discern in Adorno what I call an inchoate "metaphysics of exile," a philosophy of experience that is rooted neither in "blood and soil" nor in other less explicit, but no less menacing, expressions of nativism—indeed, a philosophy that is not rooted at all.

The historian David Hollinger's reading of the two types of modernists—the "Knower" and the "Artificer"—provides an apt model for interpreting Kraus's unique role as a critic and thinker of modernity, one who acknowledges what Hollinger calls the isolation and "secularity of modern intellectual life."[35] In Kraus's literary and allegorical endeavors, his desire to create alternative worlds that highlight the deficiencies or absurdities of our own and point, however obliquely, to exit strategies, renders him an Artificer par excellence. As does Kraus's attempt to expose the artifice behind what generally passes for objectivity. Yet in his consistent striving—however vain such an endeavor may have been—to achieve an Archimedean point of authority, whose vantage would allow him to judge the words and deeds of his fellow human beings, Kraus also shows himself to be a Knower, a seeker of truth. Occasionally, these dispositions conflict. But their coexistence in Kraus's work makes him particularly suited for analysis as both a modernist author and a theorist of modernity. His insights—some dated, some controversial, and some seemingly more germane now than they were in his own time—merit reassessment as distinct contributions as well as complements to the thought of those figures whose canonical status is undisputed. In his own time, Kraus presumed he would be misunderstood; this book offers one way to understand him.

Part 1

✦

Satire and Counterdiscourse

Chapter 1

✦

Reciting War

The Last Days of Mankind (1915–1922)

> Today "experience" can only refer to a past. Otherwise it is synonymous with "horror."
>
> —Roberto Calasso, *The Forty-Nine Steps*

> What just was will probably soon be forgotten. Only an empty, awful memory hangs in the air. . . . So of course it has remained, even up to today, as though we had not been burned badly enough.
>
> —Ernst Bloch, *The Spirit of Utopia* (1918)

In his book *Watching War* (2012), Jan Mieszkowski argues that the immanent relationship between war, mass spectatorship, reportage, and performance has its origins in the Napoleonic era, and that over the ensuing two centuries we have experienced more of a quantitative than a qualitative shift in these relations. Nevertheless, what distinguished World War I from what came before it was its introduction of the notion of "total war," which describes the by then virtually obsolete distinction between actor and acted upon, spectator and participant, soldier and civilian. This war enshrined what Mieszkowski calls "state-sponsored combat as an integral feature of the workplace," and from this point forward, the "complete militarization of existence" became routine.[1] Something of this notion is already anticipated in the preface to *The Last Days of Mankind*, in which Kraus—just prior to his disappearance into the world of the drama—introduces several distinct but interrelated discourses that are central to this text: the tragicomic representation of war; the relationship between spectator and participant; the status of memory, forgetfulness, and testimony; and the fraught question of the drama's intended audience, both present and future.[2] Kraus writes:

> The performance of this drama, which would take some ten evenings in terrestrial time, is intended for a theatre on Mars. Theatergoers on

> planet earth would find it unendurable. For it is blood of their blood and its content derives from the contents of those unreal unthinkable years, out of sight and out of mind, inaccessible to memory and preserved only in bloodstained dreams (*in blutigem Traum verwahrten Jahre*), when operetta figures played out the tragedy of mankind. The action is likewise without heroes, fractured and improbable, as it picks its way through a hundred scenes and hells. The humour is no more than the self-reproach of an author who did not lose his mind at the thought of surviving, with his faculties intact, to bear witness to such profane events (*mit heilem Hirn die Zeugenschaft dieser Zeitdinge bestanden zu haben*). He alone, compromised for posterity (*Nachwelt*) by his involvement, has a right to this humour. As for those contemporaries (*Mitwelt*) who allowed the things transcribed here to happen, let them subordinate the right to laugh to the duty to weep. (*LTM*, 9; *LDM*, 1)

Given Mars's status as the Roman god of war, the invocation of a Martian theater is far from arbitrary, and the double meaning of "theatre" as both the site of war and the venue for drama is foregrounded in the inaugural sentence: Kraus declares war against war. But this extraterrestrial reference also points to the drama's putative unstageability, through which Kraus disavows the notion of an audience that would be in any way distinct from the characters in his play, those who lived through the "Great War."[3] In this way, *The Last Days* anticipates, or provides a salient example of what Peter Szondi called the "absolute drama," in which the identity between the poet/dramaturge, audience, and characters is built into its formal apparatus.[4] For those who are watching, listening, or reading (the author included), Kraus suggests, are beholding themselves, a predicament that invokes one of what we might call the primary modes of experience under critique: that of spectatorship. What, precisely, cannot be endured, and why are these years deemed "unreal" and "unthinkable"? Why is its content "inaccessible" to memory and only manifest—as if Kraus were speaking in psychoanalytic terms—in "bloodstained" dreams?

What Kraus suggests in this opening passage is that the war that has just transpired was somehow missed by those who merely read about it, and thus that the rendering of it on stage would not be tolerated by those who managed to survive it—hence its need to be performed on Mars, whose theatergoers would be conditioned by a perpetual state of war and therefore more receptive to it. Kraus's subsequent statement that he has "portrayed the deeds they merely performed (*ich habe gemalt, was sie nur taten*)" becomes, in this context, more significant (*LTM*, 9; *LDM*, 1). Adapting and inverting a line from Friedrich Schiller's *Fiesco*—"I have done what thou—hast only painted (*Ich habe getan, was du—nur maltest*)"—Kraus has also inverted the original hierarchy implied by Schiller between performance and portrayal: the deeds of war obtain their true meaning not through their original "performance," Kraus suggests, but through his portrayal of them.[5] The repetition, in other words, is meant to supplant the original. Kraus's opening salvo thus constitutes an attempt to activate the memory of the readers who, for him, failed to process the event of war in its initial occurrence because it was presented to them as a theatrical spectacle. The preface thus poses one of the central conundrums of the entire drama: namely, the problem of portraying a war that was initially rendered and received as a performance. Kraus thereby raises broader questions about the ethics of representing a war that has been thoroughly aestheticized.

Kraus's first proposed solution is to render this historical tragedy a grotesque comedy of sorts.[6] Indeed, in her work on comedy, the Hegelian-Lacanian Alenka Zupančič has written that an event "can be terrible and devastating in its repetition, but it is no longer tragic, and this . . . constitutes a supreme tragedy of modernity."[7] For Zupančič, the very tragedy of modernity, as it were, is that it is unable to be rendered as tragedy (in any conventional form), that this particular mode of experience is no longer available to us, for multiple reasons. This position would help us understand what Kraus means when he suggests that the characters of his tragedy, namely, the actors of war, are best understood as figures from an operetta who have "played out the tragedy of mankind."[8] If the operetta is a parody of the opera, then Kraus would appear to propose a notion of tragedy in his preface that can no longer accommodate the tragic hero, a figure who traditionally elicits both fear and pity and eventually comes to acknowledge his guilt. His variant on tragedy, rather, foregrounds primarily laughable, comic figures whose very absence of subjectivity and psychological interiority constitutes their comic substance, and, to speak with Zupančič, the modern impulse of the drama.[9] Kraus's repetition of the tragedy of recent history as farce—to invoke Karl Marx (though farce would not adequately account for the range of comical and satirical techniques employed in this drama)—is thus one way that he addresses his monumental challenge. For humor grants Kraus the perspectival distance needed to turn the war into a historical artifact; humor has also allegedly prevented him from going mad over the guilt of survival, from being completely absorbed into or overwhelmed by the experience of war. In this way, humor enables Kraus to serve as what I would call a witness for posterity even as he sees himself implicated in the events on display, even, that is, as he questions his own authority. For our author admits to being not only a commentator on such "profane events" (*Zeitdinge*)—a neologism that collapses space and time—but also a guilty character in his own drama, a predicament we will see realized in the Grumbler, the play's resident satirist.[10]

And to what end are the characters portrayed in such a fashion? The preface continues with perhaps its most definitive statement about the experience of war as Kraus sees it: "It's all too easy to understand the disenchantment (*Ernüchterung*) of an epoch forever incapable of experiencing such events, or grasping what's been experienced (*niemals eines Erlebnisses und keiner Vorstellung des Erlebten fähig*) compounded by the failure to be convulsed by its collapse" (*LTM*, 10; *LDM*, 2). Exploring and indeed undoing this failure is what I take to be among the drama's most urgent impulses. *The Last Days* attempts, that is, to recite and rewrite the war in its effort to counteract the impoverished mode of experience informing its vision of a benighted modernity. Part of this critique—and part of Kraus's modernism—includes the staging of its own struggle to establish this alternative discourse, a voice of authority unsullied by the moment that has given rise to it. To better illustrate this critique and its internal predicament, I first turn to key moments of quotation and repetition in the drama, central stylistic features in which satirical contrasts and juxtapositions are most fully on display. The figures in question—primarily journalists, newspaper readers, generals, and war profiteers—are portrayed as purveyors of this spectator-oriented mode of experience. In the last part of the chapter I turn my attention to the Grumbler and his dialogue with the Optimist in order to show how the drama attempts to enact an alternative discourse and its attendant mode of experience. The Grumbler aims to rewrite this war such that its implications are adequately registered, and yet he encounters a persistent problem: to whom can he address his plaint if spectator and audience have collapsed into each other, if there is no proper "outside" of the text he claims to have written, save that of posterity? The status of witness-for-posterity betrays, effectively, the limits of the Grumbler's powers, and perhaps the limit of the satirist's powers more broadly conceived.

Linguistic Ruins

This chapter treats *The Last Days* as a single, completed text, despite the fact that it was written and published over the course of seven years (from 1915 to 1922), that there are two versions of the play (the first completed in 1917 and the second begun after 1918), and that these versions do not seamlessly correspond with each other in terms of the views they represent. The result is a highly fractured text: an admission Kraus himself makes in his introduction. Edward Timms has meticulously recorded and analyzed the shifts in Kraus's position vis-à-vis the war from being a conservative defender of state, army, and church—whose satire was directed more at the "enemy within" (i.e., journalists, and more specifically, Jewish journalists) than at the ruling classes—to becoming an arch-pacifist, whose political sympathies radically shifted toward democracy and socialism, however "reluctant" a democrat Kraus remained (*AS* 1, 371–74). This point is especially important to consider if we are trying to reconcile some of the drama's more troubling antisemitic moments (representing Kraus's early position) with its assaults on the military and state elites (informed by Kraus's later views). The inconsistencies are glaring, and yet they are essential to my approach: in treating the text as a whole rather than focusing on the vagaries of Kraus's social and political allegiances, his status as an albeit inconsistent thinker of the social totality—and thus part of his appeal to figures such as Walter Benjamin and Theodor Adorno—becomes more salient. It is not without justification that the author, critic, and Kraus-admirer Hermann Broch once called Kraus's satire "absolute," by which he meant that it was totalizing in its aims and scope.[11] In the drama's final form, hardly any position toward the war is spared from Kraus's ridicule.

Understanding the literary pretentions of *The Last Days*, including its genre classification, provides yet another challenge to its interpreters. Its montage-like constitution (an estimated half of the drama's dialogues consist of quotations Kraus culled from various news sources and conversations overheard on the streets of Vienna), incorporation of cinematic elements, and rapid scenic transitions have led some critics to label it a "documentary play."[12] In her recent study of the fundamentally ironic mode of writing that emerged in the wake of the Austro-Hungarian Empire's collapse, Marjorie Perloff has called Kraus's text "probably the first—and perhaps the most remarkable—documentary drama written," highlighting its specifically avant-garde use of cabaret song, patriotic ode, vaudeville, tableau vivant, puppet play, and photomontage.[13] On account of the biblical allusions that abound throughout, Wilhelm Hindemith called the play a "post-Christian tragedy."[14] And along similar lines, Timms has argued for an apocalyptic reading of the drama that ultimately turns against itself: "The Judaeo-Christian promise of redemption—of messianic expectation fulfilled through the life of the saviour—is retracted in the face of man's revolt against God" (*AS* 2, 69).[15] In other words, the play stages a Deus absconditus and functions as a secular rejection of messianism wrought by humanity's failure to act in accordance with divine will by waging a war against itself. The renowned East German Kraus scholar Kurt Krolop labeled the drama a "warning play," viewing it as much in terms of the horrors that it anticipated as of those it documented.[16] Yet speaking with Calasso, it would be reductive to identify *The Last Days* as either an "example of 'documentary theater' or 'epic theater' or 'political theater' or 'theater of the absurd.'"[17] The drama's action, "fractured and improbable" much like the war itself, actively resists classification. *The Last Days* contains neither images of battle nor adheres to a narrative structure that corresponds to the actual timeline of the war. It employs a polysemious use of eschatological language, ranging from the pathetic to the mordantly ironic: the intonation at the end of the drama's epilogue by the "Voice of God"—"This is not what I intended (*Ich habe es nicht gewollt*)"—is a direct quotation from Kaiser Wilhelm II, who allegedly uttered these words in 1918 as he stood with contrition over a soldier's grave (*LTM*, 770; *LDM*, 588). The irony inheres in the disjunction between the kaiser's initial intention and the end effect of a world war, but the quotation could also be read as an insignia of Kraus's general approach to quotation. Subjective intention, for Kraus, is always belied by the symptomatic nature of any instantiation of language, by the larger context in which the quotation is embedded.

Quotation (and other modes of repetition) indeed constitute a significant part of the drama's formal apparatus. Reflecting on this practice, Kraus writes in another essay that the value of his art "consists . . . in the omission of quotation marks. The life into which the words have been displaced (*in das die Worte eingesetzt sind*) is so distinct from the life from which they have been taken, that not even the trace of an inner identity remains."[18] For Kraus, quotation enacts a transformation insofar as the quoted words now assume a wholly different meaning in their new context, or their new "life," as he calls it. The plagiarism committed is merely the by-product of this gesture, censured only by those who fail to register its aesthetic, and thus for Kraus, its ethical justification.[19] But what makes this process a genuine aesthetic achievement is when the quotation marks—the material signs that signify the separation between the cited and the new text—fall away completely, and the quotation is wholly subsumed by the new text. Kraus refers to this process as one of "attainment" or "insertion" (*Einschöpfung*).[20] His originality, we might conclude, thus consists in his role as a curator of quotations, a process that becomes formally consecrated in his wartime drama. In *The Last Days*, that is, such insertions are frequently embedded into the dialogue, functioning as linguistic ruins of war: fragments of language stripped of their original contexts and subsequently preserved as artifactual evidence. To paraphrase an earlier critic, in Kraus's drama the present disappears and becomes historical time.[21] Quotations in this text—both real and invented—are instances of language in the process of becoming historical detritus, material objects to be critically reflected upon because the authority they once emitted in the form of, say, journalistic dispatches, had inoculated them against scrutiny.[22]

The major liberal and centrist press organs of the day as well as well-known journalists were, for Kraus, ripe for the process described above. Alice Schalek was one such contemporary whom Kraus viewed as representative of the lugubrious, sentimental, and celebratory war reportage that turned the war into a spectacle, and who thus functioned as a "living caricature of the Zeitgeist."[23] What had originally been a collation of direct quotations from Schalek that Kraus reproduced in issues of *The Torch* is reworked into a dialogue between the war correspondent and an unnamed officer on the southwest front:[24]

> ALICE SCHALEK. . . . Now the show (*Schauspiel*) begins—so tell me, Lieutenant, could any artist in his art produce a more thrilling, a more rousing show? Let those who stay at home call war the crime of the century to their heart's content—after all, I did, too, while I was on the home front—but those who experience it firsthand are in the grip of a passion (*Fieber des Erlebens*). Am I right, Lieutenant, as someone right in the middle of it, that many of you don't want this thrilling life to end!

OFFICER. No, no one wants their life to end. That's why everyone wants the war to stop.

(*The whistling of shells can be heard: Ssss——*)

ALICE SCHALEK. Sss—! That was a shell.

OFFICER. No, it was shrapnel. Can't you tell?

ALICE SCHALEK. You obviously find it hard to grasp that they various timbres don't yet sound different to me. But in the time I've been at the front, I've learnt a lot, and I'll learn that too.–It seems the performance (*die Vorstellung*) is over. What a shame! It was first-rate.

OFFICER. Are you satisfied?

ALICE SCHALEK. What do you mean, satisfied? That's not the word! Call it patriotism, you idealists; hatred of the enemy, you nationalists; call it sport, you modernists; adventure, you romantics; call it the thrill of power, you connoisseurs of the soul—I call it liberated humanity (*frei gewordenes Menschentum*). (*LTM*, 189; *LDM*, 140–41)

Schalek clearly views the war as an elaborate show or performance, which stands in stark contrast to the officer's curtness and unwillingness to indulge this fantasy. The satirical apogee of the exchange, however, is Schalek's concession that, despite her expertise, she has difficulty distinguishing between the various timbres that accompany combat, evincing the causal relationship between faulty perception and a faulty report. The vicious cycle begins: a perceptual apparatus skewed by the war in turn informs reportage that further contributes to the skewed perception of the war. The seamless continuity between the sound of the shrapnel ("Ssss") and Schalek's words ("Sss") suggests the way the journalist reproduces or repeats the sounds of battle in her own language, blurring the distinction between word and weapon. Recalling Mieszkowski's definition of total war, we can identify here a salient example of militarized language in a less obvious sense. For Schalek's enumeration of the various types of war supporters—idealists, romantics, athletes, moderns—culminating in the invocation of a "liberated humanity" appears vain, dehumanizing, and patently absurd when inserted into a dialogue with a thoroughly abject, confused, and demoralized officer.

Yet the drama also places Schalek's reportage in a different context—quoting its own quotation, as it were—by embedding it in an earlier conversation between two other war reporters on a battlefield who are wearing field glasses and carrying Kodak cameras. Puffs of smoke are visible in the distant background. The correspondents are discussing what they are able to discern, making occasional references to the similarities between the sounds and sights of this battle and the Balkan War, whose memory still lingers. Schalek makes a brief appearance and the conversation shifts to her impressive skills: "And the way she describes (*beschreibt*) being in a hail of bullets—formidable! Don't you feel ashamed as a man?" asks the first reporter, following it up with: "The way she describes the corpses—and the stink of decomposition is no joke!" (*LTM*, 156; *LDM*, 115). The German verb *beschreiben*, as one critic has argued, can mean either "to describe," or, quite literally, "to write upon," and suggests that Schalek (and other war correspondents) are "writing upon corpses," producing a desecration through language.[25] The point is not just that this example of aestheticizing the war is built into journalistic practice; it is also that this language enters into public and private discourse, effectively creating the official memory of the event whose trauma it has obscured. When the second reporter asks, "Am I responsible for editing the World War?"—a line that the Grumbler will invoke later in the drama in the form of an indictment—he seems to be answering his own question affirmatively (*LTM*, 158; *LDM*, 117).[26] These are, indeed, the editors of war. Reproducing Schalek's statements within this context thus constitutes an attempt to revoke the act of "writing upon" corpses and to thereby turn this language itself into a corpse ready for a postmortem.

The drama reserves, however, even more vitriol for Moriz Benedikt, the then editor-in-chief of *The New Free Press*, the most widely circulated Austrian news organ during the first part of the twentieth century and bourgeois in its orientation.[27] Referred to as the "Lord of the Hyenas," Benedikt makes his most grotesque appearance in the epilogue ("The Final Night"), as he and the other hyenas (read: journalists) partake in a dance of death around soldiers' corpses, celebrating their financial gains amidst the mounting loss of life.[28] The antisemitic undertones informing this imagery cannot be lost on the reader, then and now, and yet Benedikt's role in the text moves beyond that of offensive caricature. Two consecutive scenes in the first act juxtapose the Vatican with a newspaper editor's office, presumably the office of the *Press*. The parallel between the Vatican and the editor's office is clearly indicated through the homologous captions: from the Vatican intones "the voice of Benedict praying"; from the office, "the voice of Benedikt dictating." These two figures share three things in common: a position of great influence (the one God's vicar on earth, the other a powerful manager of public discourse); a voice that is heard and heeded by many; and, the ultimate irony, a namesake. First the Pope makes a plea to the warring nations, an excerpt from Pope Benedict XV's 1915 Apostolic Exhortation, *Allorché fummo chiamati*, which Kraus has retranslated from the milder "ghastly struggle" (*entsetzlicher Kampf*) to the more loaded "horrifying murder" (*fürchterliches Morden*):[29]

> —In the sacred name of God, our heavenly Father and Lord, and for love of the sacred blood of Jesus, which was the price of man's redemption, we appeal to you, who are ordained by divine Providence to govern the belligerent nations, to put an end to this terrible slaughter which has now been dishonoring Europe for a whole year. It is the blood of our brothers which is being spilt on land and at sea.

> The most beautiful regions of Europe, this earthly Eden, are sown with corpses and ruins. (*LTM*, 190; *LDM*, 141)

The editor then "dictates," behind which stands deliberate semantic ambiguity:[30]

> —And the fish, the lobsters and the spider crabs of the Adriatic have seldom enjoyed such good times as at this moment. In the southern Adriatic they had almost the entire crew of the *Leon Gambetta* for dinner. In the central Adriatic they subsisted on those Italians we were unable to save from the *Turbine*, while in the northern Adriatic the denizens of the deep devour ever more opulent fare. (*LTM*, 191; *LDM*, 142)[31]

Of the two statements, the Pope's appears both the more sympathetic and the more helpless: readers then and now know that the war is not going to end any time soon. The mere juxtaposition exposes the limits of modern papal authority in its confrontation with the military industrial complex and the relentless competition driving national interest: the confluence of capital and journalism has overpowered Catholicism. The Pope's desperate plea for peace thus appears naive and impotent; in stark contrast is the callous dismissal of the lives of Italian soldiers by the press mogul. Much like the case of Schalek's representation, an earlier conversation between the "Patriot" and the "Subscriber" (to the *Press*) reveals the effects of the language of the press on private discourse, as Kraus sees it. Both figures parrot and misunderstand the editor, distorting his words by reading into them a statement about the moral superiority of the Austrians over the other warring nations. In a self-congratulatory manner, the Subscriber proclaims:

> And above all, unlike them we are always humane. For example, an editorial in the *Press* even talked about good times ahead for the fish and the crustacea in the Adriatic, with so many Italian corpses to feed on (*zu fressen bekommen*). Is that not the very height of humanity, to be mindful of the fish and crustacea in the Adriatic in these bitterly hard times, when even human beings are starving! (*LTM*, 119; *LDM*, 87)

Once again the larger narrative unfolds, as information seamlessly transfers from one source to the next until it enters the private domain. Whether these combined scenes evince Kraus's longing for the restoration of Catholic authority (and were therefore written during the early part of the war) is not the point. Rather, what we have on display is an abbreviated cross-section of modernity, the waning power of religion versus the waxing power of secular authorities such as the press, an issue to be further explored in chapter 4. Authority, it seems, has merely shifted venues, its locus of power no longer the Vatican but the more modest bureaucratic office, and its target of influence is not the soul now but the tongue. Depicted in these scenes are modern authorities authorizing and editing the experience of war for those in the hinterland, and such depictions address less the crisis of authority than the way authority circulates through the particular use of words, phrases, and dictations.

These quotations thus function as a kind of intervention. For by tracing their object—language—completely and leaving no remainder, they do away with the need for any external interpretation that might otherwise influence the relationship between an object or phenomenon and the critique of that object; such an interpretation necessarily relies on a fixed position from which it derives its epistemic authority. The only external gesture vis-à-vis quotation is the dialogic, performative element that summons the quotation to life in each character in order to sentence it to death, or to banish it from the authorial present to the memorialized past.[32] The fundamental task of quotation is to foreground the very mediation of war—what Perloff has called "the mediated war"—and thereby to render the ostensibly authoritative and necessary as merely contingent.[33] Schalek's statements are no longer embedded within her narrative, nor even in the fabric of Kraus's essays in *The Torch*, while Benedikt's words are negated in their confrontation with the Pope's. The very quoteability of these words renders visible their status as having-once-been-uttered and thus their new function as testimonies that speak unwittingly against their time. If the drama's aim, to recall, is to "portray[] the deeds they merely performed," then seemingly innocuous words that once obscured or suppressed traumatic experiences can be viewed as the catalyst for a new mode of experience.

The sheer act of repetition thus thematizes the role of memory at various junctures in the text. Two nearly identical phone conversations between a General Staff Officer and a Journalist—in act II, scene 16, and act III, scene 22—revolve around the historic fortress of Przemysl, which had belonged to the Austrians since the eighteenth century, was besieged by the Russians during the first few months of the war, and was finally liberated by the Central Powers in June 1915, constituting the most protracted siege of the war.[34] Below I have reproduced an excerpt of the first of these conversations. As readers we are privy only to the General Staff Officer's part of the dialogue, not the Journalist's:

> —Hello there (*Servus*), have you got the report on Przemysl ready?—Not yet? Ah, still sleeping it off—Go and see to it, otherwise you'll be late again for the bash in the mess (*kommst wieder zum Mullattieren zu spät*). Now look here—What, forgotten everything again?—Ye gods (*Ös seids*)–Listen, and get it into your head this time—Main points: First, the fortress was absolutely worthless in any case (*die Festung war eh nix wert*). That's the key point—How's that? You can't—What, you can't get people to forget the fortress has always been the pride and joy of—My dear fellow, you can make people forget anything (*Alles kann man

> *vergessen machen*)! So listen, the fortress was a dilapidated old ruin (*lauter altes Graffelwerk*)—What's that? All the latest artillery? I'm telling you, a dilapidated old ruin, got that? All right, then. Secondly, do you hear, the loss was not due to enemy action, but to hunger, OK? (*LTM*, 274; *LDM*, 203)

And below an abridged version of the conversation in act III:

> —Hello, have you got the report on Przemysl ready?—Not yet? Ah, still sleeping it off—Go and see to it, otherwise you'll be late again for the bash in the mess—yes, it is on—Now look here—What, forgotten everything again?—Listen, here are the main points: Everyone knows we lost Przemysl because our garrison was at starvation point, remember?—now the situation is quite diffic (*jetzt ganz was andreas*)—different—the enemy succumbed to our superior strength, no way did he succumb to hunger, the enemy was never starving! Only we were! The Russians always had plenty of provisions—but they couldn't withstand the vigorous assault of our brave troops, stands to reason—the force of our attack—Moreover: the fortress is completely undamaged, we took possession of it intact—and all the latest artillery—What? We can't make people—just old junk? No, no, of course we don't say that anymore (*jetzt nicht mehr natürlich*)! My dear fellow, you can make people forget anything! (*LTM*, 364; *LDM*, 271–72)[35]

At stake in the two exchanges is nothing less than the fate of a collective memory, or the recording of an experience whose existence threatens to be removed from history. The issue is not merely how propaganda functions, or how information is manipulated, but the role that the mediation of this information plays in the process of memory-formation and memory-destruction. In these nearly identical conversations (and future dispatches), the General of Staff makes clear that as long as the event is reported in such a way, Austrians will just as easily forget that this dilapidated fortress had once been the pride of their nation as they will remember it as soon as it has been recaptured: "My dear fellow, you can make people forget everything," the General of Staff assures his interlocutor in both scenes. Yet the doubling of this key phrase in the two conversations works against the intention of its speaker, insofar as it reminds its readers not only not to forget, but not to forget that everything can be so quickly forgotten. Phrased otherwise: the two scenes actively work against the act of forgetting that is framed in the drama as central to the war's very means of persistence. The subsequent alteration of the narrative from the first to the second monologue regarding who was starving and who succumbed due to sheer force renders the General of Staff a figure of authority, wholly capable of editing a collective memory that pertains to something as allegedly significant as one's national heritage. But if this forced forgetting is tantamount to the erasure of a collective experience, its recording in the drama would be an attempt at its preservation—the issue at stake is not the fortress, but memory itself.[36]

Through various modes of textual repetition, the drama addresses the experience of temporality during the war. *The Last Days* maintains only a loose correspondence to the war's historical unfolding, a not insignificant formal feature. Kurt Krolop has for this reason characterized the structure of the play as a "time frame (*Zeitraum*) without 'origin' and without future."[37] In other words, the play treats the war as if it had no marked beginning and no foreseeable end, a thought reinforced, as we will see, by some of the Grumbler's own comments. Here it would make sense to recall Kraus's use of the term *Zeitdinge* in the prologue, a vision of spatialized time filled with events that collapse into each other and become indistinguishable; this, the drama suggests, is one way in which the war is being experienced. The frequent reprisal of scenes with only minor differences thus functions as a critique of this experience: the longer the war drags on and the more exacting its toll on the populations affected, the more glaring (to us as readers) is the sameness in its representation to the public—and yet, paradoxically, the less that sameness is perceived by the drama's characters, who have adjusted their response mechanisms to this form of representation. This phenomenon is perhaps best represented in the opening scene of each act of the play, which commences with a newspaper vendor in Vienna shouting out the latest headline in the same manner, followed by a nearly identical conversation among various passers-by. Below are excerpts from the opening scenes of acts III, IV, and V:

> FIRST NEWSPAPER VENDOR. Ex-tra-aa edi-shun—! Venice bombarded! Eye-talians routed! (*Schwere Niederlage der Italiena!*) . . .[38]
> FIRST OFFICER (*to three others*). Evening Nowotny, evening Pokorny, evening Powolny—the very man! You know all about politics. Come on, tell us, what d'ya say to Romania? (*LTM*, 323; *LDM*, 240)

> FIRST NEWSPAPER VENDOR. Ex-tra-aa edi-shun—! Eye-talians annoyilated! (*Varnichtete Niedelaga der Italiena!*) . . .
> FIRST OFFICER. Evening Nowotny, evening Pokorny, evening Powolny—the very man! You know all about politics. Come on, tell us, what do you think about America? (*LTM*, 425; *LDM*, 318)

> VOICE OF A NEWS VENDOR. Evening paper—eight o'clock edition! (*Der Aabeend, Aachtuhrblaad!*)
> FIRST OFFICER (*to three others*): Evening Nowotny, evening Pokorny, evening Powolny—the very man! You know all about politics. Come on, tell us, what d'ya think about Bulgaria? (*LTM*, 553; *LDM*, 418)

For the drama's stock characters, these headlines essentially present the same event having repeated itself with only minor differences. The dialogue that ensues in each iteration mirrors the temporality of the war as it is being *reported*. Time, and the plot that appears to be wedged within it, is at a standstill, and the potential experience of such events in their utter singularity has been foreclosed. Helmut Arntzen has, accordingly, argued that unlike traditional dramatic dialogue, the plot is not pushed along via thesis and antithesis, but rather by the "stage-prop effect" (*Kulissenhaftigkeit*) of the events transpiring. These characters do not engage in dialogue so much as an "idiomatic parlando," prompting the reader to make independent judgments regarding what has actually happened.[39] The headlines above are the sole determinant of the discourse that ensues in each successive scene, producing the impression that the events reported exist in a temporal vacuum, isolated and contingent rather than the product of agency and action. The nonidentical is rendered identical (Romania becomes America, which becomes Bulgaria), a discourse that will resurface in my investigation of Adorno's dialogue with Kraus in chapter 5. Symptom and etiology collide as the headlines translate into public discourse, which, in turn, gets translated back into headlines. And yet: the sheer repetition of these scenes challenges the medial representation of war by making salient this coerced identity and the concomitant impression of an endless, exitless present.

On the one hand, then, the drama features operetta-like figures that lack subjectivity and are absorbed into the war to such an extent that they are barred from an experience of its violence—their mutilated condition is only evident in their speech. Running parallel to this feature of the drama, however, is a dialogue between the Grumbler and the Optimist, the former of whom tries to create space for reason and critique despite the mounting chaos and his increasing despair. The Grumbler, in other words, tries to establish an alternative discourse that radically challenges the mode of experience described above. In aiming to rewrite the war, he casts his gaze away from the present and toward posterity.

Pledging to Posterity: The Case of the Grumbler

In his work on early modern English satire, Fredric Bogel has written that while satirists "often seem to be devoted to a lucid and purely oppositional single-mindedness, the shadow of connection [to the object of ridicule] is always there."[40] In other words, for Bogel, satirist and satirized are not as diametrically opposed as would appear to be the case. We encounter this predicament in the figure of the Grumbler. Both the anchor of the drama as well as its self-proclaimed author—"I have written a tragedy whose doomed hero is mankind," he claims—the Grumbler cannot escape the world he subjects to relentless critique (*LTM*, 671; *LDM*, 509).[41] He is not a mere commentator on the plot or a modern analog to the ancient chorus, and he should not be conflated with Kraus himself, as some critics have argued, for that would undermine the role of artifice in the drama's structure.[42] Fundamental to his position is his insistence that those who "describe" or "edit" the war create the false impression of being distant to it, a distance that forecloses awareness of their own implication in that which is being described. Insofar as the Grumbler suffers with the reality he confronts, he cannot remain apart from it, and this mode of self-awareness marks his discourse as distinct from the Journalist's.[43] He would be incomplete, however, without his counterpart, the Optimist, whose consistent interjections throughout their dialogue represent the broken remnants of "healthy common sense" that the Grumbler finds plagued from the outset.[44] Perloff thus compares the Optimist to the naive interlocutor in Plato's dialogues (subsequently made familiar by Denis Diderot in *Rameau's Nephew*), and yet the Optimist is the only character that acknowledges and engages with the Grumbler, attempting—if failing—to understand his arguments and positions.[45]

In a key dialogue appearing toward the end of the first act, the Grumbler thus aims to distinguish his position from others around him. He first juxtaposes the Optimist's insensitivity to the war's implications against his own eye, which "perceives the contours" that others do not see, and his own ear, which hears the noises "that others don't hear": "For the moment, I can only tell the public I am keeping silent, and if possible, what I am keeping silent" (*LTM*, 224; *LDM*, 166). In other words, the Grumbler claims to have heightened senses that allow him to perceive things that go unnoticed by others, whose imaginations have failed them: he is no augur or prophet, but rather a careful observer. For the Grumbler, it is a matter of listening and seeing more clearly than others, as if reason could be achieved by refining one's sense apparatus, which he clearly feels has been damaged by modern institutions, technologies, and political endeavors. Characterizing the Optimist as the "prompter" of his own thoughts, the Grumbler needs only a few words to hold court. And if the Optimist is the mouthpiece of official discourse, remaining optimistic despite the mounting catastrophes befalling the Central Powers, then the Grumbler aims to parry this logic with what he calls silence, which I take to be an indication of the unspoken truths that inhere in the Optimist's own logic. The Grumbler's monologues qua dialogues are the platform for his dialectics, as he counters each and every defense of the war by making explicit what such a defense expresses implicitly. This process further contributes to his attempt at creating a counterdiscourse to journalism, an utterly distinct mode of language. This would explain why the Optimist's misunderstandings only increase as the drama (and the war) spirals further into chaos: "Again, I don't follow you," he helplessly claims, indicating not only his cluelessness, but also the Grumbler's resolute refusal to more straightforwardly communicate with his interlocutor (*LTM*, 409; *LDM*, 307). If the latter undergoes any sort of development in the drama, it must be identified in the ever-widening gap between these two competing discourses, in which reason and unreason, common sense and madness, have become thoroughly intertwined. It is worth examining some of these exchanges to gain a sense of the content of the Grumbler's discourse.

Early on in the drama, the Optimist tries to explain to the Grumbler that during war, unintended consequences invariably arise and that certain adjustments in our expectations need to be made regarding the status and quality of human life. As is usually the case, the Optimist cannot seem to follow the Grumbler's train of thought. For the mordant Grumbler, "Heroic death hovers in a cloud of gas, and we experience only the choked wording of a communiqué! The bodies of 40,000 Russians twitching on the barbed wire were simply a special bulletin." This war, he goes on, is a force of total negation insofar as it reduces all individual "qualities" to indistinguishable "quantities." To the question of what remains, he thus responds:

> There are quantities which are mutually self-destructive in equal measure (*die sich gegenseitig gleichmäßig vermindern*), as they attempt to prove that they are no match for quantities transformed into mechanical energies. In other words, that massed troops can be obliterated by mortars (*daß der Mörser auch mit Massen fertig werden*). It was only the lack of imagination remaining after the transformation of mankind into mechanical energy that made this experiment possible and provided the proof. (*LTM*, 210–11; *LDM*, 156–57)

By drawing attention to violence rather than heroism, the alliterative features of the Grumbler's language (*Mörser* and *Massen*) polemicize rather than aestheticize. Indeed, the loaded concept of the "hero's death" (*Heldentod*) received considerable attention from Kraus, as it indicated the extent to which anachronistic, romantic ideas of war were integrated into the propaganda machine.[46] In the statement above, the concept is brutally ironized through its glaring contrast to the impersonal death that results from gas and machine warfare. If, for Robert Musil, modernity has produced men "without qualities," for the Grumbler, war has produced quantities without men, a world in which the individual has been completely liquidated and yet is still celebrated as a hero.[47] Looking closer, he also calls this war an "experiment," placing it within a trajectory of Enlightenment, progressivist thinking that has gone awry of its own making. His larger point is that modern warfare entails no epiphenomena, but only various expressions of the same phenomenon. This war was not to be viewed as a caesura, but rather as the event that made visible the implications of modernity's regressive, violent, and shortsighted impulses, and of its "transformation of mankind into mechanical energy."[48] For the Grumbler, this process has led to the suspension of human agency (since it has led to the suspension of the human as such) along with the destruction of the distinctly human faculty of imagination. In this way, the Grumbler envisions a war that emerges from the relationship between unfettered technological "progress" and a damaged sensory apparatus, a vision that has rendered it increasingly difficult to experience any world beyond the confines of this war.

In light of this predicament, the existential concerns that emerge for the Grumbler are formulated as questions and accusations regarding guilt and responsibility.[49] To whom or to which institutions can the responsibility for the war be ascribed when, as the Grumbler states, "we were prepared to live and breathe in a world which wages wars for which it can make no one responsible" (*LTM*, 412–13; *LDM*, 310)? This statement appears in the context of a conversation in which the imperial foreign minister, Leopold Berchtold—a major player in the war—is invoked, but the indictment is a self-indictment, as the Grumbler suggests that it is "we" who have created the conditions of possibility for such "rogues" to play this dangerous game. On the one hand, he identifies the destructive forces in collusion with each other—journalists, bureaucrats, generals, statesmen, scientists, poets, and war profiteers—on the other, he must concede that he belongs to this very world, that he played an instrumental role in its formation. Indeed, his concession of guilt appears to be the only thing that grants him the authority to make such definitive claims about the guilt of others. In response to the Optimist's earlier question about what the Grumbler must keep silent about (quoted earlier), the latter responds:

> . . . That this war of today is nothing but an outbreak of peace, and that it cannot be ended by peace, but by the war of the cosmos against this rabid planet! That innumerable human beings had to be sacrificed, not to be lamented simply because an alien will drove them to the slaughterhouse, but as tragic victims compelled to atone for an unknown guilt. (*LTM*, 224; *LDM*, 166)

It would seem that for the Grumbler, the tragedy of the war is not only that those fighting it are alienated from its cause and the powers who are waging it, though this is certainly a significant component that elicits the Grumbler's sympathy. Equally tragic is the reality that the soldiers have become sacrifices for, or victims of the war and still must atone for a guilt of which they remained wholly unaware, since they were invariably participating in acts of violence and thus contributing to the war machine. The Grumbler is ultimately speaking about a kind of alienation from both the state apparatus and from one's own conscience—another "by-product" of war that is really one of its expressions.

Yet just after he claims that the only way the war could end would be through another war waged by the cosmos against the entire planet, the Grumbler's tense crucially shifts from present to past, suggesting that he is beginning to view this war from the perspective of posterity looking backward, or from that of a historian paradoxically speaking both to and from the moment he is addressing. This feature of his discourse is crucial to further understanding his function in the drama, and it is one of the central ways in which the Grumbler relates the madness of a war to something like a collective death wish.[50]

For the discourse of the press, the Grumbler substitutes an address to posterity; for the inability to experience the war in the full range of its impact, his own experience; and for criticism of the enemy, a relentless self-critique. Yet if the Grumbler envisions a world beyond that which currently exists, he refuses to renounce his Austrian citizenship and the responsibility this entails, an issue that will resurface in chapter 2. In another conversation with the Optimist about the irresponsibility of the various heads of state, and more specifically about the criminal misdeeds of Count Berchtold, the Grumbler interjects with equal parts pathos and irony: "They knew not what they did, none of them. . . . The Germans are the innocent instigators, the Austrians the fleecy lambs (*mir san die reine Lamperln*). Neither can help it" (*LTM*, 409; *LDM*, 307).[51] Turning Austria's claim to innocence against itself and rendering Germany's aggression a result of Austria's prodding, the Grumbler undermines the legitimacy of both parties. That neither "can help it" is precisely the problem. This is a war that produces an immeasurable death toll but no remorse, immediate goals but no endgame, and actions executed that exceed the imaginative capacities of their executors.[52] For the Grumbler, this war thus portends the "real war" that will erupt in the future, when such a mentality will have come to define the standard of normalcy:

> The returning warriors will break through into the home front and launch the real war. They will grab for themselves the successes they had been denied, and the impact of war—murder, pillage, rape—will be child's play compared with the peace that will then break out. May the god of battles protect us from this coming offensive! A terrible agitation, liberated from the trenches and no longer constrained by any system of command, will start wielding weapons and seeking sensual gratifications in every sphere of life, and more death and disease will come into the world than could ever be contrived by the war itself. May heaven protect the children from the sabres that will serve as canes for spanking, and from the grenades brought back for them as toys. (*LTM*, 207; *LDM*, 154)

As a prelude to the postwar mood that Kraus had anticipated as early as 1915, this passage would certainly confirm Krolop's labeling of Kraus's play as a "warning play." But there is more to excavate from this passage. First, the Grumbler appropriates the language of war in order to ironize it: in pleading for protection from the god of battles against the coming offensive, he suggests that only a warlike mentality will be able to defend Europeans against the paradoxically violent peace that will soon break out. Second, the Grumbler again points to the egregious lack of foresight that went into declaring and fighting this war. The returning soldiers will become the *Freikorps* (the right-wing paramilitary militias consisting largely of World War I veterans that formed as a result of the German Revolution of 1918–1919), and their children, the soldiers of World War II, but the Grumbler does not have to intuit these actualities in order to predict that the belated effects of the war might outweigh its immediate consequences. When the Optimist naively replies without hesitation that it is, indeed, dangerous for children to play with grenades, he reveals a blatant misunderstanding. The two competing modes of discourse directly confront one another: on the one hand, the Grumbler's attempt to turn the language of war against itself, and, on the other, the Optimist's commentary, which restates a truism while betraying the absence of genuine comprehension. Again, the Grumbler does not augur as much as he draws attention to detail, suggesting that the future will be hardly more than an extension of the present. This insight, once again, recalls the term *Zeitdinge*, Kraus's nightmarish vision of modern temporality as an ever-expanding present, the collapsing of time into space that precludes the possibility of a genuine future. This he opposes to the ideology responsible for marketing the war as the crowning achievement of technological progress.

The Grumbler thus wants to depict this image from outside the catastrophe, as it were, but also realizes that he cannot speak from any such position, since he despairs over the possibility that there could be an end to the war in sight. And yet, by virtue of his utterances, he secures a place for critique in an effort to detotalize this war, to speak and write against it. One brief exchange that makes this predicament particularly salient presents us with a frustrated Optimist who cannot light his cigarette due to a faulty match. The Grumbler attributes this failure to the ultimatum on Serbia, confounding the Optimist, who fails to see the logic. "I said, the match won't light!" the Optimist asserts, to which the Grumbler confidently replies, "And I say, that's because we managed to set the world alight (*die Welt in Brand zu setzen*)!" (*LTM*, 658–59; *LDM*, 500). It is impossible to light a match—let alone an entire torch—when the whole world has been set ablaze. Assuming guilt for the war when nobody else will, the Grumbler simultaneously sees himself as merely another "noise" produced by it and implicated in its production, despite his desire to unravel its plots and machinations and assign blame to various actors and agents. At the border between intelligibility and insanity, he sits at his desk and finally proclaims:

> And if the times no longer hear, surely an ear above shall hear. I have done no more than condense the scale of mass murder (*diese tödliche Quantität verkürzt*), taking the measure of the amorphous alliance between the age of journalism and the journalism of the age (*die sich in ihrer Unermeßlichkeit auf den Unbestand von Zeit und Zeitung beriefe*). Its blood was merely ink—now the writing will be in blood! This is the World War. This is my manifesto. *I have weighed everything*

> *in the balance* (*Ich habe alles reiflich erwogen*). The tragedy, fractured into scenes reflecting mankind's fallen state (*die in Szenen der zerfallenden Menschheit zerfällt*), I have taken upon myself, so that it may be heard by a spirit that takes pity on the victims, even if it had renounced forever all connection to a human ear. Let it hear the keynote of these times, the echo of my bloodthirsty obsession, which makes me complicit (*mitschuldig*) with these cries. Let it be an act of redemption!
>
> (*From outside, at a great distance, the cry:—"Ex—traaa!"*) (*LTM*, 681; *LDM*, 516)

Apocalyptic pathos blends with ironic quotation, effectively combined in Franz Josef's notorious wartime proclamation, "I have weighed everything in the balance," which the Grumbler has incorporated—*eingeschöpft*—into his monologue and imbued with new meaning. His parting words consummate his monumental attempt to rewrite this war, and in so doing, to declare war on the World War itself.[53] Perhaps the Grumbler's sense of guilt stems from the realization that he can only undertake an act of rewriting. And yet while it is too late for him to intervene in any meaningful way, it may not be too late to be heard (or read) by a future generation.[54] This tension is also visible in the Grumbler's pathos, which can only be sustained until the distant cry of the newsvendor interrupts it, an interruption suggesting that the Grumbler's words and his claim to authority are lost on his contemporaries. In his inability to remain detached, or, like the Journalist, merely "describe" the events that have transpired, the Grumbler is eventually consumed by madness. His attempt to posit an alternative discourse to the newspaper and to mediate a more authentic experience has failed, at least in his own eyes. All he is capable of is repeating the sounds of war, which is why the "keynote" of the era—that which unites all of the minor notes into one resounding and lasting sound—is the echo of *his* "bloodthirsty obsession," and not vice versa. This declaration once again raises the question of the Grumbler's audience.[55]

For while he has renounced his age (*die Mitwelt*), the Grumbler simultaneously sees it as his charge to preserve the language of war for a future generation, one qualitatively distinct from his own: a genuine posterity (*die Nachwelt*). Kraus already hints at this notion in his preface, and there are similar indications throughout the text that this is his intended audience:

> And it is to be feared that some future age, sprung from the loins of this desolate generation (*wüsten Gegenwart*), will have no greater power of understanding, despite being at a greater distance. Yet an unqualified admission of guilt at belonging to mankind, as it currently exists, must at some place and time be welcomed and valued. (*LTM*, 10–11; *LDM*, 2)

Despite its pessimism regarding the next generation's ability to comprehend the crimes of Kraus's generation, the passage also contains the faint hope that a humanity of a different era might one day recognize his atonement and therefore the moment to which such an admission of guilt belonged. This curious admixture of hope and cynicism carries over into the Grumbler's own discourse, evidenced once again in his parting monologue, when he makes his pledge to posterity: "I have preserved documents for an epoch that will no longer comprehend them or will say that I forged them, so remote will they be from today. But that day will never come for there will be no survivors" (*LTM*, 671; *LDM*, 509). The Grumbler welcomes the possibility that his words will one day be illegible to an audience because its reality is so radically distinct from the Grumbler's. At the same time, he is convinced that no true survivors will emerge from this catastrophe, and thus that there will be no genuine audience for his message. And yet the Grumbler still claims to be preserving documents, rendering himself a witness not only to the war, but to those who bear false witness, those who transmit a distorted version of the experience of war to both the present and to posterity.[56] False testimonies are consumed daily; the words of the witness might only be understood by the Grumbler's imagined future audience. At stake is the very legacy of the war itself.

The Grumbler's greatest fear is that the war and everything it entails will never come to an end; that his moment, in other words, will never become posterity and thus part of history, leading him to meditate on the phenomenon of historical amnesia (a central focus of the next chapter). He declares:

> [This war] didn't play out on the surface of life, but in its very core. The fighting front has expanded back into the hinterland. There it will stay. And our same old mental attitudes will be applied to an altered life—if there still is life. Like the sun, the world will set, and we won't notice. All our yesterdays will be forgotten; we will not see what today means; nor fear for the future. We will have forgotten that we lost the war, forgotten that we started it, forgotten that we waged it. That is why it will never cease. (*LTM*, 659; *LDM*, 500)[57]

The repetition of the word "forgotten" resonates with the earlier scenes between the General of Staff and the Journalist regarding the capture and recapture of the Przemysl fortress and thus could be read as a commentary or reflection on those exchanges and the type of historical consciousness they evoked. But we also have to read this statement in the context of the Grumbler's final words: if the war never ends, neither will the Grumbler's grumblings, insofar as his very intelligibility depends on the war's continued existence, in whatever form it may take.[58] As he had claimed earlier, the peace that is to come will be nothing compared to the war that will have just ended. The paradox is that he longs for a true posterity, which, however, would consist of an audience for whom his language would be unintelligible, since merely to recognize it would be to betray one's own implication in it. But in order to become this posterity, he implicitly admonishes his audience not to forget the war, lest it continue without end and intensify in its expression. This predicament highlights one of the text's central critical-philosophical concerns: At what point does a *Mitwelt* become a *Nachwelt*, both within the text proper and in terms of modernity's temporal modalities more broadly conceived? A liminal figure at the threshold of these two worlds, the Grumbler believes he is writing a text that will never end, while hoping to be proven wrong. Unable to comprehend his age any more than it is able to comprehend him, he ultimately merges with the insanity he has diagnosed around him.

This perspective is, finally, important for interpreting the Grumbler's self-consciousness of his paradoxical position within and outside of his text, a position best illustrated in a scene involving a postcard of the recently hanged Italian politician, Cesare Battisti, and next to him, his gleeful executioners. This arresting image (see next page) also serves as the frontispiece to the published drama, demonstrating the emblematic value it contains beyond the scene in which it is directly invoked. To the Optimist, the Grumbler states:

> For as some were being hanged, others were posing for the camera (*es wurde auch gestellt*); and photos were taken not only of the executions, but also of the spectators, and even of the photographers. The consequence of our bestiality (*Scheußlichkeit*) is that enemy propaganda has no need to photograph our deeds, since instead of lying it now simply reproduces our truths, having to its surprise discovered our own photos of our deeds at the scene of the crime. Thus it has a comprehensive picture of us, utterly lacking in self-awareness (*Ahnungslosigkeit*). . . . For it is not the fact that [the criminal] is a killer, nor that he photographed his crime, but that he photographed himself as well (*daß er sich mitphotographiert hat*), and that he photographed himself photographing it—that's what makes this type an imperishable (*unvergänglichen*) snapshot of our civilization. As if what we have done did not speak for itself! (*LTM*, 510; *LDM*, 385)[59]

For the Grumbler, this photograph provides an image of the concentric circles of complicity fueling the war. At the center stands the deed of execution, but just as reprehensible are the grinning perpetrators who surround the victim; more incriminating, their pose for the camera; and worse than that, the photograph and the photographer that capture the entire scene. Finally, we can add, there is the Grumbler offering the interpretation while holding the photo in his hand. The image reappears once again as one of the last "apparitions" prior to the drama's convulsive epilogue, "The Last Night."[60] These truths, the Grumbler concludes, are the real lies, which speak louder than the conventional lies told by the enemy nations. But it is also useful to conceive of this "imperishable" photograph—the photograph that, quite literally,

The hanging of Cesare Battisti (1916).

is *unable* to become the past—as a metonymy for the historical moment itself, which only threatens to grow more expansive without ever becoming history proper. The preservation of the photo alone guarantees, the Grumbler hopes, that such an image will not be forgotten, since it at the very least confirms that the event portrayed actually took place.[61] The inability to intervene in this scene is thus compensated by the vanishing but nonetheless residual plea that the photograph will be seen by a future generation; in this way, the Grumbler gives a quasi-phenomenological reading of the image as a piece of evidence that testifies against its time.[62] And yet the photograph also speaks to the paradox just elaborated, in that the genuine posterity the Grumbler anticipates would be one for which the content of this photograph, too, had become unrecognizable. Such a posterity would understand neither the crime portrayed nor the Grumbler's interpretation of it because the conditions that necessitated its existence would have all but disappeared. For posterity in the robust sense can only emerge once this entire historical epoch is understood as a discrete moment—an artifact—severed off from the moment that succeeds it. The Grumbler wants this moment to both perish *and* be recorded for posterity, and these tensions and paradoxes that thoroughly inform his character and function in the drama contribute to the drama's modernist sensibility.

To be sure: I have not attempted to provide an exhaustive account of *The Last Days*, having ignored some of its more formal innovations (such as the way it anticipates Brechtian epic theater).[63] Rather, I hope to have provided an insight into the way this text stages a tension between competing discourses, and what the implications of this tension are within the framework of the drama's larger critique of experience. On the one hand, journalistic discourse and its widespread influence are cited in order to put on display the entire apparatus at work, including its understanding of the *time* of war. At stake is not simply the juxtaposition of true and false accounts of the war, but the desire to show how the war was being staged and edited and therefore recorded for those in the hinterland; with this, Kraus anticipates the phenomenon of "coordination" (*Gleichschaltung*) that he would mercilessly critique in the context of National Socialism. The quotations in the text—both real and invented—are the drama's evidence of how the war was making its way from the battlefield to public to private discourse, incurring further harm to an already damaged sensory apparatus that could perceive suffering as spectacle. The Grumbler's function, in part, is to rewrite this war by attempting to convey his experience to members of his own milieu who were guilty of, at best, watching the war from afar, and at worst, profiting from it. His unyielding belief in the ability to generate empathy constitutes one of the drama's central ethical impulses. But the Grumbler faces his own internal conflict in the dual realization that he, too, is a cocreator of the world he renounces and a failure in his attempt to offer a total account of the war—he thereby points to the many complexities entailed in the attempt to critique the whole of which one is ineluctably a part. His enduring, if weak, hope is that he is transmitting a message in a bottle.

Chapter 2

✦

On Birds, Wars, and Fragile Republics

Cloudcuckooland (1923)

> It is, certainly, a question of filth. But because the bird who finds his own nest befouled, the bird whose own nest befouls him, wishes to cleanse it, since he has the longing and possesses the courage for this labor, the other birds, who feel quite comfortable and at home in the filth, say that he 'befouls' the nest.
>
> —Karl Kraus, "The Bird Who Befouls His Own Nest" (1928)

> But to where does one flee when the earth itself no longer offers sanctuary?
>
> —Emil Schinck, "Introduction," *The Birds: A Comedy by Aristophanes* (c. 1880)

Among the first questions provoked by *Cloudcuckooland*, Kraus's 1923 adaptation of the ancient Greek comedy *The Birds* (414 B.C.E.), is why Aristophanes, a figure who occupies a relatively minor—though not entirely negligible—role in Kraus's work?[1] And why this allegory, in particular, to address Austria's postwar experience? *The Birds*, in brief, opens with two disgruntled former Athenians, Peistetaerus and Euelpides, seeking out a new home, free of the ills of city life. Athens, they declare, has become burdensome and corrupt; what they desire is a freer and more peaceful abode, where their desires are immediately gratified. In their perambulation they encounter the half-man, half-bird Tereus, who has been living among the bird community for a while, and Peistetaerus proposes the construction of a city in the sky as a solution to their earthly problems. The more ambitious of the two, Peistetaerus delivers a resounding speech to the initially reluctant birds—who believe humans to be their natural enemy—that convinces them of his plan and of their inherent divinity, which they accept as superior to that of the Olympian gods. To these gods they will no longer offer sacrifices. During the construction of "Cloudcuckooland," however, Peistetaerus receives a series of unwanted visitors, each trying to sell a service or a product and thus contributing to the creation of a city that resembles precisely that which it was supposed to replace: Athens. The ethereal city is finally completed and the gods are unsatisfied. Eventually, Prometheus notifies Peistetaerus of the gods' recent bird-induced starvation and desperately pleads for a treaty with the birds. Peistetaerus concedes, but only under certain conditions. The leader of Cloudcuckooland easily negotiates with the half-witted delegates sent to represent the Olympians, and the play ends—in accordance with the conventions of Old Comedy—in celebration, with the erstwhile wanderer Peistetaerus regaled with the scepter, Zeus's girlfriend, and the throne.[2]

Kraus's "fantastical verse-play," which he dedicated to his friend Berthold Viertel, transposes the basic premise and structure of *The Birds* against the background of the contemporary political moment, allegorizing the early years of Austria's First Republic.[3] Unthinkable apart from the lingering memory of war and the Dual Monarchy—that is, from the specters of the recent past—Kraus's foray into the world of Attic comedy can also be viewed as a pendant to *The Last Days*.[4] For while it is ostensibly set in ancient Greece, *Cloudcuckooland* begins, in one sense, where *The Last Days* concludes: namely, after a war has ended and a republic has been founded. Yet in a radical departure from the Aristophanean original, Kraus's version stages, in its third and final act, a war between the birds and the gods, thereby also taking place prior to and during the "last days of mankind." Its temporal structure is indeed one of its formal peculiarities. A hesitant but committed supporter of the First Republic (until the political situation got significantly worse, a moment to be explored in chapter 3), Kraus conceived of his drama as an affirmation of what he called the "republican thought," performing his most cherished and celebratory reading in front of a group of workers.[5] But, as he declared during a 1929 reading in Berlin, his "republican festival drama" was simultaneously, and, perhaps, primarily, intended as a protest against "a monarchical entity smothered in blood and excrement" (*D*, 384).[6] It was thus meant to be as critical of the past as it was affirmative of the future.[7] But what specifically does the play negate and what does it affirm?

Like most of Kraus's dramatic endeavors (aside from *The Last Days*), the play has received limited—and largely negative—critical attention. Franz Mautner, for example, provides a close philological analysis of *Cloudcuckooland*, but he discusses its allegorical significance only briefly. The play, he argues, is essentially a "Viennesation" of the original, with both felicitous and awkward results. On the one hand, Kraus's "bird-world" is more developed and more colorful than Aristophanes's (bird-related metaphors and puns abound), while, on the other, the presence of Viennese dialects and World War I-derived jargon often conflicts with its ostensible setting in Athens.[8] The central contradiction Mautner thus identifies in the play is between what he calls the "satirist of great style" and his decidedly *un*satirical engagement with politics.[9] In a more recent evaluation, Bernhard Greiner argues that while Aristophanes's original produces pleasure through its carnivalesque transgressions and inversions, Kraus's decidedly more satirical adaptation is limited in the way it seeks to clarify its political positions and construct oppositions. Greiner's argument is that comedy—at least Old Comedy—enables a fullness of, and an indeterminacy within meaning that Kraus's satire forecloses, which relies on ridicule and the delineation of clear boundaries to produce its effect.[10] Greiner's argument effectively amounts to a (not entirely uncommon) critique of modern satire; because, the argument goes, Kraus's play devolves into violence (departing from Aristophanes in tone and content), Kraus must ultimately aim at total annihilation, a solution Greiner rejects as aesthetically facile.

Neither of these readings, however, sufficiently addresses the relationship between the two satirists "of great style" who were writing at the twilight of their respective empires (Athens and Austria-Hungary). And neither is sensitive to what I view as the constitutive ambiguity of Kraus's political allegory.[11] Thus perhaps more helpful for our purposes would be the reading of Aristophanes's play offered by Heinrich Heine in the nineteenth century, who viewed *The Birds* through a very different lens. For Heine, the play does not end in jubilation as it appears to do, but rather in the celebratory union of folly and power; from his perspective, there is nothing more tragic than that.[12] Kraus's adaptation foregrounds, I argue, a similar tension between its dystopian and its utopian impulses. To be sure, its aesthetic inconsistency occasionally reveals traces of having been written in haste; my aim is not to redeem this drama as an overlooked masterpiece.[13] Yet we would be remiss to ignore how *Cloudcuckooland* is interested—both on the level of its allegorical structure and on that of its recurring themes—in the experience of renewal and thus in the conditions of possibility for the emergence of a political tabula rasa. Kraus's textual rearrangement offers both insightful reflections on the yet-to-be-fulfilled promise of social democracy, as well as a warning about the precarious relationship between Austria's recent past and its potential future.

"All the Birds Are Here Again"

> Idiocy will blame the Republic. For in longing after the times that made everyone dumb, the Republic may no longer be capable of completing the shortest train of thought, which goes something like this: the monarchy brought us the war, the war brought us the ruin, the ruin brought us the Republic. But no, republicans perceive only the simultaneity of Republic and ruin: the Republic has brought us the ruin. Going backwards will be easier—and if at all possible, let's omit the way station: the ruin shall bring us the monarchy.
>
> —Kraus, "Specters" (1919)

> *Die Dummheit wird der Republik die Schuld geben. Denn sie, die in Sehnsucht nach den Zeiten lebt, die sie dumm gemacht haben, vermag den kürzesten Gedankengang nicht mehr zurücklegen. Etwa so: Die Monarchie hat uns den Krieg gebracht, der Krieg den Ruin, der Ruin die Republik. Nein, sie gewahrt nur die Gleichzeitigkeit von Republik und Ruin: die Republik hat uns den Ruin gebracht. Zurück gehts leichter—somit tunlichst mit Auslassung der Zwischenstation: der Ruin soll uns die Monarchie bringen.*
>
> (*F* 514, 23, 1919; *BL*, 11)

In the opening scene of *Cloudcuckooland*, the two disgruntled Athenians—now Ratefreund ("trustworthy friend") and Hoffegut ("good hope")—have, like their dramatic predecessors, defected from Athens, though it appears to be a republican, post–Peloponnesian War Athens.[14] "Are we far from, or near to / our eagerly anticipated goal (*heißersehntem Ziel*)?" inquires Hoffegut during the opening exchange between the two protagonists (*D*, 111). With this he poses arguably the central question of the drama, for at this point they do not know what their goal or destination is, nor would they necessarily be able to recognize it should they stumble upon it; they simply know that returning home is not a viable option. It soon becomes clear (to us) that the Athens the two have abandoned resembles postwar Vienna in several ways. For one, the two friends out themselves as former aristocrats who detest the social and economic policies introduced by the new state. Since the war has ended, apartments are nearly impossible to come by, even for the rich. The prewar days are clearly an object of longing and desire.[15] Hence Ratefreund's early monologue, expressed in rhymed verse like much of the play's dialogue:

> They pluck the raisins from the dough;
> we're doomed to watch while on strike they go.
> Simply gawking makes everyone grey
> and our misfortune is the eight-hour day.
> Moreover, I said this the last time we met,
> we'll have to deal with unemployment benefits.
> The middle class, the landlord, the retiree-
> The tax burden weighs on us eternally.
> To our lord almighty we can only pray
> that he protects us from prol' and plague.
> What do you know, you birds of prey,
> you don't have any war loans today!
>
> *Sie klauben die Rosinen aus dem Teig;*
> *wir können zuschauen, jene machen Streik.*
> *Nur zuzuschaun, ist schon genug der Plag'*

und unser Unglück der Achtstundentag.
Dazu, ich sagt' es in der letzten Sitzung,
kommt noch die Arbeitslosenunterstützung.
Der Mittelstand, die Hausbesitzer, Rentner–
es liegt der Steuerdruck auf uns wie Zentner.
Wir können nur zu unserm Herrgott beten,
er schütze uns vor Pest und vor Proleten.
Was wißt denn ihr, ihr Geier, Reiher, Weihe,[16]
ihr habt doch alle keine Kriegsanleihe! (*D*, 118)

What initially appears as a utopian desire to discover a piece of "human-free earth" reveals itself as a lament about the dissolution of social hierarchies, the shorter workday, widespread disease, and war-incurred debt. It is clear that these are the factors that have driven out the two ex-patriots in the first place. But more importantly, it is clear that Ratefreund has failed to identify the proper relationship between the causes of war and the current state of their forsaken city; subsequently, the two reject the new Athens entirely, recalling the mentality (the "idiocy") Kraus had invoked in his 1919 essay "Specters" quoted above. The logical fallacy that equates the present misery with the current regime informs the thinking of Ratefreund and Hoffegut, but it is significant that neither of them has yet proclaimed a desire for restoration. Seeing themselves as victims who have been forced to take on the economic burdens of a burgeoning republic, they claim to want something new. They will soon project all of their desires onto the ostensibly untainted bird community, a community free of human intervention: a fantasy world of unfamiliarity and nonmimetic otherness that the itinerants view as everything Athens and the Athenians are not. The actual motives of Hoffegut and his "trustworthy comrade" (whose name, according to Leo Strauss, could also be rendered "persuader of his comrade") are thus from the beginning unclear, but the question of whether their desires can transcend their horizon of experience is implicitly introduced.[17]

As in Aristophanes's original, the two "bad luck birds" (*Pechvögel*)—one of the many ornithological puns littered throughout the drama—soon encounter Zaunschlüpfer (a Eurasian wren) and his master, Wiedehopf (a Eurasian hoopoe; in *The Birds*: Tereus), the bird-human hybrid who, having successfully assimilated into the bird community, would presumably have sympathy for their plight. Wiedehopf, however, rightly identifies them as aristocrats who are escaping the misery they helped instantiate, despite their claims to being republicans and to simply want to live as they do in "Cockaigne," the mythical land of plenty (*D*, 117). Wiedehopf is thus a crucial character in the drama—and, I would add, the first stand-in for Kraus qua political convert, insofar as he represents the very possibility of radical transformation on the individual level. He was once a human (perhaps even a former aristocrat) who then underwent a seemingly genuine conversion to the bird world. As Ratefreund claims: "As a human you recall our suffering and strife; / as a bird you have an overview of life" (*D*, 116). Wiedehopf's first speech is, accordingly, a bitingly ironic indictment of postwar Athens. It is ironic because he outwardly claims not to understand why Hoffegut no longer harbors love for his former city, while his message bespeaks a more keen awareness of the city's ills and thus the reasons why its inhabitants currently suffer. He inquires:

> How come? For among Athens's various treasures
> are its commonly popular musical pleasures.
> Even their misery they trumpet and cherish
> for we know the Athenian will never perish.
> They say that after the Peloponnesian War
> death's been embraced like never before,
> and being promoted in part for national glory,
> and in part to boost the tourism industry.
> They bestow honor upon those who don't matter
> while their robbers and thieves get obediently fatter.
> Their strength lies in their glaring weakness
> and thus the world adores their uniqueness.
> All day long they speak about money
> and how they're dreaming of milk and honey.
> In everything they see ornamentation
> and call such a form of decay sanitation.
>
> *Wie das? Dort wohnen doch die weltbekannten*
> *und allgemein beliebten Musikanten.*
> *Selbst Trübsal blasen sie dort fesch und munter*
> *und der Athener, sagt man, geht nicht unter.*[18]
> *Man sagt, nach den peloponnesischen Kriegen*
> *genießen den Tod sie in vollen Zügen*
> *und opfern teils nationaler Ehre,*
> *teils aber auch dem Fremdenverkehre.*
> *Sie verehren zumal ihre Zeitvertreiber*
> *und mästen gehorsamst ihre Räuber.*
> *Ihre Stärke liegt in ihren Schwächen*
> *und eben darum liebt sie alle Welt.*
> *So dürfen sie den ganzen Tag von Geld*
> *und was sie sonst nicht haben, sprechen.*
> *An allem Wesen sehn sie die Verzierung,*
> *und solches Siechtum nennen sie Sanierung.* (*D*, 117)

Ornament, greed, tourism, materialism, verbal incontinence: these are the problems afflicting postwar Athens, problems that, as we can see, can be easily beautified and thereby obscured through song and rhyme. But neither Ratefreund nor Hoffegut perceive the irony and continue their lament. Their desire to live among the "bird people"—where supposedly, when it rains, "one's already in the clouds" (*D*, 119)—is thus presented as an escapist fantasy, but we know that this is an escape from civic responsibility and from the dilapidated, immiserated, bureaucratic world these figures were instrumental in creating. Ratefreund and Hoffegut patently refuse, or are unable to recognize, their own implication in the social and political ills that Wiedehopf diagnoses, and their initial impulse is defection. What is their proposed solution? To colonize the heavens.

The idea of building a city in the sky comes to Ratefreund in a flash, but he first has to convince Wiedehopf that the birds—content as they are, living freely and "in flight"—will not know true happiness until they create a state recognized by international law (*Völkerrecht*): in other words, until they cease to live like birds (*D*, 120). This, of course, is not how Ratefreund presents his case; instead, he argues that it is only natural for the birds to build castles in the sky and to essentially take over the "heavenly" kingdom that they had previously only been renting. The irony is that Ratefreund has to sell the idea to Wiedehopf and, soon thereafter, the birds themselves, that the birds' new state will be a bulwark against the intrusion of humanity as well as the parasitic gods who have been regularly extracting sacrifices from their aviary subjects. The birds have indeed lived in a subordinate relation to the gods, and this aspect of their existence becomes the selling point of Ratefreund's plan, who convinces them that the gods will be finished once the birds have starved them (*D*, 121).[19] As the spokesman of the bird community who claims to have taught them how to speak, Wiedehopf is the first to embrace the plan; the promise of unprecedented status, of reversing the relationship between the birds and divinities, and of starving the latter is attractive. It is the "cunning" nature of the plan to block the passageway to their city-state and charge the gods a tariff for their sacrifices that Wiedehopf cannot resist, subtly hinting at the ways in which human motivations still play a role in his world (*D*, 121). After being introduced as a skeptical observer of the true motives and circumstances informing his visitors' self-imposed exile, Wiedehopf abandons this skepticism for the promise of power, a concept that appears to be wholly alien to the birds. Clearly overlooked or ignored by all parties involved is thus the crucial fact that the birds are already largely satisfied with their lot in life (apart from their subordination to the gods).

The birds are an ambiguous group, and their interpretation hinges on their allegorical indeterminacy. On the one hand, they are presented as crude, indistinguishable as a flock (despite being comprised of various bird species), prone to violence, and lacking in self-confidence: the silver-tongued Ratefreund convinces them both that humans are good and that they should become like them (*D*, 134). On the other hand, they elicit immediate sympathy insofar as they are promised something that should have reasonably belonged to them all along, and which they should therefore reasonably embrace: the right to self-determination and freedom from their subservience to the gods. They are, after all, older than the gods, and supposedly even older than the earth itself. As Hoffegut explains to the leader of the chorus of birds: "And once you've become master, there's no groveling at their feet; / then before every greenhorn Zeus will have to retreat. / For today we're entitled to self-determination, as I like to repeat!" (*D*, 131)[20] Ratefreund and Hoffegut entice the birds with dreams of power over both the realms below (the humans) and above (the divinities), making the plan more appealing by invoking the popular right of self-determination (*Selbstbestimmungsrecht*), however hollowed-out a term that may be for the former aristocrats.[21] Wiedehopf, however, appears not to understand the term, prompting Ratefreund to explain it metaphorically as the moment "when the chain breaks / and the prisoner becomes the jailer. / For in the life of a people it often succeeds, / that an erstwhile tyrant falls to his knees" (*D*, 131).[22] Ratefreund's more cynical definition of this term, we should note, presupposes the continued existence of a prison and thus the relationship between prisoner and jailer, concealing an ominous warning about what his intentions are, or least what might transpire despite his stated intentions. Can the cycle of power and subjugation be broken? The birds, Ratefreund eloquently argues, have become slaves to the gods; it is time for them to reverse this hierarchy and for their own divinity to be recognized. Even if he does not entirely endorse what he is saying, he is still able to articulate revolutionary fervor in an appealing and sympathetic way—he would, it seems, like to become half-bird just as Wiedehopf has. Indeed, he feels that this process would not be complete were he and Hoffegut to remain featherless (*D*, 139).

It is still, however, unclear regarding what sort of society is to be formed out of this previously stateless community, which is in some sense both prehuman and posthuman in its constitution. For it has not yet been determined whether the world whence the two Athenians originated—the world prior to the war and still under monarchical rule—will reproduce itself in the city in the clouds, even if there are clues that Ratefreund and Hoffegut's intentions are not wholly aligned with the aspirations of the birds. Will the birds found a kingdom, a state, or a genuine "bird city," something completely of their own design? After their initial hesitation, they embrace Ratefreund and Hoffegut's plan, but not without warning from their own chorus leader. Played by an eagle, the figure of "Adler"—presumably a reference to the founder of the Socialist Party in Austria, Victor Adler—expresses concern that everything will remain in the end as it once was, that the humans will always see the birds as "ravens" and never as gods (*D*, 136).[23] Yet his warning goes essentially unheeded and the first act ends on a largely optimistic note. It concludes with the song of the nightingale Prokne, whom I view as the second stand-in for Kraus, this time his position as observer and participant. She waxes lyrically on the nature of the bird community and its relationship to the human world, proclaiming the essential difference between human and bird:[24]

> Ye have the law, but the world is ours
> and we may without scathe
> take joy in our powers.
> O come and have faith!
> We are lovers of lovers.[25]
>
> *Ihr habt das Gesetz, wir haben die Welt*
> *und uns ist erlaubt,*
> *was uns gefällt.*
> *O kommt und glaubt!*
> *Wir lieben Verliebte.* (*D*, 142)

It is a strength of the allegory that the birds appear to represent a conglomeration of several not entirely reconcilable elements or ideas. They are at once an underclass that has been repeatedly exploited by humans and gods alike; an ancient agricultural society yet to be sundered by the modern fabrications of race, state, nation, and law; an anarchical, utopian, quasi-Christian community bound by unconditional love (the nightingale's perspective); and a mythical representation of immortality, more divine than the gods themselves. "You children of men . . . / perish so quickly! / And we are forever," the nightingale declares (*D*, 141). But from the perspective of the human figures in the drama, they lack collective self-consciousness and have yet to be shaped into a concrete political entity. In turn, they have hitherto defined themselves in opposition to the humans—whom they associate with mendacity and political corruption—and the gods, their primary exploiters, who remain powerful by virtue of their supposedly natural divinity (we can read the gods allegorically in relation to the birds as stand-ins for the aristocratic class, holdovers from a bygone era who still retain their self-image as natural rulers). Thus, given the constitutive indeterminacy of the bird community, it remains as yet unclear how the proposed bird revolution will transpire and what will result from it.[26]

Cloudcuckooland

Ratefreund and Hoffegut appear in the beginning of the second act donning "grotesque" bird masks. Asked what the name of their city will be, the former declares that it shall be called "Cloudcuckooland." In line with the original drama (and more broadly, with the structural conventions of Old Comedy), this act presents a series of visitors to the new city, each representing a vice of

"Athens" that they want to introduce and that Ratefreund and Hoffegut had hoped to escape: religion (read: Catholicism), journalism, sophistry, literary celebrity, psychoanalysis, kitsch, bureaucracy, and spiritualism. This certainly presents a moment of allegorical slippage: of all these respective vices, only the last two could be said to have equal relevance to ancient Athens and modern-day Vienna. The others are time- and context-specific, evincing the difficulties involved in the attempt to adapt an ancient drama for a contemporary audience while also making a polemical point about the ease with which Athenian vices can be simply substituted by Viennese ones. The question of how one builds a republic from the ground up without intrusion from the outside or interference from the past is foregrounded. This issue is clearly at stake in the first visitor, a bullfinch (*Dompfaff*) and likely an allegory of the Austrian prelate-turned-chancellor from 1922 to 1924 and again from 1926 to 1929, Ignaz Seipel.[27] His two assistants, a raven and a crow—birds of prey—consume everything in the sacrificial basket such that nothing remains but skin and bones.[28] The meaning of the allegory is more stable here, with the dubious attempt of Austrian clericalism to reinstate its authority in the democratic republic lingering in the background. Ratefreund sees through his guest's "averted face" and decides that the new state will not have a religious foundation, that the priest has no business meddling in its affairs: "The gods won't get anything / and even the priest has nothing to gain," he claims, showing himself to be committed to a secular state, or at least one unencumbered by the pretentions and pieties of religion (*D*, 146).

Next in line is the journalist and his ambitions to establish a periodical, *The Free Bird*, and obtain access to all of the details of the new city, lest he is forced to extract them out of Ratefreund—an obvious reference to the corrupt journalistic practice of blackmail that Kraus reported on with great zeal (whereby, for example, a tabloid press would threaten to publish a reputation-destroying article about a particular business or institution unless it received the information it desired).[29] He and Ratefreund thus make a deal, and the journalist already refers to the new citizens of the bird city as his "subscribers," producing an intertextual reference to Kraus's "Subscriber" character from *The Last Days*, who does nothing but parrot newspaper headlines (*D*, 148). A poet described as a "modern composer" (*Neutöner*) next approaches and begins to recite what appears to be a parody of an Expressionist poem, leaving the chorus leader in a state of consternation. The poet claims to want to imbue the new city with a fitting *Weltanschauung*, but in so doing estranges himself from the mentality and desires of the city's primary inhabitants.[30] As the leader of the chorus confesses in response to the poem: "I am far removed from the issue at hand; / the idiom he speaks exceeds my command" (*D*, 150).[31] Though expressed with some naïveté, the question he raises is significant: How can those who have played no part in the founding or the construction of Cloud-cuckooland have anything meaningful to contribute to it? Fully attuned to, and familiar with the motives of these visitors, an irritated Ratefreund is in the unique position to mediate between them and the birds, who find the visitors unintelligible, obnoxious, or unnecessary. Ratefreund and Hoffegut may have abandoned Athens, but Athens, it appears, has not abandoned them.

Indeed, nothing of the bird city is of the birds' own doing apart from its physical construction, the labor that brought it into existence and is now being ignored by the city's intruders. At the same time, however, the news of Cloudcuckooland has spread to the human world, serving as a source of inspiration and imitation. Progress is in the air, as it were, foregrounding one of the drama's fundamental questions regarding the experience of political transformation: Is it possible to shed all traces of the old order and start anew? If not, what remains of the past? The birds, as far as we can tell, have no past in which they held political dominion. We do not know of their history (or whether they have a history to speak of), and thus what they desire—power and self-determination—is sympathetic only insofar as these constitute forms of life that are entirely new for them. But Ratefreund and Hoffegut have experienced life under both a monarchy—in which their class held all the power—and a burgeoning democratic republic, which rendered them obsolete at best, and harmful at worst. How much are they motivated by a desire for restoration, despite claiming to want to convert the bird community into a self-determining state? The appearance of the all too recognizable visitors is certainly annoying to Ratefreund, but it does not bode well for the future of the bird city. This is registered by the dove, a chorus-like figure who appears toward the end of this scene and proclaims to all what she observes in earthbound creatures:

> Man flies free in the abyss of slavery,
> and thus accustomed to his idols dethroned
> he's able to replace them with mortals alone.
> Though conquering nature with a power so free,
> he lives in permanent captivity . . .
>
> *Der Mensch fliegt frei in tiefster Sklaverei,*
> *und so gewohnt an die entthronten Götzen,*
> *kann er sie durch sie selber nur ersetzen.*
> *Wie er Natur besiegt mit freier Kraft,*
> *lebt er in steter Kriegsgefangenschaft* . . . (D, 164)

For this traditional bird of peace, the human being is cyclically trapped in a state of war, slavishly driven by "blood and money" and incapable of experiencing genuine sympathy for fellow human suffering. When the dove observes, "they hear the message, it is their faith that is lacking," she transforms Goethe's line from *Faust* into a political statement: what prevents humanity from undergoing the self-overcoming it can envision is its lack of faith in itself to become something other than it (currently) is (*D*, 164–65).[32] The dove thereby portends a bleak future for the bird city so long as it remains under the control of its founders, who can only pretend to be one of them, who are incapable, in other words, of shedding their aristocratic feathers. Much like the misunderstood bird in Kraus's earlier inversion of the common metaphor, the dove speaks as a member of the community that has always been subordinate to human and god alike; her authority derives from her ability to see how power functions without having ever been in a position to exercise it, and this is key to understanding what the birds are beginning to represent and what Ratefreund overlooks or ignores in them.

For replacing a dethroned idol with himself is precisely the course of action that Ratefreund undertakes. In response to some resistance from the divinities, who, through their messenger, have begun to complain about the recent dearth of sacrifices, Ratefreund ultimately declares a "defensive war" against them, shifting the terms of the allegory to the present-day context in this reference to World War I.[33] Without hesitation he proclaims that "we" are now the gods who must be served, and it is clear that the birds will soon be reinscribed into the violent cycle of human history described by the dove. Indeed, toward the end of the second act, Ratefreund declares to Wiedehopf that in preparation for this war, the birds will be trained in the ways of man: "Human convention (*Menschensitte*) we'll re-instantiate, / by showing them how to live, die, and celebrate!" (*D*, 167).[34] Just like the soldiers in *The Last Days*, the birds are to become *einrückend gemacht*—"compulsorily enlisted"—since for Ratefreund, the only way to unite his subjects under the collective category of Cloudcuckoolanders is to mobilize them against the gods, whose status has suddenly shifted from allegorizing the aristocracy to representing the Allied Powers of World War I (*D*, 173).[35] Ratefreund and Hoffegut, in turn, have gone from being disgruntled aristocrats to becoming the leaders of a dual monarchy who intend to plunge their bird subjects into a war they never wanted.

The drama begins, in a sense, anew, and this is where Kraus's play diverges most drastically from its predecessor text. In Aristophanes, Peistetaerus peacefully negotiates with a tribunal of gods in order to secure his power; in Kraus, diplomacy yields quickly to violence, and the drama effectively restages the war of words that constituted the content of *The Last Days*. The times, this aesthetic decision seems to suggest, have changed since ancient Greece. But the drastic shift in character and tone raises the question of whether Ratefreund had ever intended to abandon Athens in the first place. Was he an exile seeking refuge or a colonizer seeking new subjects? Either way, it is clear that he cannot truly imagine what a new city or a new form of communal life would look like; within the limits of his imagination, he can only restore the status quo. Like *The Last Days*, *Cloudcuckooland* thus also aims to expose state-sanctioned violence as, in part, the product of the lethal combination of historical amnesia and a resolute lack of imagination: forgetting, once again, emerges as a salient theme. But this insight is perhaps more effectively expressed in the allegory than in the "documentary drama" because of the former's recursive structure: Ratefreund and Hoffegut abandoned a city that had just experienced war. Did Ratefreund's willful ignorance of his complicity in creating the Athens he renounced set him on the path toward the very catastrophe that drove him out in the first place? Was the experience of war not enough to steer him elsewhere precisely because he never truly experienced it, or because he experienced it only from the perspective of one who had lost power? His drive for power is then not natural or instinctual, but rather a function of his desire to avenge the condition of being exposed to a temporary period of powerlessness. The dual monarchs can only think of the state as an instrument of power.

Rearrangements

> Time moves ambiguously (*doppelsinnig*); we will suddenly again be where we just were. And by contemplating the example of Karl Kraus, I will speak about past futures (*vergangene Zukünftigkeiten*) and, at the same time, about future pasts (*zukünftige Vergangenheiten*).
>
> —Berthold Viertel, *Karl Kraus: Ein Charakter und die Zeit* (1921)

The third act begins, accordingly, in the middle of the war—seemingly at a point before the drama technically began—but this time the birds are substituting for the Athenians. The bird world is in a war-induced frenzy despite the increasing starvation besetting it. Amidst the cries of patriotic glory in the final act is the sparrow's lone voice of opposition, the most obvious analogue to the Grumbler and another Kraus stand-in. Regurgitating wartime propaganda, the turkey enjoins the sparrow to be silent "in these great times," reminding him that the sparrow is god, commanding him to quiet his pacifism and defeatism, and reiterating that the war is both a "chalybeate bath" (*Stahlbad*) and a "strength-renewer" (*Krafterneurer*), terms taken straight from the lexicon of World War I (*D*, 174–75). The sparrow is thus accused by his fellow birds of being a traitor and an enemy of the state, while himself claiming that the military and the state are the legitimate enemy. Both the sparrow and the birds that extol the virtues of war are, we should note, united in their birdness; the sparrow does not speak from any position of authority. If the sparrow thus criticizes the bellicosity the birds have adopted, he does so as a member of the community they once were, or still could be, for the birds were never a militarized entity until they allowed human intruders to turn them into one. The sparrow is in solidarity with the birds prior to the existence of Cloudcuckooland, the birds whose labor was first exploited in the act of constructing the city and who were then conscripted into a war they did not will. Something had to be done; the birds could not serve the gods forever and live in a permanent condition of unfreedom, if the implications of the allegory can be further abstracted. But for the sparrow, their striving for emancipation and self-determination was not fated to culminate in a war whose sole purpose was to reverse this hierarchy. The third act thus stages the consequences of state-sponsored violence, a violence that leaves its subjects in abject misery. The sparrow laments: "We sacrificed ourselves for heroic grandeur (*Heldenwahn*). / Now look around, we're wretched and poor!" (*D*, 175).[36] Regardless of how merciless the sparrow is in his critique of his fellow birds, his aim is ultimately to reveal the state as the true betrayer of its own subjects.

"Clusters form" in this act, echoing a recurring stage direction from *The Last Days* and reminding us that endemic to the mood induced by war are the attendant phenomena of groupthink and group formation, which Roberto Calasso argues are decidedly not an "expression of democratic spontaneity" (*D*, 183).[37] In keeping with the historical allegory, the heads of state and military—Ratefreund/Hoffegut and Flamingo von Fahnenfeld, respectively—refuse to accept the negative outcome of the war, framing their impending defeat as merely the beginning stages of a protracted but inevitable victory. When they finally do admit to defeat, Flamingo immediately scapegoats the inner enemy, referring both to this "dastardly sparrow" who has weakened morale from within and to the "cunning" and "backstabbing" hinterland, who has robbed the birds of their victory (*D*, 186). Clear in this statement is a thinly veiled reference to the socialists, the republicans, the Jews, and the "stab-in-the-back" legend that took root in rightwing consciousness after World War I and became firmly implanted in Nazi ideology. Ratefreund's subsequent statements, separated only by a page of text—"I have weighed everything in the balance" and "This I did not will"—make salient his identification with the kaiser, confirming that these wanderers brought with them more of their recent past than they were willing to admit (*D*, 186–87). The entire war has been essentially condensed into a few key gestures and phrases, as Ratefreund, the kaiser, God (from *The Last Days*) and, indeed, Kraus, all unite in this one voice.

The drama's most prescient moment, however, emerges in the penultimate scene, when Ratefreund, stripped of his erstwhile power, becomes—finally—a victim of the political process. Two "helpers" appear from nowhere more specific than the earth, introduced by the falcon as their potential saviors and described by him as "strange figures" (*D*, 187). The first identifies himself as a "legitimist" coming to aid in the regime change, and we are led to believe that they might be representatives of a new republic. But upon Ratefreund's inquiry into their motives and plans for reform, the first helper ambiguously responds: "Very simple: in order to construct something, / we must naturally destroy (*vernichten*) something; / to get things rearranged (*um herzurichten*), someone's gotta hang" (*D*, 188). It would first appear that the helper is referring to the fate of the monarchy, which must be fully destroyed in order for a new republic to be erected in its place. Yet his use of the verb *herrichten* connotes more the notion of "rearranging" or "renovating" than radically reconstructing. The statement thus ominously suggests that sacrifices must be made in order for such a rearrangement to take place; in order, that is, to start over without *completely* starting over, without the ostensibly destructive element—the "inner" enemy—that led to this catastrophe in the first place. It is easier, the helper implies, to turn to the right than to the left when a power vacuum emerges and needs to be filled.[38] This is confirmed when the two helpers out themselves as a monarchist and a fascist, the former advocating the restoration of the dynasty by invoking the Double-Headed Eagle (*Doppeladler*), the latter speaking from the "Aryan point of view" and advocating violence against potential traitors of the state, namely those with "crooked beaks" (not so obliquely referring to the stereotype of Jewish physiognomy). The second helper intervenes:

> Train your people in national hate
> Ask about race while you calculate.
> What's *fortunately still lacking*—wait, I meant to say:
> what's *still unfortunately lacking* in your Fatherland,
> is what's required in our stormy days
> for the sake of order, a very strong hand. [. . .]
> To clarify my plan, let me repeat:
> it's terror tactics that we must defeat.
> The best defense is a pre-emptive strike,
> Wielding your clubs as wildly as you like.
> Behold, out of this twisted form
> the sacred swastika is born.[39]
>
> *Erzieht das Volk zum nationalen Hasse,*
> *zählt es und fragt nach der Rasse.*
> *Was euch zum Glück noch fehlt—nicht doch, ich wollte sagen:*
> *was euch noch fehlt zum Glück in euerm Vaterland,*
> *das ist in solchen sturmbewegten Tagen*
> *zum Ordnungmachen eine starke Hand. [. . .]*
> *Wenn ihr es noch nicht wißt, sei's euch gesagt:*
> *der Terror ist es, was wir stets beklagt;*
> *und um ihm noch beizeiten vorzubaun,*
> *braucht man mit Knütteln nur herumzuhaun.*
> *Ihr werdet sehn, es wirkt enorm,*
> *das Kreuz gewinnt die Hakenform.* (*D*, 190–91)

Of significance are the third and fourth lines of the first of the two stanzas: the fascist unreflectively admits that the people would be better off *not* succumbing to the will of a "strong hand," but then corrects himself immediately, as if the original formulation were merely a Freudian slip. Perhaps even he is not fully committed to the idea he propounds; perhaps his thought has already been coordinated. Either way, he suggests that good fortune will arise only through their own "terror tactics" and through the adoption and transformation of the cross—symbol of the Catholic foundation of the monarchy—into the swastika.[40] This scene clearly points to the hidden, but nonetheless burgeoning alliance Kraus detected between reactionary clericalism and Nazism in the newly created Austria.[41] The first helper, who claims to represent a less radical solution, nonetheless hints at the eventual unification of Austria and Germany, evidenced by his request that Ratefreund and Hoffegut consider "coating the yellow beak with a touch of black (*D*, 191). It does not take much to convince Ratefreund that this advice should be heeded, but the error in his thinking is his insistence that the birds will remain birds if they follow this course of action; he does not see that they were already coerced into renouncing their birdness when they fought this war, indeed when they agreed to build a new city in the sky. He still subscribes to the illusion that he is part of the bird community and is convinced of the birds' desire to be human:

> I see we birds will victors remain,
> so long as mustard gas is part of the game;
> we must progress with our regress,
> like man through the hazy double-mist.
>
> *Ich seh', wir Vögel werden Sieger bleiben,*
> *wenn teils Chemie wir, teils Romantik treiben;*
> *wir müssen vorwärts mit dem Rückschritt gehen,*
> *im Doppeldunst dem Menschen gleichzusehn.* (*D*, 193)

The emphasis on how war and violence are encouraged through the mutual appeal to romantic ideals and technological progress is a recurring motif in Kraus's writings. In this iteration, it appears that the former monarch has his eyes set on the unity of the two former empires, even as he is aware of how this move is politically reactive—one cannot see through a double mist. Indeed, this passage articulates one of the central insights of the play, insofar as it foregrounds the absurdity of equating progress with war. The war that has destroyed Cloudcuckooland and its inhabitants will beget more terror and more violence, much as the first war that drove Ratefreund and Hoffegut out of Athens had planted the seeds for the war waged by the bird leaders against the gods: Athens will, as was suggested earlier, never perish. Unimpressed with Ratefreund's now meaningless claim to divinity, the second helper soon assures him that "Wotan" will win the battle against Zeus (*D*, 194). In the battle of divinities, in other words, the Teutonic will defeat the Greek; the old will become the new again, but either way, divinities will remain at the foundation of the state and thus violence will remain endemic to it.

The drama has thus staged the danger inherent to a misguided nostalgia that believes the past contains all the solutions to the discontented present, or that longs for power to be consolidated under the leadership of a "strong hand." The potential utopian unity between bird and man ends in utter failure; Ratefreund and Hoffegut are stripped of their crowns, and the foreign ministry demands their extradition. They are deemed traitors who taught their subjects to hate like men. After announcing the transition of the benighted monarchy into the "provisional State Council of the Republic of Cloudcuckooland"—a reference to the title of the first government of the rump state of German-Austria formed in 1918/19[42]—Wiedehopf declares that the two human leaders poisoned the thought of the bird world, corrupted their morals, introduced "ambiguous" elements into their political life, and ultimately drove them into a hopeless war against the gods (*D*, 199). Yet even in his denunciation of the two monarchs and their short-lived reign, Wiedehopf speaks in a bureaucratic tongue that is alien to the bird population. The language of the new republic, that is, is still not in full harmony with those it governs, raising the political-philosophical question once again regarding the potential for genuine self-determination. *Cloudcuckooland* appears to celebrate the accomplishments of the early First Republic—and there were many such accomplishments—while remaining skeptical of the elements from within that threatened this experiment and suspicious of the remnants of Austria's past that had not been fully exorcised. Indeed, when Wiedehopf finally announces that the effigies of the "evildoers" will be used as "scarecrows" in the fields in order to protect the bird community from future invasions, it becomes clear that the shadowy existence of the two monarchs will continue to function as a specter—a *Gespenst*, to invoke Kraus's earlier essay—in the lives of the birds (*D*, 200).

"The Air Is Pure"

> In a republic, to begin with, people are as bad and as dumb as they are, but they are not prevented by any barrier from changing the situation. The monarchical power, in order to exist, must make people stupider and worse than they are.
>
> —Kraus, "Obituary" (1919)

Articulated in the statement above—and in *Cloudcuckooland* more generally—is an uneasy admixture of cynicism and hope, however weakly the latter is insinuated.[43] An analysis of this dramatic allegory would thus not be complete without acknowledging the implications of the consonance between the political "rearrangement" introduced by the monarchist and the fascist "helpers" in the final act, and Kraus's own aesthetic rearrangement of Aristophanes's precursor text. Perhaps aligning himself on a world-historical level with the Greek poet who, too, laughed away his empire's follies and vices, Kraus suggests that a political tabula rasa is a pure fantasy.[44] Indeed, his drama turns Aristophanes's comedy into a decidedly dark affair, as Greiner has argued. But such an adaptation also shows that there is no necessary form such a rearrangement of this sort must assume. The raw material might remain fixed, but it can be shaped in different and unexpected ways; new conventions can be sought, shedding light on the pliability of the material itself. We are thus reminded, through Wiedehopf and his shifting function throughout the play, that a genuine conversion to the bird world was at least at one point possible. Unlike Ratefreund and Hoffegut, he was able to live among the birds and become one of them (even if he, too, was earlier convinced of the need to build the city in the sky—perhaps because his erstwhile humanness had never fully disappeared).[45]

Returning, finally, to the birds themselves—who are virtually absent from the explicitly political moments in the third act until the act's final scene—we are compelled to ask what *Cloudcuckooland* is ultimately affirming and what political vision it is committed to upholding. What more can be said, in other words, about what this bird community represents? The lark's parting song—the bird of daybreak and the counterpart to the nightingale that closed the first act—addresses these questions in poetic terms. In the middle of her lyrical monologue, which begins with uncertainty regarding who the subject and who the object of this "dream" were, she offers an interpretation of the allegory that reads like the moral of a fable:

> If they have dreamed this dream with us together,
> then they, if all-too earthly minds can still
> receive from other spheres an allegory,
> may see themselves in us, and see that force
> in conquest nothing can fulfill, but makes
> all desolate. We would not, that as gods
> they honor us, but honor pay themselves
> as men! This is the dream's import.[46]
>
> *Wofern sie diesen Traum mit uns geträumt,*
> *so haben sie, wenn allzu irdisch Denken*
> *aus anderer Luft ein Gleichnis noch empfängt,*
> *in uns ihr Tun erkannt und daß Gewalt*
> *den Raum der Welt erobernd nicht erfüllt,*
> *nur leert. Nicht wollen wir, daß sie als Götter*
> *uns ehren, aber sich als Menschen! Dies der Sinn*
> *des Traums.* (*D*, 203)

For the lark, the birds wanted neither to be nor be treated like gods, pleading only that their former rulers treat themselves with the dignity commensurate with their own humanity, here understood in the most generous of ways.

Models for humanity and the winged alike, she implies, need no longer be divinities, a polemical statement in the context of the political mythology represented in this play. This is her fundamentally secular gesture, if it is also to be read as a more specific polemic against the influence of Austrian clericalism and its attempt to wield power in the new republic. What Kraus thus also takes over in his rearrangement of the Aristophanean comedy is the impulse to slay false idols, even if the gods in this drama are indexed to different historical referents at different junctures. The drama is decidedly opposed to the monarchical idea and the notion of divine dispensation on which it rests. The lark continues: "At last we are awake. We bless the happy hour. / The life of the Republic destroys the dream of power!" (*D*, 203).[47] With this she posits another possible rearrangement and an outright challenge to the vision of Flamingo von Fahnenfeld, the "helpers," and Ratefreund, leaving open-ended the political future of this collective, in whom the traumatic memory of war and its driving forces are now firmly lodged. Speaking on behalf of the birds, the lark hints at a republic *in potentia*: a speculative community based on an unsullied vision of self-determination, not one that presupposes the continued existence of a jail, let alone a jailer. The lark's last line (and the last line of the drama), "The air is pure. Mankind is gone!," thus contains, on the one hand, an apocalyptic element, insofar as it heralds the end of a humanity destined to repeat its violent tendencies because it has not (yet) transcended social domination—Ratefreund and Hoffegut could not help but subject the birds to their will, since that is all they knew (*D*, 203).[48] On the other hand, with these words the birds declare themselves to be free to realize their freedom, to establish a republic of their own making and befitting of their own kind, and thus to become themselves models for an improved humanity. The birds are now liberated from their servitude and no longer constrained by external limitations, recalling Kraus's cynical yet hopeful definition of life under a republic quoted above. As suggested earlier, the birds cannot be tethered to any existing faction, party, or class; they represent, rather, the *possibility* of a political future freed from the burdens of the past, or rather, a future in which the past has been registered in its actual relationship to the present. More than anyone else, the birds experienced the war against the gods and the massive suffering it incurred. The lark's emphatic and poetic declaration to put an end to war and power as such thus carries more weight than Wiedehopf's rote political declaration, which was read aloud and thus merely interpellated. She—like the nightingale and the sparrow before her—speaks as a member of the bird community.

Thus just as the drama allegorizes a vision of the political life of Austria between the end of the war and the early years of the First Republic—and of how the republic might continue to develop if its politically regressive impulses are not curbed—so does it offer, finally, a reflection on how to interpret Kraus's response to the accusation of being a "bird who defiles his own nest," quoted at the outset of this chapter. The commonly held view (also invoked in *The Last Days*[49]) is that the satirist tears down the existing infrastructure without offering any positive content in its stead. Kraus's point, by contrast, is that only from the perspective of the actual nest defilers does it appear that the figure who attempts to address—and thereby clear away—the filth is the one responsible for producing it. His inversion thus not only links the satirist to genuine patriotism; it also challenges the view of causality informing this inadequate vision. For the nest cleanser, as Kraus sees it, does not feel at home in the filth in which he is compelled to linger: the dirty nest was there prior to the cleanser's arrival, who nonetheless has to breathe in its air in order to apply the deep cleansing the nest now needs. Invariably, the nest cleanser looks filthy. Self-censure—if we interpret the self in this context as both a metonymy and a metaphor for the nation (Austria)—and patriotism are not, for Kraus, mutually exclusive dispositions. Indeed, on this reading, the only genuinely "filthy" act is the decision to force one's subjects into an unwanted war, a decision that ultimately destroys the nest altogether. Those who would accuse Kraus, the Grumbler, or the sparrow of being a nest defiler are thus of one mind with those who long for the restoration of the past: they see only the simultaneity of misery and politics, and are in want of the kind of historical consciousness that *Cloudcuckooland* seems to summon. The self-identified nest cleanser identifies historical amnesia as the primary culprit, for the problems that have accompanied life under the republic, the play suggests, must be understood as a product of the monarchy that led its people into war and self-destructed: the nest had been defiled prior to the arrival of the supposed nest defiler, who wants nothing more than to build it anew.

Chapter 3

"Where Illegality Becomes the Law"

Third Walpurgis Night (1933/1952)

First we saw with satisfaction
Only wildness, folly, error.
Suddenly, unthought of, then
Enters a new Emperor!
Now proceeding as they're told
Through the land the people troop
Following en masse the unrolled
Lying banners—like sheep.
—Johann Wolfgang von Goethe, *Faust: Part II* (1832)

As discussed in the last chapter, Kraus publicly aligned himself with the Socialists and the First Republic during the immediate postwar years and found the lingering nostalgia for a monarchy that had plunged its people into a total war entirely suspect. From the mid-1920s onward, however, it became increasingly clear to him that despite the early accomplishments of Austria's Social Democratic Party—particularly in the realms of culture and education (*Bildung)*—the party had distanced itself from its revolutionary promises and was becoming more "bourgeois" in its practices.[1] Kraus became wary of both the growing complicity of the party with journalistic corruption on the one hand, and of the ability for the Social Democrats to handle threats from the right on the other.[2] This once potentially fruitful alliance between Kraus and the Social Democrats was curtailed. Kraus's critiques of the political sphere are rarely structural; as Edward Timms has pointed out, they focus more on the "mentality" of the bourgeoisie and on the widespread "corruption" of the political system than on systemic deficiencies of social democracy or capitalism as such.[3] And yet there were particular events during the interwar period to which Kraus responded that render his controversial response to National Socialism and subsequent decision to endorse Austro-Fascism more intelligible, if not entirely sympathetic.

One such watershed event has become known as the July Revolt of 1927. Three right-wing war veterans opened fire in a small Austrian town in 1927, killing a veteran socialist and a child—and were acquitted. The shooting and subsequent acquittal (the "Schattendorf Verdict") became symbolic of the growing tension between the Social Democrats and a right-wing alliance in Austria, which included industrialists and the Catholic Church. In response to what was widely perceived as an unjust court decision, hundreds of workers led a general strike against the then Christian Socialist–led government, convening in the streets of Vienna and ultimately setting fire to the Palace of Justice. The Viennese chief of police, Johann Schober, was authorized by the chancellor, Ignaz Seipel (allegorized in Kraus's *Cloudcuckooland*), to suppress the unrest with force, which effectively resulted in the militarization of the police. Eighty-five civilians were killed and hundreds more were wounded. In response to this revolt and the ensuing massacre, Kraus took a highly publicized and politicized stance against what he perceived to be an authoritarian police state developing within the womb of a weakened republic. Not only did he compose a series of polemics in *The Torch*, he also launched an open campaign against Schober, printing hundreds of placards demanding that Schober resign and posting them all over Vienna.[4] Elias Canetti, then at the height of his obsession with Kraus, recalls this series of events vividly in *The Torch in My Ear*, the second volume of his three-part autobiography:

> In the following days and weeks of utter dejection . . . when the events you had witnessed kept recurring over and over again in your mind, haunting you night after night even in your sleep, there was still *one* legitimate connection to literature. And this connection was Karl Kraus. . . . His posters were the only thing that kept us going in those days. I went from one poster to another, paused in front of each one, and I felt as if all the justice on earth had entered the letters of Kraus's name.[5]

Not without its element of fantasy, Canetti's evocation of Kraus's singular relationship to the political scene of that moment—*the* relationship between literature and politics, as he phrases it—will be important to bear in mind when we turn to Kraus's response to National Socialism. For Kraus, it was enough that innocent blood had been shed, that what was thoughtlessly referred to as "the masses" and the criminal elements of society were being blamed, and that neither the rule of democracy nor its staunchest political party was able to do anything to combat this confusion, deceit, and egregious abuse of power. State violence committed against the state's own people had become sanctioned and could rely on the press for its support.

This crisis would serve as a symptom for Kraus of both the increasing instability of the republic and the powerlessness of the Social Democrats, who were implicated in the massacre precisely because of their perceived inaction. Kraus would continue to distance himself from this party, identifying in their leadership a willingness to compromise with the Austrian elite. In his most significant polemic of the 1920s, "The Bastion of the Republic," Kraus carefully arranged a montage of quotations documenting both the suffering that occurred as a result of the police brutality and the insensitivity of those in power to such suffering.[6] At one juncture, he quotes the vice chancellor: "Stop spreading lies about the 100 deaths when the number was 85!," underscoring the measures taken by those in power to downplay the severity of this act of violence (*F* 766, 3, 1927; *SG*, 239). The text highlights, in other words, "the political fanaticism and moral vacuousness of Seipel, Schober and their supporters" (*AS* 2, 341).[7] The republic had, for Kraus, suffered a serious and irreparable wound, as Kraus essentially concluded that Schober protected "the glory of the Republic by massacring its citizens."[8]

Kraus's relationship to social democracy over the course of the 1920s and early 1930s was the "most complex, contradictory, and problematic" of all of his political alliances, and is in no way here being given the attention it deserves.[9] But for our purposes, it is important to acknowledge that Kraus's disillusionment would continue to grow as he was keeping a close eye on the related issues of Austrian independence, Pan-German unity, and eventually, the rise of National Socialism across the border. Such disillusionment would eventually lead him to endorse the Austro-fascist Engelbert Dollfuss and his Catholic-corporate state, which, in Kraus's eyes, was the only legitimate bulwark left against the threat of German annexation.[10] Kraus's farewell to social democracy was most trenchantly formulated in a speech he gave in October 1932 entitled "Both Sides of the Border" after the National Socialists had gained over 230 seats in the Reichstag.[11] In this polemic, he deemed the Social Democrats a moral and political failure for their inability to both confront the threat of Nazism and protect Austrian independence. Kraus was also suspicious of the rhetoric of a "common destiny" (*Schicksalsgemeinschaft*) uniting Germany and Austria, a position endorsed by members on the left and right. Talk of Pan-German unity, he felt, would play into the hands of the National Socialists and indicated a glaring blind spot within the Social Democratic leadership, whose policy of "muddling through" these difficult times was certain to lead to self-destruction. In the same piece, Kraus also denounced communist and Marxist intellectuals, many of whom had once extolled Kraus as a revolutionary figure.[12] Their "intellectual life," he claims, was reducible to the vacuous inscriptions on a beer mug, which, by implication, prevented them from perceiving the actual implications of Nazism and German annexation (*F* 876, 14, 1932; *HD*, 176). Thus apart from the cowardice of the Social Democrats, as evidenced by their capitulation to the Pan-Germanists, a major source of Kraus's frustration was the seeming incapacity of all the major parties and players occupying the landscape of social democracy to truly comprehend the threat of National Socialism. The experience of an impending political, and, indeed, humanitarian catastrophe was, once again, being obscured by bourgeois party politics. Everything related to the socialists had become, for Kraus, "counter-human" (*widermenschlich*), a sentiment he articulates in the opening salvo of "Both Sides":

> And though this world, with swastiklers filled (*Und wenn die Welt voll Hakenkreuzler wär'*)—a creation primarily indebted to social democracy, on both sides of the border—we must finally wise up to the fact that ever since humanity let itself be betrayed by politics, there has never been a greater miscarriage (*Mißlingen*) than the actions of this party, and that the violation of countless ideals they touted in order to partake in the bourgeois world (*um mit der Bürgerwelt teilen zu können*) has finally been consummated. (*F* 876, 1; *HU*, 165)

Combining an allusion to Martin Luther's "A Mighty Fortress Is Our God"—the Protestant battle hymn, whose third stanza begins with the line, "And though this world, with devils filled" (*Und wenn die Welt voll Teufel wär'*)"—with the iconic emblem of National Socialism, Kraus polemically insists that the Social Democrats are largely responsible for not preventing the circumstances under which the Nazis had come to power.[13] They were, for Kraus, blind to the actual threat of Nazism, which far exceeded their imagination. A political system, Kraus furthermore suggests, fueled by the betrayal of its own ideals, by internal corruption, and by a compromised relationship to the liberal press had created a set of conditions ripe for the Nazi seizure of power.

"Faust-Natures" and Kraus's *Third Walpurgis Night*

Kraus composed *Third Walpurgis Night* in 1933 but purposefully withheld it from publication, apart from excerpts of it he published in *The Torch*; the full text was not published in book form until 1952.[14] In many respects, this text is even more fragmented than *The Last Days*. Within the framework of a long, satirical essay, other voices constantly intervene and interrupt Kraus's monologue: newspaper reports detailing barbaric acts of cruelty committed by the storm troopers (*Sturmabteilung*; hereafter referred to by its abbreviation, SA) against Jews, communists, socialists, women, and animals; quotations by prominent Nazi leaders that underscore the linguistic degradation of Nazi discourse; passages from Shakespeare's *Macbeth* and *King Lear* that are thematically linked to the events unfolding in Germany and Austria; and, most significant for my purposes, passages from Goethe's *Faust: The Second Part of the Tragedy* (*Faust II*) that are both embedded in the essay and visibly set apart from Kraus's language.

The *Third Walpurgis Night* attempts to address the experience of Nazism: its language, its ideological incoherency, and its violence. Kraus, I argue, thus identifies one aspect of National Socialism as a function of the social, political, and cultural conditions whence it sprang; the Nazis succeeded because their methods of ideological dissemination were continuous with the methods of modernity. The Nazis were journalists who wrote "with blood" and "feuilletonists of the deed" (*DW*, 307). This is what rendered them discursively intelligible and susceptible to being exposed as the liars and charlatans they were. But the Nazis simultaneously embodied, for Kraus, a historical break—a caesura—which deprived even language "of a secure foundation."[15] How was one thus to respond in language to a historical experience that was, in a sense, beyond experience? The *Third Walpurgis Night* is Kraus's most sustained literary response not only to the phenomenon of Nazism, but to this predicament itself. What constitutes its literariness—and, more specifically, its modernism—is the tension it reveals between the intelligible aspects of Nazism on the one hand, and the virtually unrepresentable dimensions of Nazi violence on the other. This tension is most salient in Kraus's intertextual engagement with yet another precursor text: namely, *Faust II*, one of the more perplexing, ambiguous, and violent works of the modern German canon, a drama that resists facile interpretation.[16] In his complex engagement with the second part of Goethe's tragedy, Kraus attempts, I argue, to articulate an experience that no historical precedent could make recognizable and no single linguistic register could make representable. At the same time, by invoking the domain of literature and myth—the domain of linguistic singularity—Kraus, paradoxically, arrives at insights regarding this political regime that few recognized at the time.[17] Kraus, indeed, had plenty to say about Hitler and the Third Reich; his concern was identifying the form of language to properly contend with this new form of life.

Faust II weds individual desire to political expansion and destruction, combining grotesque violence and sexuality in its portrayal of a collision between the ancient and modern worlds. These are also salient features of Kraus's reading of National Socialism, leading one critic to conclude that this bleak vision of humanity binds the two authors in question.[18] Goethe's political satire of the French Revolution and the Reign of Terror—events that inspired fear and fascination in the poet—also resonate with Kraus's own vision of revolution. Thus in his comparison of Kraus's use of Goethe with his use of *Macbeth*, Timms argues that Goethe represents one side of Kraus's moral ponderings vis-à-vis the irruption of National Socialism and Shakespeare the other. Shakespeare, for Timms, still operates within a universe in which the characters are aware that they will be judged in moral terms; Goethe entertains the more unsettling idea that nature sanctions *all* forms of violence. Macbeth's intentions and ambitions are political, while Faust's are "existential" (*AS* 2, 505–7). By combining the two literary interlocutors Kraus is thus able to weave together competing moral, political, and philosophical worldviews without ever coming to a resolution. A valuable insight, Timms's view nevertheless overlooks how the formal experimentation with Goethe's tragedy speaks directly to the challenge of representing Nazism with which Kraus's text is engaged. Indeed, toward the beginning of the essay, Kraus writes: "Um zu sagen, was geschah, kann es die Sprache nur stammelnd nachsprechen" (*DW*, 16), which could be rendered as, "In order to say what happened, language can only repeat it as a stammer." In other words, language qua pure repetition—Kraus's preferred satirical method up until this point—has reached its critical limits and can only shudder or stammer when faced with the task of articulating the events that have just unfolded. But the use of the word "es" to refer to "was geschah" also enacts this very paradox: the sentence both points to the surplus of experience that cannot be contained by language and attempts to name it. Phrased otherwise, this sentence both suggests the need for quoting the language of Nazism in order to expose its obscenity and contains the insight that pure repetition will (in this case) fall short of its aim, that something in this movement and its intentions cannot be adequately mediated through this method alone. Broadly stated, Kraus seeks out other ways to engage the relationship between word and deed.[19]

Kraus's original intentions for the final layout of this text remain unknown, but what he referred to as the essay's "motto"—a montage of quotations culled from act I, act IV, and the "Classical Walpurgis Night" in act II of Goethe's tragedy—was only appended to the beginning of the 1989 Suhrkamp edition and here appears before the drama's (in)famous opening line: "To me, Hitler brings nothing to mind (*mir fällt zu Hitler nichts ein*)" (*DW*, 12). This arrangement represents the most credible attempt to fulfill authorial intention, especially given its general consistency with Kraus's poetics.[20] Many of these quotations reappear later on in the essay, embedded within Kraus's own commentary and juxtaposed against documentary quotations testifying to acts of violence committed by the SA. While thematically united in their reference to a political, natural, or mythological monstrosity, the quotes from *Faust* are not arranged in any immediately intuitive order, undermining the impulse to discern from this arrangement a coherent narrative. From the outset, we can thus identify a mimetic moment constitutive of Kraus's method: the experience of Nazism, as Kraus sees it, cannot be easily narrated, despite the transparency of certain elements of its self-presentation. Nonetheless, more than "nothing" had, in fact, already occurred to Kraus.[21] For about the motto itself and its relationship to the present situation, Kraus writes elsewhere that this "most German event" has been "preformed" by this "most German poem."[22] Kraus is not, or at least not primarily interested in exploring the Faustian character and its relation to the German spirit. Rather, his concern is the relationship between the poem itself and the unfolding of this historical moment. The preformation of which he speaks must, accordingly, be understood as a relationship of correspondence, not between fate and character, as it were, but between a formally and politically ambiguous text on the one hand, and its function and legacy in the context of National Socialism on the other.[23]

We can thus first turn to the tenth passage of Kraus's opening motto, excerpted from act I of *Faust II*, where it is set in the throne room of a late medieval or early Renaissance imperial palace. The Chancellor (accompanied in this scene by the entire state council, including Mephisto) is addressing the Emperor, informing him of the instability of his empire and the violence that may ensue. The Emperor is concerned about the financial condition of his empire, only to be reassured by Mephisto that money can easily be fabricated to fix the problem; there are clear resonances between this scene and the contemporary crisis of inflation in Germany. The Emperor's concern will ultimately be validated in the fourth act, when civil war breaks out. The scene has been read as an allusion to the conditions in France prior to the revolution, raising the possibility that Kraus identifies an analogy between the French Revolution and the contemporary moment to which he bears witness, thereby speculating on the discourse of revolution in times of crisis.[24] It is important to point out that the excerpt from the Chancellor's speech quoted in *Walpurgis* appears, in Goethe's drama, just after these crucial lines (which are omitted from Kraus's text): "If fever runs in rage throughout the state / And evils further evils propagate?"[25] Below is the passage that appears in *Walpurgis*:

> Whoever looks below from this high room
> Into the wide realm, he thinks it a bad dream
> Where one deformity couples with another
> And illegality is the law
> In a whole world of rampant error.[26]
>
> *Wer schaut hinab von diesem hohen Raum*
> *Ins weite Reich, ihm scheint's ein schwerer Traum,*
> *Wo Mißgestalt in Mißgestalten schaltet,*
> *Das Ungesetz gesetzlich überwaltet,*
> *Und eine Welt des Irrtums sich entfaltet.*[27]

The isolated words *Reich* and *schalten* resonate with the self-designation of the regime as the "Third Reich" and with its most effective accomplishment to date: "co-ordination" (*Gleichschaltung*), a word that appears approximately forty times throughout Kraus's text. Less clear, however, is how to interpret the deformities that couple with other deformities. Would pre-Nazi Germany be the first deformity in this formulation, in which case Nazism would be rendered as an intensification or culmination of the conditions already in place, rather than an actual revolution as its exponents insisted—and as Kraus seems to affirm in other passages? Or does the inclusion of this passage translate into a claim about how power begets power and produces more destructive manifestations of itself, a process inaugurated by Hitler's initial transformation of illegality into law? The allusion certainly allows for ambiguity, and the quote introduces an immanent relationship between certain motifs in Goethe's drama and the first few months of Nazi rule.

> Yet because this transaction cannot satisfy every demand, and with the thirst for blood the hunger is nowhere near being stilled, the safe bed of evolution grants no one a peaceful sleep. Elements trample on the plan. Shaken by the illusion with which the state was made. Take a look at what hides behind. Faust-natures threaten to become complete, where illegality becomes the law. And as it's been decreed—
> Meanwhile rebellious turmoil waxes
> Horribly into savage spate.[28]

> *Da jene Erledigung nicht alle Ansprüche befriedigen kann und mit dem Blutdurst beiweitem noch nicht der Hunger gestillt ist, so gewährt das sichere Bett der Evolution keinen ruhigen Schlaf. Elemente treten auf den Plan. Rütteln an der Illusion, mit der Staat gemacht wurde. Schauen nach, was dahinter steckt. Faustnaturen drohen zu vollenden, wo Ungesetz gesetzlich überwaltet, und wie auch verordnet sei—*
> *Indessen wogt, in grimmigem Schwalle*
> *Des Aufruhrs wachsendes Gewühl.*[29]

This and the following passages form a collage of literary and documentary texts, all of which, as Simon Ganahl has pointed out, require deciphering.[30] The "safe bed of evolution" is a reference to a statement made by Hitler during a speech in 1933 that declared the end of the revolutionary stage of National Socialism. Kraus quotes this passage from its reproduction in the *Arbeiter-Zeitung*, the primary mouthpiece of the Austrian Social Democrats. He is dubious of Hitler's promise that social change will take effect gradually, and that anyone affected by this process will be granted a "peaceful sleep"; he may also be embedding an allusion to Faust's long slumber and eventual awakening with which the second part of the tragedy commences. Skeptical of any clear end to the "revolutionary" (and therefore violent) stage of this coup d'état, Kraus furthermore anticipates a claim made by Hannah Arendt regarding the nonteleological aspect of the National Socialist movement in *The Origins of Totalitarianism* (1951), coincidentally published one year before Kraus's text. In her trenchant analysis, Arendt writes, "The practical goal of the movement is to organize as many people within its framework and to set up and *keep them in motion*; a political goal that would constitute the end of the movement simply does not exist."[31] By undermining the ideological coherence of the movement, Kraus, too, questions whether the violent usurpation of power has a political end in sight—that is, whether it has any goal apart from the total annihilation of its enemies.

This insight is buffered—and further complicated—when Kraus invokes the "elements" and the tone and register of his passage shift. On the one hand, he is referring to the *social* elements—that is, the men who have been lured to join the party by the ostensibly "socialist" aspect of National Socialism only to be disillusioned and to subsequently take out their resentment on the more vulnerable members of society. By suggesting that these elements "trample on the plan," Kraus thus hints at the developing conflict between the members of the SA and the party leadership. But the shifting of rhetorical gears from the analytical mode to the language of pathos makes the reference to the elements simultaneously appear more tethered to the natural or mythical world. The verbs become infinitives (*rütteln*)—renouncing their discursive force—and the literary-mimetic mode takes over as Kraus hints at the dimension of violence and suffering he feels has not been properly registered. His language, in other words, yields to Goethe's at precisely the moment he invokes utter lawlessness and the "savage spate" of Nazi violence, as if to suggest that this is where *he* must fall silent. And yet, his falling silent—and this could be one way of interpreting the essay's opening line—does not amount to the total renunciation of critical insight. For the indented quotation that follows the announcement of the Chancellor's decree (also derived from the same speech in the opening act) again emphasizes that while all of the attention is being directed at the issue of state power and at the highest levels of leadership, savagery and unruliness are becoming increasingly rampant. The word "meanwhile" (*indessen*) from Goethe's drama adds an additional layer of meaning to Kraus's essay, as it almost casually draws attention to the consequences of this misdirected attention, whether one is on the outside or on the inside. Kraus's critique, to be sure, is also about the dangers that inhere in focusing on the wrong thing; *Faust* provides him with a language to make this critique more salient. For even if the violence itself is beyond representation, it is its acknowledgment that *Faust* helps Kraus articulate.

To further explain: that the Nazi state has been produced by the selling of illusions and that its seemingly united front conceals its inner contradictions are valid political insights, as is the idea established in the motto that illegality has become the law.[32] The revolution is not over, in other words, if revolution is equated with lawlessness. But the use of the term *Faustnaturen* points, finally, to another central claim of the text: namely, that Nazism is to be understood as an "elementary event" (*Elementarereignis*), or as the violent expression of drives and desires that can neither be hindered nor easily explained away by a straightforward analysis of the political situation (*DW*, 307). As Ganahl has shown, there is, to be sure, a tension running throughout the text regarding Kraus's views of nature: at one point, Kraus calls National Socialism a "natural event" (*Naturereignis*), and in the very following sentence, he suggests that "nature the judge" (*die Richterin Natur*) might one day avenge the crimes committed against her (*DW*, 20).[33] Perhaps Kraus is hitting upon a dialectical understanding of nature à la the Frankfurt School, but either way, this tension between the understanding of nature as both cause of, and solution to this catastrophe is never fully resolved.

And it does not need to be. For in the context of the longer passage quoted above, it would appear that the most terrifying aspect of Nazism, for Kraus, is that despite the internal conflicts that may end up bringing about its ruin, the worst is yet to come: the Faust-natures are only threatening to become complete.[34] Here, even while hinting at the possibility that the movement will be destroyed from within, Kraus thus falls on the side of Nazism qua natural event, an event that continues to manifest itself in ever more grotesque forms. Taken as a whole, this passage provides an illustration of how the form of this "incommensurable" poem—Goethe's term to describe his literary creation—found, for Kraus, its corresponding incommensurable content.[35] The Faust-natures cannot be properly named or described; Kraus can only suggest that we have not yet seen what they are capable of becoming.

The spate of quotations that proceed this passage all derive from the same dialogue between the Chancellor and the Army Chief, and all are interrupted by brief Krausian commentaries. The focus has now shifted to a discussion of the burning of the Reichstag, and how this event has inaugurated a new instantiation of violence that is unable to be sated. Kraus transposes what he calls this "German violence" onto the Army Chief's prescient warning to his Emperor:

What madness raves in these wild days!
Kill and be killed on every hand,
The soldiery beyond command. [. . .]
The mercenary is malcontent,
Loud in the mouth demands his pay,
And if we settled our account
There and then he'd run away.
Stop people doing as they please
Is poking in a hornets' nest.
The realm they owe protection lies
Plucked and plundered, laid to waste.[36]

Wie tobt's in diesen wilden Tagen!
Ein jeder schlägt und wird erschlagen,
Und für's Kommando bleibt man taub . . . .
Der Mietsoldat wird ungeduldig,
Mit Ungestüm verlangt er seinen Lohn,
Und wären wir ihm nichts mehr schuldig,
Er liefe ganz und gar davon.
Verbiete wer, was Alle wollten,
Der hat ins Wespennest gestört;
Das Reicht, das sie beschützen sollten,
Es liegt geplündert und verheert.[37]

Faust appears to prophesize the historical trajectory of this regime: the mercenaries (i.e., the SA) are becoming impatient, and their violence increases in direct proportion to the time they are waiting to be compensated. Insanity has become the norm, evidenced by the unrestrained aggression that has been let loose. Yet the most visionary moment in the quotation is also the grimmest, as Kraus suggests that outside interference in this event is futile, and what lies ahead is an empire in ruins. Kraus's genuine plea to the world abroad finds him returning to the same speech by the Army Chief. "And abroad?", Kraus wonders:

> They have the freedom to run riot,
> Half the world's already lost,
> There are still kings in the Empire but
> None thinks it is his business in the least.[38]
>
> *Man läßt ihr Toben, wütend Hausen,*
> *Schon ist die halbe Welt vertan;*
> *Es sind noch Könige da draußen,*
> *Doch keiner denkt, es ging' ihn irgend an.*[39]

Addressing the non-German world, Kraus imagines that leaders abroad (the "kings in the Empire") would have to be forcibly dragged into a conflict before being convinced that the political unrest in Germany is a worthy concern. Again, Kraus has arrived at a sound insight regarding Nazism's ability to remain largely ignored by the international community, despite having committed criminal acts of violence against communists, homosexuals, and Jews, violence that has been well documented. But formally speaking, this set of quotations from *Faust II* supplements such documentary evidence through their mimetic reproduction of the terror that is invoked simply in the realization of the parallels between Goethe's drama and the contemporary political situation. They thus function affectively in Kraus's text as a catalyst for the reactivation of a dormant sensory apparatus that can no longer experience pain. At one point, Kraus is very explicit about this process:

> This newspaper-conception (*Zeitungsbegriff*) of a humanity, which has prostituted misfortune (*Unglück*) into a market cry and which still lies when it's telling the truth, corresponds entirely to the habitus of a readership that can only resume its relationship to humanity once it is capable of feeling a thousandth of that which it does not believe. Strike when in doubt (*Hiebe im Zweifelsfall*), so that they believe in violence! (*DW*, 111)

The "strike" above could be read as both a reference to Nazi violence and as a self-reference: Kraus's use of *Faust* would be, accordingly, the strike that attempts to induce belief in a violence that continues to be denied or ignored. In a kind of second-order mimetic reflection, the *Faust* quotations both point to the contradiction between National Socialism's words and deeds and reproduce the terror of the latter, otherwise (for Kraus) obscured to the reading public.

How, finally, does *Faust* assist Kraus in providing a critical vantage onto the problem of representing Nazi violence? Kraus turns, I suggest, to Raufebold, Habebald, and Haltefest, Mephisto's three henchmen introduced in the fourth act, where civil war has broken out, power politics is the context, and reactionary and revolutionary elements are hard to distinguish. These are the figures, we should recall, who murder the elderly couple, Philemon and Baucis, to make space for a Faustian dictatorship. In *Walpurgis*, they have become stand-ins for the SA, and Kraus thus weaves their dialogue into his own discussion of the violence-training to which Austrian youth are being subjected and of the fate of several Jewish doctors and lawyers from Breslau who were brutally assaulted. Here, as elsewhere, Kraus insists on understanding this violence as a revenge fantasy. But this episode has a prelude earlier in the text, and it is worth calling attention to the two distinct textual strategies Kraus employs in order to make his larger point. In the earlier episode, Kraus mentions a Dr. Ernst Eckstein and the work he performed "for" a concentration camp in Breslau. Heavily ironized in this section is the egregiously misleading term, "protective custody" (*Schutzhaft*), applied to those individuals who were removed from society and placed into these camps because their lives—on account of having been either a Marxist or a Jew—were deemed to be imperiled by this society (*DW*, 204–8). Giving the lie to this euphemism, Kraus splices in horrifying newspaper reports about the brutal treatment to which Eckstein was subjected by the "beast of Breslau, the murderer and police chief Heines" while under ostensible protection.[40] It was later reported that Eckstein committed suicide in his cell; other reports testified to the critical wounds and contusions found all over his body. In the later scene involving Mephisto's henchmen, Kraus alludes to this earlier episode, but here Heines has morphed into Raufebold ("Thug"). He writes: "But Thug steps forward and reports his accomplishments in Breslau," then quotes Thug's lines from *Faust*:

> The man who looks at me, before he can
> Look anywhere else I pulp his face and bash
> The back of the head of any man
> Who turns away into a bloody mush.[41]

> *Wer das Gesicht mir zeigt, der kehrt's nicht ab*
> *Als mit zerschlagenen Unter- und Oberbacken;*
> *Wer mir den Rücken kehrt, gleich liegt ihm schlapp*
> *Hals, Kopf und Schopf hinschlotternd graß im Nacken.*[42]

"The man" above has no options: perceived audacity (making eye contact) and perceived insolence (turning away) are deemed equally punishable crimes. In the end, his body will be nothing but a loose conglomeration of parts—the reference to the *Schopf* is especially resonant, since it evokes images of stereotypically Jewish hair.[43] We are thus presented with an image of brute, naked violence, executed by those whose names, Kraus writes, are not merely "allegorical" references to their character: "Thug," "Grabber," and "Tightfist" (*DW*, 303). The allegory has become reality when it "was previously all a metaphor" (*DW*, 141).[44] Combined, these two related moments in the essay constitute their own form of documentation. The literary intervention has become, in a sense, a more faithful reportage in its attempt to reproduce the terror of National Socialism while pointing to the limitations of discursive-descriptive language in its capacity to render certain dimensions of this experience intelligible. To understand Heines as Raufebold works in this context precisely because the latter is both an embodiment of grotesque, singular violence—violence incarnate, which is one way Kraus understands Nazism—*and* a quasi-mythical creature that resists discursive representation. The passage from *Faust II* that Kraus appropriates itself consists of contorted syntax, in a sense mirroring the violence to the body it describes.

Evolution and Revolution: The "Classical Walpurgis Night"

There is yet another way in which Goethe's drama provides Kraus with a unique vantage onto the problem of Nazism and its representation. Specifically, we can turn to Kraus's references to the "Classical Walpurgis Night," the long scene in the second act of *Faust II* that depicts a grotesque encounter between antiquity and modernity.[45] Among other moments from this scene that make their way into Kraus's text is a debate between two pre-Socratic philosophers, Thales and Anaxagoras, both of whom are trying to convince the Homunculus (who has joined Faust and Mephisto on their journey through the underworld) of their respective views on the origins of life and matter.[46] Thales promotes what has been referred to as a gradualist cosmology, the idea that life emerged slowly from water or from "dampness": "Things that live are engendered in the wet (*im feuchten*)."[47] Anaxagoras, for his part, envisions life as the product of a violent, volcanic eruption. This debate had been waged anew in the early nineteenth century under the respective guises of "Neptunian" and "Vulcanist" geology. Goethe was more sympathetic to the former, which better aligned with his gradualist politics and fear of revolution; accordingly, this scene is resolved with a victorious Thales and a Homunculus who shatters his vial and is ultimately absorbed into the sea in pursuit of human form.[48] It is important to emphasize that this debate not only pertained to the realm of geology, but also contained political and philosophical implications of which Kraus was clearly aware. In *Walpurgis*, Anaxagoras's words first appear in the motto, where Kraus invokes his ecstatic claim: "No nearer, orb of menace, or you lay / Waste our lives and all land and sea!"[49] A parallel is thus immediately perceptible between the menacing orb that Anaxagoras believes he has summoned to earth and that will bring only destruction, and the otherworldly eruption that is National Socialism, which, too, destroys all that it touches. Thales is left out of this picture.

The debate between Thales and Anaxagoras—not presented as such in Kraus's text—is later embedded within a series of critical passages juxtaposing three distinct figurations: the ideological misuse of Nietzsche's doctrines by the party elites; the notorious Nazi thug, Manfred von Killinger; and a newspaper report detailing the violence committed against, and humiliation suffered by communists, socialists, and Jews inside a concentration camp. This last report in particular, a harrowing section of which I have reproduced below, helps situate the context in which Kraus then turns to the two Greek philosophers. Kraus first quotes from the report; he then interrupts his own quotation:

> The camp was divided into several classes. The communists and the radical socialists in the third class had it the worst. The Jews were, indeed, provided for by the Jewish community, but they had to perform the most degrading services, scrubbing the toilet, cleaning the boots of the SA-men, kissing their feet or licking their boots on command. If they refused, the rubber bludgeon helped. I saw how their hair was torn out such that pieces of scalp were torn along with it. . . . Many suffered nervous breakdowns, others became ill . . .
>
> No, no philosopher can have willed that. (*DW*, 74–75)[50]

For Kraus, it is clear that Nietzsche would never have endorsed the atrocities committed in his name or in defense of his "will to power," a sentiment that Kraus does not share about Martin Heidegger—an issue to which I will return in chapter 5.[51] His point is that such brute force can in no way be justified by any philosophical doctrine worthy of the name; the sources of this violence must be sought elsewhere. Kraus thus quotes a police chief's promise to enact a "pogrom" the likes of which the world has never seen, along with invoking an ominous "retribution" that will make what has already occurred look like child's play. But just following Kraus's reference to Nietzsche above, he inserts a line from Anaxagoras's dialogue with Thales: "Tell me, O Thales, whether you ever did / In one night bring such a mountain forth from mud?", relating the question of the origins of matter to the violence just discussed.[52] Like Goethe, Kraus appears to be either conflating the realms of politics and nature or treating them as analogous to one another. This is, to be sure, a dialectical insight, insofar as Kraus implicitly raises the question whether nature sanctions or condemns politically charged violence, which, in the current context, is being carried out under its sign.

Timms has accordingly argued that Kraus was aware of the "vitalistic strain in German thought, which pictured nature in terms of conquest and violence, not harmony and balance, and his aim is now to bring out the ideological implications of this controversy, which are only hinted at by Goethe" (*AS* 2, 503–4). Yet the picture presented might even be more complicated. For while with Goethe, it is clear both who is speaking and whose theory ultimately prevails (Thales), in *Walpurgis* neither of these features is clearly demarcated.[53] In *Faust II*, it is Thales who first proclaims:

> The living flux of Nature was never bound
> To days and nights and the hourly round.
> She shapes all things after her ordinance.
> And even in the large there is no violence.[54]
>
> *Nie war Natur und ihr lebendiges Fließen*
> *Auf Tag und Nacht und Stunden angewiesen.*
> *Sie bildet regelnd jegliche Gestalt,*
> *Und selbst im Großen ist es nicht Gewalt.*[55]

Anaxagoras then interjects with "But here there was!" before launching into his opposing theory about the emergence of a mountain through fire. By contrast, Kraus omits the markers of dialogue, along with any indication that he is invoking two distinct speakers (*DW*, 75). *Walpurgis* thus inhabits both positions at once without necessarily privileging one over the other. This omission is significant for several reasons. By converting an erstwhile dialogue into a monologue, Kraus foregrounds the tension between continuity and discontinuity. Thales speaks to the aspect of the regime that is the product of a gradual process and is therefore more legible in its origins and trajectory—in this way there is a relationship between Thales's position and the earlier quotation about one "deformity" coupling with another, if we understand the latter to be hinting at the relationship between liberalism and National Socialism. Thales would, on this reading, embody not so much a normative understanding of political change that Kraus endorses (á la Goethe) as he would a vision of Nazism's continuity with a modernity it outwardly disavows. This modernity, for Kraus, is intimately connected to the power of the press and the liberalism that spawned it. Kraus will say as much when he claims toward the end of his essay that National Socialism "did not annihilate the press; it is the press that has created (*erschaffen*) National Socialism. Seemingly as a reaction alone, but in truth as fulfillment (*Fortsetzung*)" (*DW*, 307). Goebbels, Kraus reminds us, was trained on the techniques of modern journalism, and it is he who appears as the real protagonist of the text. Without this

Mephisto-like figure wielding his black magic in order to stir up a dormant, violent sentiment in the masses, there would be, for Kraus, no proper movement to speak of.[56] For Goebbels

> is familiar with all the trendy terminology which rootless intellectual authors are no longer able to use. He has attitude and empathy, he knows about stimulus and impetus, application and implication, dramatic presentation, filmic transposition, flexible formulation and the other aids to radical renewal, he has experience and perspective, indeed for both reality and vision, he has life-dynamics and world-philosophy, he approves of ethos and pathos, but also mythos.[57]

> *ist ein Kenner aller einschlägigen Terminologie, deren Verwendung dem Asphaltschriftum nicht mehr möglich ist. Er hat die Einstellung wie die Einführung, er kennt den Antrieb wie den Auftrieb, die Auswertung wie die Auswirkung, die szenische Aufmachung, den filmischen Aufriß wie die Auflockerung und was sonst zum Aufbruch gehört, er hat das Erlebnis und den Aspekt, und zwar sowohl für die Realität wie für die Vision, er hat Lebensgefühl und Weltanschauung, er will das Ethos, das Pathos, jedoch auch den Mythos.* (*DW*, 54)

Especially evident in the original German, Kraus imitates the linguistic flourishes of journalistic writing as he identifies Goebbels as one of its master practitioners.[58] In so doing, he exposes the sheer familiarity of Goebbels's techniques. In this way, Goebbels represents the more Thalesian aspect of National Socialism, its gradual formation out of the loins of modernity. On the other hand, Goebbels's ability to smuggle myth into his appeal indexes the seemingly asynchronous element of this movement, that which radically sets it apart from other political systems. Goebbels is thus able to synthesize modern form (his methods of propaganda) with archaic content (his appeal to myth, or the occult and repressed elements of the movement, whose violent return is being summoned). When Kraus quotes Anaxagoras without naming him—"But here there was [violence]!"—he suggests that sometimes nature simply erupts unannounced and in unforeseeably violent ways. Anaxagoras peers into nature and portends violence, chaos, and spontaneity. His presence in Kraus's text supplements the merely discursive accounts of the violence that is endemic to this movement. In a word, Kraus thus points both to the evolutionary (Thales) *and* the revolutionary (Anaxagoras) dimensions of National Socialism by foregrounding the various relationships that emerge between the literary, the natural, and the political.

"The Figment Risen Up Against Us"

Just before Mephistopheles, Faust, and the Homunculus depart on their journey to the underworld of the Walpurgis Night, Mephistopheles declares *ad spectatores*: "In the end we are dependent on / Creatures we ourselves have made."[59] Appearing toward the end of Kraus's essay, this line stands out in relief against the flurry of *Faust* quotations involving Mephisto's henchmen and their belligerence. It suggests, in this context, a view of the Nazi regime as a product of the epoch's own making, a self-indictment similar to those found in *The Last Days* and in *Cloudcuckooland*. And yet a regime man-made can also, Kraus suggests, collapse due to internal or external causes. The senseless suffering of the individual, Kraus concludes—without attaching metaphysical meaning to such suffering[60]—will cease when "the good spirits of a human world are brought to life for the deed of retribution (*aufleben zur Tat der Vergeltung*)" (*DW*, 327). Such unflagging humanism thus reasserts itself in Kraus's insistence that the world that has just erupted is far from the human world, which is nonetheless capable of avenging the misdeeds committed against it.[61] The passage that follows—the very last words of *Walpurgis*—however, belongs to the Emperor. Kraus quotes from a scene in the fourth act in which the Emperor is addressing Faust, pleading for the downfall of the recently arisen "Anti-Emperor" and the restoration of his empire:

> And the figment risen up against us
> That calls himself Emperor, prince of our territories,
> Our vassals' lord, our army's chief, I'll thrust
> Him down among the dead with my own fist.[62]
>
> *Sei das Gespenst, das gegen uns erstanden,*
> *Sich Kaiser nennt und Herr von unsern Landen,*
> *Des Heeres Herzog, Lehnsherr unsrer Großen,*
> *Mit eigner Faust ins Totenreich gestoßen!*[63]

The Anti-Emperor alone believes himself to be an emperor; in truth, he is no more than a "figment" or a specter that has risen up against his people. David Constantine has translated the personal possessive in the passage ("*Mit* eigner *Faust*") such that the fist in question refers the fist of the Emperor as opposed to that of the Anti-Emperor, but the original German is less clear. In view of Kraus's admonition, the passage suggests that some kind of brute force (a literal "fist") will be needed to combat the established reign, though it is unclear whether this is supposed to come from within or without. Either way, it is fitting that Kraus concludes his literary response to Nazism not with an analysis but with an ambiguous allusion, not with his own words, but with Goethe's.

Not all cultural inheritances, Kraus thereby suggests, need to be simply redeemed from external abuse (i.e., the Nazi appropriation of the Faust legend) or given a final interpretation, especially when their linguistic and political ambiguities provide insights into modern experience where other words have failed.[64] Much like National Socialism itself, Faust and the Faustian character, for Kraus, cannot be reduced to a single image, trait, or phenomenon, even if there are clear resonances between Faust's insatiable drive toward domination and Nazism.[65] *Walpurgis* attempts, rather, to oppose the grand, myth-making project of Nazism by turning another myth against itself—that is, not by reducing a literary text to the ostensible essence of its central character, but by deploying it as a modernist assemblage of quotations that is both continuous with Kraus's commentary and disruptive. If Kraus declared that he was taking a "stance" against Nazism as opposed to a "position" (*DW*, 14–15),[66] perhaps we can understand this as akin to what Jean-Luc Nancy has called the modern writer's "interruption" of myth: quite literally, Kraus interrupts the staging of Nazi mythology by invoking another myth.[67] In this way, his text functions as a mimetic reflection of the phenomenon under critique, for Kraus's use of *Faust* evinces the very tensions and inconsistencies that underlie National Socialism, both in ideology and in practice. Kraus treats the "Third Reich" as the realization of a fantasy or the enactment of a reality both more inconceivable than the literary-mythological world that "preformed" it and yet most faithfully represented through recourse to this world. He has created, in effect, a third installment of the Faust tragedy, while raising the troubling question of what it means to be the inheritor of such a tradition—another iteration of the question the Grumbler earlier posed regarding his own complicity in *The Last Days*.

What final conclusions can be drawn? As the instantiation of a new form of life—distinct even from other contemporary fascist movements—Nazism, for Kraus, demanded a singular form of representation.[68] In this respect, the formal experiments of *Walpurgis* anticipate another claim made by Arendt in which she explicitly distinguishes Nazism from Italian fascism and other authoritarian movements that developed in Central and Eastern Europe. Mussolini, for example, never established a totalitarian regime and was satisfied "with dictatorship and one-party rule."[69] Quoting Goebbels on the difference between fascism and National Socialism, Arendt thus argues that the latter penetrated the "roots" of its members, demanding total identification and conformity, and destroying the capacity for *individualized experience*.[70] If focusing more on its violent inclinations, Kraus similarly treats Nazism as distinct from both fascism and bourgeois party politics, but through his use of *Faust* he goes one step further in attempting to show how the transition from a politics of the *word* (i.e., social democracy) to a politics of the *deed* (Nazism) was both gradual and revolutionary. The radicalism of the Nazi movement consisted in the absolute consummation of this transition, such that what emerged was a world of pure cant and pure violence: "In every domain of social and cultural renewal we catch sight of the awakening of the phrase to the deed (*Aufbruch der Phrase zur Tat*)" (*DW*, 141). Nazism provoked a response in Kraus that, accordingly, moved beyond conventional satire. His dialogue with Goethe's last drama most explicitly conveys the tension introduced earlier: between the characterization of Nazism as, on the one hand, a civilizational caesura, and, on the other, as a product of modernity that can be parsed, analyzed, and undermined from within. An amalgam of allusion, historical documentation, and incisive critique, this late text is Kraus's testament to the limits to, and potential of, both discursive and literary language to grasp experience under the conditions of totalitarianism.

Part 2

Dialogues

Chapter 4

"A Monstrous Nonentity"

Kierkegaard, Kraus, and Benjamin

> [Journalism is] an incurable sore which will become more and more cancerous, more and more insufferable; and the greater the evil, the more it will be tolerated, until the day comes when, thanks to their abundance, the newspapers will be in a confusion like that of Babel. We know, the whole lot of us, that the papers will go further in ingratitude than kings, further in speculation and calculation than the dirtiest kind of commerce, that they will rot our intelligences by selling us their mental fire-water every morning.
>
> —Honoré de Balzac, *Lost Illusions* (1837–1843)

> It is impossible to discern whether this "public opinion" has come about by way of public communication or through opinion management, whereby it must remain undecided again whether the latter refers merely to the enunciation of a mass preference incapable of articulating itself or to the reduction to the status of a plebiscitary echo of an opinion that, although quite capable of attaining enlightenment, has been forcibly integrated.
>
> —Jürgen Habermas, *The Structural Transformations of the Bourgeois Public Sphere* (1991)

Criticism of the press and of journalism has a long tradition of its own. Balzac ventriloquizes his hatred of journalism through the embittered Claude Vignon of *Lost Illusions*, himself a journalist filled with shame over the disreputable social role to which he has been reduced. Balzac's point is twofold: first, that the press's integration into society and subsequent influence on that society knows no limits; and second, that there is an inverse relationship between the press's influence and the intelligence and suggestibility of its readers. Balzac speaks of "confusion" and "commerce" as the defining features of this enterprise.

Over a century later, Jürgen Habermas addressed the genealogical unfolding of the concept of "public opinion" in its constitutive relationship to the press. Denoting either the inability for a public to articulate anything more than a general preference, or the imposition of an opinion generated by private interests on the public, public opinion, for Habermas, has not always been what it ostensibly claims to be. In his study of the "transformations of the bourgeois public sphere," he argues that the liberal press—an indispensable forum for reflecting on and disseminating public opinion, and thus a thoroughly political instrument of liberalism—would undergo a major transformation in the second half of the nineteenth century. Broadly stated, Habermas is concerned with the extent to which certain institutions served to expand or interfere with the space in which "critical reason," absent of political domination, could be articulated and negotiated. The press is one such institution, and his discussion of its internal transformations warrants our attention:

> The history of the big daily papers in the second half of the nineteenth century proves that the press itself became manipulable to the extent that it became commercialized. Ever since the marketing of the editorial section became interdependent with that of the advertising section, the press (until then an institution of private people insofar as they constituted a public) became . . . the gate through which privileged private interests invaded the public sphere.[1]

The press—primarily in France, Germany, and Great Britain—effectively began as a profit-*losing* endeavor; its publishers gave free reign to their respective editors, who, in turn, frequently shared in the profits. Habermas's narrative, however, is one of increasing depoliticization: an institution that "evolved out of the public's use of its reason" eventually became a "medium for culture as an object of consumption."[2] Hundreds of daily papers emerged during the first decades of the nineteenth century, each with its own political position and each struggling to insert its voice in the officially sanctioned political public sphere. With the establishment of the bourgeois constitutional state, however, such an enterprise was "released" from the pressure to be a political instrument and could focus solely on its growth as a business enterprise.[3] In other words, when commerce began to dominate and profit margins began to determine the content of the news, the nature of the press shifted fundamentally. The ill-repute into which this institution—and the journalist in particular—fell in the eyes of a certain segment of society skeptical of the press's growing influence over the public sphere thus appears to be rooted in the historical development of the institution itself.

Indeed, in his 1919 lecture "Politics as a Vocation," the economist and sociologist Max Weber argued that the journalist "shares with all demagogues and lawyers (as well as artists) the fate of being denied a fixed place in the social structure. . . . He belongs," Weber continues, "to a kind of pariah caste that in the eyes of 'society' is always judged socially by its lowest representatives from the point of view of morality."[4] While Weber ultimately defends the integrity of the profession and critiques this unbalanced view that he sees as prevalent in modern societies, his point about the constitutively unstable position of the journalist vis-à-vis the social structure is an important one. For it is not simply that the demagogue, lawyer, and journalist are denied this "fixed place," but that such figures appear to exert a disproportionate amount of power and influence within the very social order responsible for relegating them to this unstable position. Thus, while Balzac was concerned with the immorality of journalists and the rotting intelligence of the newspaper-reading public, and Habermas focuses on the relationship between capitalism/liberalism and the press qua institution, Weber is interested in understanding, in sociological terms, how the figure of the journalist came to represent what he represents in the eyes of the public. In light of these theories and reflections (of which there are many more), what comes into view is the reality that the history of the Western, liberal—and what Walter Benjamin will call the "bourgeois"—press is nearly coeval with the history of the suspicion directed at its function and influence in modernity.[5]

Kraus's critiques of the press constitute an important chapter of this narrative, though they are distinct from both the sociological perspectives of Habermas or Weber and the more reactionary, distanced position represented by Balzac (even if Kraus quotes Balzac as an authority). Kraus had his own interlocutors, implicit and explicit, and my central claim in this chapter is that Kraus's positions on the press are best illuminated when brought into dialogue with two figures not necessarily known for their reflections on this institution: Søren Kierkegaard on one side of the historical divide, and Walter Benjamin on the other. In what I will argue to be their respective searches for an alternative public discourse—a *counter*discourse, to invoke a concept I developed in chapter 1—Kierkegaard and Benjamin provide a pre- and posthistory to Kraus's polemics. More specifically, Kierkegaard's reflections on the nature of public opinion and the "chatter" of the "present age" not only offer insight into his own theory of modernity, but also anticipate what Kraus later identifies as the press's fundamental threat to the imaginative capacities of the modern reader. Kraus's condemnations of the relationship between the press and World War I provide, subsequently, a rereading of Kierkegaard. Benjamin's writings on both Kraus and the press, in turn, reveal the dialectical, and, indeed, Marxist implications of Kierkegaard and Kraus, implications that are most salient in Benjamin's theories of public opinion and journalistic language under capitalism.

The critique of the press we find in both Kierkegaard and Benjamin is not to be viewed, I argue, as a peripheral feature of their work, but rather as a necessary component of their broader theories of subjectivity and authority. For both of these figures are concerned with the dialectic between privacy and publicity, and with what happens to the voice of the modern subject within this dialectic. Kraus serves as a linchpin connecting these two figures, otherwise separated by distinct and even opposing philosophical, theological, and political commitments.

Kierkegaard's *Two Ages: The Age of Revolution and the Present Age: A Literary Review* (1846, hereafter *A Literary Review*) sets the philosophical tone for what follows. In it, Kierkegaard probes the relationship between the press, the public, and modern subjectivity. In this sense, the text constitutes an early foray into media critique by drawing attention to the function of the press as a conspicuous medium within the modern social totality. This text is particularly significant because it was translated into German by Theodor Haecker in 1914, who was primarily responsible for introducing Kierkegaard to the German-speaking world. In the introduction to his translation, Haecker makes explicit the affinity between Kraus and Kierkegaard; he is thus a crucial figure for understanding the historical context in which this relationship first becomes intelligible.[6] While Haecker's translations are the source of Kraus's explicit invocations of Kierkegaard during the war and again in the 1920s, Kierkegaardian motifs are evident throughout Kraus's oeuvre. Accordingly, I next turn to Kraus's 1912 essay "The Downfall of the World through Black Magic" before offering a reading of Kraus's anti-war oration, "In These Great Times" (1914). It is here, indeed, where Kraus invokes, á la Kierkegaard, the trope of silence before launching a merciless assault against the journalistic era that has created the conditions of possibility for this war.

Benjamin's reflections on these discourses constitute the last part of this chapter. For Benjamin—who, like Kraus and Kierkegaard, partakes of broad-brush attacks on the press that require qualifications from our perspective—the "bourgeois" press exists to further its class's political and economic interests. In accordance with both his investment in the shifting nature of authorship and his Marxist approach to new forms of mass media, Benjamin scrutinizes the effects of the press on reading habits and, ultimately, on the formation of modern subjectivity. He is, in other words, concerned with the effects and vicissitudes of language under the regime of commodity capitalism. Benjamin, too, subjects the concept of public opinion to a critical lens, exploring its paradoxical structure. For him, Kraus embodies a self-reflective moment within the press that hints at its latent, redemptive dimension. Krausian authority thus offers an ephemeral glimpse into what language might look like beyond the spell of the commodity.

Kierkegaard's Phantoms

As a thinker of subjective truth, Kierkegaard's work, often ventriloquized through pseudonyms and other ironic devices, explores various modes or stages of subjectivity (the aesthetic, the ethical, and the religious) as a means to elucidate the varying degrees of truth one embodies at each respective stage.[7]

Kierkegaard advocated a radical vision of Christianity that addressed the subject qua thinking individual—hence his frequent and analogous invocation of Socrates, who, similarly, waged a campaign against a corrupt universal (ancient Greek religious life) in the name of inner subjectivity.[8] Truth, for Kierkegaard is to be embodied or experienced in order to be affirmed as such, not merely comprehended as a concept (as he saw in G. W. F. Hegel) and perceived as external to subjective experience.[9] Kierkegaard is thus supremely invested in the fate of the modern subject and in the existential burden of freedom that she bears. These broad philosophical-theological concerns are relevant because they fundamentally inform his polemical interventions into matters concerning the public sphere and the role of journalism within it. Thus while Kierkegaard's attention to the press was at least partially motivated by his involvement in a nasty affair with an influential satirical weekly in Copenhagen—it is important to situate his critique within the context of his broader understanding of what he termed the "present age."[10]

A Literary Review is Kierkegaard's nominal attempt to write a literary review of the Danish novel *Two Ages* by Thomasine Gyllembourg, first published in 1845.[11] He uses this platform, however, to explore the meaning of the eponymous "two ages" as he conceives of them: the "age of revolution," which he describes as passionate, erotic, decisive, and as having form; and the nihilistic "age of reflection"—or, the present age—which he describes as torpid, indecisive, and formless (*KW* XIV, 60–64).[12] The age of revolution has "*not nullified the principle of contradiction*," and is thus able to become "either good or evil," but either way, its passion renders perceptible the progress or regress of its actions (*KW* XIV, 66). This is all in contrast to the present age, which hovers in a state of indecision and is neither progressive, nor conservative, nor destructive.[13] Its most salient characteristic is its "leveling" tendency, which refers to the elimination of all qualitative distinctions among individuals—the destruction of individuality—and to the impoverished reduction of the concept of equality before God to mere sameness. As Alastair Hannay writes, "Kierkegaard takes 'levelling' to be the nemesis of his age, . . . a blocking off of the only viable path to human completion. It is also able, if carried to its extreme, to produce a crisis that reawakens individuals to their possibilities."[14] To explore this dialectical moment in Kierkegaard I have reproduced a longer passage from his review, which addresses the social conditions that both inform and issue from the emergence of leveling:[15]

> For leveling really to take place, a phantom must first be raised, the spirit of leveling, a *monstrous abstraction*, an all-encompassing something that is nothing, a mirage—and this phantom is *the public*. Only in a passionless but reflective age can this phantom develop with the aid of the press, when the press itself becomes a phantom. There is no such thing as a public in spirited, passionate, tumultuous times, even when a *people* wants to actualize the idea of the barren

> desert, destroying everything. There are parties, and there is concretion. In such times the press takes on the character of a concretion in relation to the division. But . . . a sedentary reflective age devoid of passion will produce this phantom if the press is supposed to be the only thing which, though weak itself, maintains a kind of life in this somnolence. The public is . . . a monstrous nonentity . . . a corps, outnumbering all the people together, but this corps can never be called up for inspection; indeed, it cannot even have so much as a *single representative*, because it is itself an abstraction. (*KW* XIV, 90–91)[16]

This reads as an indictment. For in contrast to the genuine, or "concrete" leveling that Kierkegaard suggests is the provenance of true religion, the leveling described above is a function of the anonymity that defines the "public" in the present age. Kierkegaard understands this "abstraction" to be both infinitely larger than the sum of its parts and a deformed reflection of those parts, which would explain why he calls the public "monstrous." By distinguishing between "abstract" and "concrete," Kierkegaard reveals the Hegelian residues in his thinking, according to which the abstract would be the one-sided, contentless entity whose mere existence is at odds with, or in contradiction to, its self-understanding. The public, in other words, is an abstract entity because it consists of an anonymous mass; it is in contrast to the idea of a concrete "people," which, in age of revolution, is mobilized for a specific cause and thereby reconstitutes itself as a higher form of collective subjectivity. A people has form and will in contrast to the public, which is formless and lacking in will. And its lack of conviction means that it survives in contradiction to itself.

In drawing out the implications of this diagnosis of the present age, Kierkegaard explores what it means to exist "in contradiction to oneself," and in so doing, he refers to the language of public discourse as "chatter," defined as the "annulment of the passionate disjunction between being silent and speaking." Only, we read, "the person who can remain essentially silent can speak essentially, can act essentially. Silence is inwardness. Chattering gets ahead of essential speaking, and giving utterance to reflection has a weakening effect on action by getting ahead of it" (*KW* XIV, 97). To chatter is thus to avoid speaking and acting with any significance. Peter Fenves understands chatter in Kierkegaard as that gesture that "suspends disjunctive judgment," reducing chatter to the condition of language in a postlapsarian state and raising the question of whether any speech act at all can be distinguished from "inactive, inert, and thus idle talk."[17] Yet this position seems to ignore the way Kierkegaard views chatter as distinct from essential speech, even if the latter belongs exclusively to the habitus of the passionate age. Kierkegaard is clearly concerned with chatter's anticipatory, suspended, and contradictory character. It is contradictory because it is an utterance that appears to say nothing; it has no telos other than its own self-perpetuation, hence its relation to indecision and formlessness. And for Kierkegaard, chatter finds its most socially sanctioned articulation in the press—above all, the tabloid press—which is never silent, but does not know the value of essential speech.

This philosophical exploration of chatter as a symptom of modernity is ultimately what brings Kierkegaard's concerns closer to those of Habermas and, ultimately, of Kraus. For in chatter, the "distinction between what is private and what is public is *nullified* in a private-public garrulousness. . . . For the public is public opinion that is interested in what is utterly private" (*KW* XIV, 100). Public opinion, for Kierkegaard, is a misleading concept—much like it will be for Kraus and Benjamin—for it entails both the publicity of the private sphere and the privatization of the public.[18] This term should therefore not be confused with the will of the people. If Kierkegaard wishes to maintain a distinction between the public and private domains, it is because he thinks that they need to be first thought of as discrete domains before they can be thought of in relation to each other. For where else, he implies, would subjective inwardness—that quality decidedly lacking in the present age—develop, if not in the private sphere? Kierkegaard's point, I take it, is that the press conceals this contradiction: in its chatter and its attendant role as a generator of public opinion, it is antithetical to the development of inwardness, which would be, in turn, necessary for the emergence of a robust people and a concrete politics. The public and the press are thus mutually reliant on one another, and both work toward the destruction of individual subjectivity, an absence that is necessary for the public and its press.

Kierkegaard's reflections on the public and the press amount to a social theory about modernity, which he views as splintered and extending in various, irreconcilable directions. Enumerating a series of dispositions that define the present age, he thus highlights how its salient features are, in effect, contradictory compromises between two subjective modes of experience that are internally consistent. The lover and the debauchee, for example, are united by their equally passionate commitment to Eros, if manifested in distinct ways. The philanderer, by contrast—an embodiment of Kierkegaard's nihilistic modernity—flirts with both ends of the spectrum without committing to either (*KW* XIV, 100–103).[19] The more an individual's actions fall into contradictions of which he remains unaware, the more he disavows inwardness and thus the ability to recognize contradiction—and the more he is able to remain anonymous and therefore unwedded to any position or view. In illustrating the relationship between anonymity, modernity, and the press, Kierkegaard describes a dog who is repeatedly encouraged to attack a prominent figure, but over whom nobody will claim ownership—the philosopher is clearly reflecting on his own bitter experience as the butt of a series of anonymously authored satires and caricatures published in *The Corsair*, a Danish mass-produced satirical journal. It is precisely this form of anonymity that Kierkegaard elevates as central to the public and its press, even if it is only visible in the tabloids. Accordingly, he criticizes the "unrepentant" subscribers of newspapers for never claiming ownership over the opinions expressed therein (*KW* XIV, 95). The subscriber just as easily attaches himself to a reigning opinion as he detaches himself from it when that opinion becomes unpopular. The press, to be sure, contains the inchoate potential to be something other than what it currently is—recall what Kierkegaard asserts in the long passage above regarding its political potential in an age of revolution. In its present form, however, it sanctions inaction and anonymity and it dissolves any potential distinction between a public and a private sphere.

Leveling, chatter, contradiction, anonymity: these are the symptoms of Kierkegaard's modernity, a modernity that has unwittingly paved a path toward self-destruction and has done so without *essentially* acting, speaking, or making a decision. In its idleness and indecision, Kierkegaard's "reflective" age thus quietly brings ruin upon itself. In referring once again to the effect of the press in the present age, his tone becomes apocalyptic:

> An age exhausted by a flash of enthusiasm will relax all the more readily in indolence, and even if we were to imagine that the press would become weaker and weaker for lack of events and ideas to stir the age, leveling becomes all the more a decadent urge, a sensate stimulation that excites momentarily and only makes the evil worse, the rescue more difficult, and the probability of destruction greater. (*KW* XIV, 94)

It is precisely during moments such as this, Kierkegaard admonishes his readers, that the press's leveling tendencies have the most deleterious effects on its readers, whose resistance to momentary excitement has been weakened on account of their diminished capacities to think as individual subjects. With an eye toward journalistic sensationalism, Kierkegaard thus sees his age as teetering on the edge of crisis. What makes his critique modern and helpful for clarifying the stakes of Kraus's and Benjamin's positions is that it emphasizes the threats to modern subjectivity even if it does not name structures and events such as capitalism, liberalism, or war. If Kierkegaard presupposes that the press is a product of modernity's emancipation from bygone institutions of authority, he is also aware of its underside, of the illiberal forces unleashed within a liberal framework. His views, I argue, are subsequently transformed and radicalized by Kraus.

Haecker, Kierkegaard, Kraus

> When the context has become meaningless . . . the best thing to do is to scrutinize the particular parts of what is said. When the mouth blathers pure drivel, it is futile to try to deliver a coherent discourse; it is better to consider each word by itself.
>
> —Kierkegaard, as quoted by Theodor Haecker in "The War and the Leaders of Spirit" (1915)[20]

The German author, satirist, translator, and Protestant-cum-Catholic theologian Theodor Haecker is largely responsible for bringing Kierkegaard to Kraus's attention and for making the most explicit connection between these two figures.[21] As a translator of Kierkegaard, Haecker can be credited with spreading the philosopher's influence within the German-speaking world during the prewar era. While Haecker's relationship to both Kierkegaard and Kraus was transformed on account of his conversion, Kraus remained an important figure for him throughout his life, a model satirist, if, in the end, a non-Christian who was therefore irredeemable. Haecker's prewar writings, however, mark the period when he viewed Kraus as the closest living descendent of the Danish philosopher. In *Søren Kierkegaard: Philosophy of Inwardness* (1913), he writes:

> Among all the living, Kraus was regaled with the strongest *vis comica*, and yet with him it stands in the service of the Idea. He is the only great, ethical (*durch Ethik gedeckte*) polemicist and satirist of the age; he alone—and no one else—would have the right in his works of hatred (*Werke des Hasses*) to quote Kierkegaard's terrifying words about the journalists.[22]

For Haecker, Kraus's vitriol elevated him into the same ethical sphere as Kierkegaard, which made it possible for them to be discussed in the context of their shared scathing critique of the press. He writes that Kraus "is the most courageous man living today, for he stands with his work in the *glaring light of the public*. It is indeed still less demanding to search for God, who is spirit, while hiding or among the bees and flowers, than it is not to lose sight of him in the city streets among the grimaces and larvae."[23] Haecker valorizes Kraus's role as a quintessentially public figure, who neither hides nor escapes into the realm of privacy or romantic, aesthetic longing, and who thus risks everything in his unwavering commitment to an idea, which Haecker calls "God" or "spirit." Here, Haecker views Kraus through a Kierkegaardian lens. For while Kraus has not achieved the religious stage that Kierkegaard (and Haecker) extols as the highest stage of existence, he has nonetheless obtained ethical status amidst an "aesthetically" saturated culture—that is, a culture of hiddenness and anonymity, precisely the sort of culture Kierkegaard diagnoses in *A Literary Review*.[24] For Haecker, Kraus's relationship to Kierkegaard is thus not only based on the continuity of an ethical tradition, but also on Kraus's commitment to a certain notion of public life that rejects anonymity and its implications.

In the afterword to his 1914 German translation of Kierkegaard's essay, *The Present Age* (the second part of *A Literary Review*, the essay discussed in the previous section)—which Haecker translated as *Kritik der Gegenwart* ("critique of the present"), aligning his age with Kierkegaard's—Kraus goes unmentioned but lingers in background.[25] After quoting an important passage from Kierkegaard—"Leveling does not come from God" (suggesting that "leveling" is not to be equated with genuine equality)—Haecker turns his attention to his own specific present.

> Who rules the world today? Every child, every chorus girl, and especially every minister knows that the press does, even if they cannot grasp what that means, although the minister should know exactly what it means. We can recognize a European people from its newspapers, at best from its most successful ones. . . . The comical unity of the talented smarminess is all there, for the feuilleton is contained in politics, and politics is contained in the feuilleton.[26]

The Krausian resonances are salient not only in content, but also in Haecker's satirical tone and use of chiasmus to identify a formal identity between the feuilleton and politics—the pretensions of the former match the shallowness of the latter.[27] The press embodies, furthermore, the absence of inwardness characteristic of this age and its tendency toward self-deception or even self-delusion. We can thus conclude that, for Haecker, Kraus fulfilled a role that Kierkegaard had once occupied: he is the inwardness of the present age; his work the counterdiscourse to the press. Indeed, in his postconversion essay, "The Catholic Writer and Language" (1927), Haecker rhetorically asks his readers, "What else will remain from our time apart from its genuine satire? Black magic or *The Torch*?"[28] He thereby invokes Kraus's concern discussed in chapter 1: Which discourse will outlive its time and be received by posterity?[29] And yet from Haecker's now Catholic perspective, satire was to be effectively "overcome" and Kraus was ultimately a "despairing," "impatient" idealist, whose "love of unbelief" was inferior to Christian love.[30] Haecker's reception of Kierkegaard, Kraus, and the relationship between the two (both before and after his conversion) is thus unthinkable without his investment in matters of faith and Christianity.[31] What I want to argue, however, is that Kraus and Kierkegaard can be thought together beyond the framework of either Protestantism or Catholicism.

It would thus be helpful to turn our attention to the spate of Kierkegaard quotations that Kraus reproduces in successive order in a 1916 issue of *The Torch*, under the heading "Kierkegaard on the Journalists." Two related passages, in particular, merit analysis (neither of which, to be sure, comes from *A Literary Review*):

> Woe to the daily press! If Christ came to the world today, as sure as I live he would not attack the high priests, etc.—he would attack the journalists.
>
> God in heaven knows that bloodthirst is alien to my soul, and I believe that I also have a concept of a responsibility to a God that is appalling, but yet, yet would I in the name of God take the

> responsibility to give the order if I first of all, with the precaution of the most anxious conscience, had convinced myself that there was not one single other man facing the rifles—yes, not one single living creature other than—journalists.[32]

These severe—and, from our perspective, rather unsettling—words were uttered by Kierkegaard in the context of the *Corsair* affair, which would explain their impassioned and violent undertone. Yet Kierkegaard's reference to the "high priests" suggests a provocative analogy between the Pharisees of antiquity and contemporary mainstream journalists, both of whom, for Kierkegaard, represent examples of unwarranted and abused authority. It is, furthermore, important to read Kraus's response to these quotations in the context of World War I, when the repercussions of journalistic unscrupulousness were, for Kraus, far more serious than what they were in Kierkegaard's time:

> And after seventy years, when [what Kierkegaard envisions] would be seventy times more desirable because there are seventy times as many gun barrels and journalists, the latter no longer stand in front of the barrels but, rather, behind them; they've helped with the loading and then stand by as we show them the shooting guns and the blood that runs (*wie es schießt und fließt*), waiting for them to arrive so that they can describe it all. What a responsibility the earth—which wills and bears this—takes upon itself in the name of God![33]

Kierkegaard functions in this context as a valid authority who, in a sense, grants Kraus permission to reproduce and expand upon this violent fantasy. Both figures converge on the image of the journalist as a secular high priest. But Kraus's response also suggests that Kierkegaard has become more than a mere predecessor, for his point is slightly different than the philosopher's. If Kierkegaard fantasizes about eradicating the journalist because he exercises false authority over a passive reading public, Kraus sees the journalist's powers as having increased seventyfold: today, the journalist both stages *and* reports the event; he is both a cause and an effect, rendering negligible the distinction between the two. Having today assumed a position "behind" the barrel, the journalist, for Kraus, is as much an agent of war as the general in battle. We have returned to familiar territory.

That Kraus viewed himself as aligned with Kierkegaard can, finally, be confirmed by turning briefly to one more issue of *The Torch*. Amidst Kraus's long-standing polemic against Imre Bekessy, the Hungarian-born proprietor of the tabloid paper *The Hour* (*Die Stunde*), Kraus published a piece entitled "Kierkegaard and *The Corsair*" (1925), invoking the philosopher once again. Kraus's campaign against the sensationalism, extortionary practices, and general corruption of *The Hour* culminated in one of his most memorable slogans—"Throw the villain out of Vienna!"—and eventually resulted in Bekessy's shameful departure from the Austrian capital.[34] This result was, in Kraus's eyes and the eyes of his public, a victory for the city of Vienna.[35] It also evoked comparisons between his situation and Kierkegaard's polemic with Meir Goldschmidt—the editor of *The Corsair*—which had once rendered the philosopher the laughingstock of the city. Reproducing Kierkegaard's journal entries that addressed this affair (Haecker's translations), Kraus suggests a strong parallel between their respective feuds, despite the fact that Kierkegaard suffered much more humiliation from his affair with Goldschmidt than Kraus did from his with Bekessy. The inaccuracies of the analogy notwithstanding, however, Kraus found Kierkegaard's 1854 definition of the daily press compelling enough to reprint: "Here people are demoralized in the shortest possible time, on the largest possible scale and at the cheapest possible price" (*F* 706, 24, 1925).[36] The avarice and immorality of the boulevard press—specifically, the type responsible for rumormongering and gossip—are brought together in this pithy definition, but even more important is Kraus's suggestion that the press's primary threat is not to the individual per se, but to the moral health of the city at large. This perspective allows us to view a play such as *Cloudcuckooland* in slightly different light, but it also provides a glimpse into Kraus's self-understanding as a defender of the demos—a purifier of the city's scourges—and, in this sense, an inheritor and transformer of Kierkegaard's legacy.[37] Next worth exploring, then, is how certain aspects of Kraus's thinking can be identified as Kierkegaardian even when the philosopher plays no explicit role in their articulation.[38]

Words, Deeds, and War

> The government cannot outlaw the natural powers that a man possesses, but it can forbid the possession of firearms because these are much too powerful and beyond the domain of the human. In the same way, the government cannot prohibit spoken communication . . . , but it could very well prohibit the daily press, because it is far too powerful as a means of communication.
>
> —Kierkegaard, reprinted in *The Torch*, no. 706 (1925)[39]

Anticipating Benjamin's reflections on the matter at hand, Kierkegaard contrasts the potential for spoken communication with the degradation of language in the daily press, a sentiment to which Kraus also clearly subscribes. On more than one occasion, Kraus suggests that in the mid-nineteenth century—during a time of revolution and civil unrest—journalists still had the dignity to report on events, even if they exaggerated the truth. To offer a conceptual distinction that works better in German than in English, we could say they were *Journalisten*, not *Publizisten*. In his essay, "The Destruction of the World through Black Magic" (1912), Kraus expands upon this claim:

> The newspaper ruins all powers of the imagination:[40] directly (*unmittelbar*), insofar as it spares its receiver any mental effort by serving up fact with fantasy; indirectly (*mittelbar*), by making the receiver unreceptive to art and making art unappealing (*reizlos*) to him because it has robbed art of its surface value (*Oberflächenwerte*). The newspaper is a dishonest competitor who burgles his neighbor and commits violence against the customer. When the old journalistic type went to war, he lied. But he was satisfied with simply communicating untrue facts. The new journalist is not even capable of that and in addition, steals moods (*Stimmungen*). Of course, these moods immediately decay into clichés. (*F* 363, 4, 1912; *U*, 425)

Kraus writes of the different ways the newspaper destroys the imagination of its readers, rendering them incapable of making judgments or distinctions. Essentially, he is speaking to a process that has led to a type of reader, or rather "receiver," who is not attuned to differences in language that belong to distinct semantic domains (in the case above, literature and reportage). In manufacturing a uniform response from its receiver, the newspaper thus contributes to the process of leveling. But the distinction between the old and the new journalist demands further unpacking. Kraus argues that the journalist has always participated in deception, but that the nature of this deception has shifted over time: in the past, the journalist simply falsified or distorted the facts, whereas the contemporary journalist manipulates language to such an extent that he can no longer claim to be a mere "messenger"—he has become, rather, a "poet of deeds" (*F* 363, 22; *U*, 445). In other words, the new mode of journalistic language evinces a fundamental shift in the role of the press from observer/reporter (*Journalist*) to actor or agent (*Publizist*) that codetermines the fate of peoples and nations—we saw this transition first enacted in *The Last Days* and then consummated in *Third Walpurgis Night*.[41] In "Destruction," Kraus thus writes about the press's coverage of the war in the Balkans—which turned out to be a prelude to World War I—in part to show how easy it is to make people receptive to the idea of war precisely by making them *un*receptive to the reality it entails. "War and peace are still thoughts," Kraus writes, "and one still thinks thoughts individually (*Gedanken denkt man noch selbst*) rather than subscribes to them" (*F* 363, 22; *U*, 445). Kierkegaard's earlier critique of the subscriber who renounces his own responsibility to think and enters the sphere of public opinion finds in Kraus another incarnation. This is not to say that there can be no coincidence between "subscribing" to a thought and producing it individually, but it is the potential discrepancy—and the implications of this discrepancy—that Kierkegaard and Kraus foreground.

Kraus's essay would prove to be an augur of sorts, since the "Great War" was, for Kraus, sold to its subscribers and never truly imagined. Kraus did not start work on *The Last Days* until 1915, but his first considered response to World War I was also delayed, giving him time to reflect on his own silence. He delivered the speech "In These Great Times" in November 1914 and published it in *The Torch* a month later. As the title suggests, the piece ironizes the self-proclaimed grandiosity of the times that produced this war. It is a critical examination of the "unimagined" war, the war that had exceeded the limits of the human capacity to imagine it, a condition which, in turn, created the conditions of its own possibility (*AS* 1, 282). Thus more important than Kraus's attacks on individual journalists or editors (including Moriz Benedikt, also a prime target in *The Last Days*) is his assault on the journalistic "apparatus" as a whole.[42] Kraus, indeed, places language and speech at the forefront of his reflections on the problem of confronting this war with words:

> In these times in which things are happening that could not be imagined and in which what can no longer be *imagined* must *happen*, for if one could imagine it, it would not happen; in these serious times which have died laughing at the thought that they might become serious; which, surprised by their own tragedy, are reaching for words . . . in these times you should not expect any words of my own from me—none but these words which barely manage to prevent silence from being misinterpreted (*das eben noch Schweigen vor Mißdeutung bewahrt*). Respect for the immutability, the subordination of language before this misfortune is too deeply rooted in me. In the realm of poverty of imagination where people die of spiritual famine without feeling spiritual hunger, where pens are dipped in blood and swords in ink, that which is not thought must be done, but that which is only thought is unutterable (*muß das, was nicht gedacht wird, getan werden, aber ist das, was nur gedacht wird, unaussprechlich*). . . . He who encourages deeds with words desecrates words and deeds and is doubly despicable. . . . Those who now have nothing to say because actions are speaking continue to talk. Let him who has something to say come forward and be silent! (*F* 404, 1–2, 1914; *WG*, 9; *GT*, 70–71)

Alluding to both the biblical and Faustian relationship between word and deed (a recurring motif in Kraus's works), Kraus conflates the two as if to suggest that in the context of this war, the language of the press and the violence on the battlefield are mutually constitutive, that the one continues to produce the other.[43] Words and deeds have collapsed into one another and have collectively formed the chatter of war: neither contains an end apart from its own self-perpetuation. Kraus articulates, furthermore, a seemingly paradoxical disjunction between, and conflation of, thought and deed: the deeds being committed are indistinguishable from the words that encourage them (whether in the form of journalistic propaganda or war-enthused poetry), while the deeds that need to be done require a type of thinking that appears to be unavailable. And what *is* actually thought is converted into such a horrifying deed that it *ought* to be unspeakable. For Kraus, those who currently opt to speak—poets, journalists, and other public figures—have no respect for the silence that, for him, must precede any words that aim to adequately address this catastrophe, hence his demand that those who have something to say come forward and "be silent." Kraus thereby offers his version of the antinomies of essential speech and absolute silence as a way to frame the realm of possible responses to the war, wary of the idea that all utterances risk becoming another noise that can be assimilated into the cacophony of war. How, Kraus implicitly asks, does one produce a register or mode of language adequate to the magnitude and scale of this war, a war that erupted because it could not be imagined?

To address this question it is worth further investigating what the implications of Kraus's notion of silence are in terms of his thinking about the relationship between the press and war. At one point in his speech Kraus invokes the "unlimited promptness" (*maßlose Promptheit*) of the reporter's "machinery" (*Apparate*), which "has made it unnecessary for mankind to have any ability to experience and to extend experience intellectually," and yet still allows the reporter "to instill into [his report] that death-defying courage with which mankind is rushing into this war" (*F* 404, 9; *WG*, 14; *GT*, 76). The journalist, that is, rarely hesitates to report immediately after the event, and there is a relationship between this lack of hesitation (the "unlimited promptness") and the rendering superfluous of individual experience. Silence, for Kraus, means pausing before speaking such that speaking contains genuine thought. In this sense, Kraus and Kierkegaard both present a critique of the desire for immediacy that retards the development of what the latter calls "inwardness" and the former calls "imagination." Kraus establishes thereby an equivalence between press and machine, effectively suggesting that both entities are utilized to the same end—in this case, the perpetuation of war—and both have come into existence without the extended use of their capacities being fully comprehended (certainly part of Kraus's more comprehensive critique of progress). The press, for Kraus, seduces, generating the mentality needed to endure such a war by instilling the "death-defying courage" that creates heroes out of men. This is the kind of "momentary excitement" that I take Kierkegaard to be hinting at when he writes of the press's suggestive powers: the war as relief from the collective boredom that has befallen Europe. What further concerns Kraus is the idea that once the imagination has been irrevocably damaged, the ability to discern the difference between an individually derived experience and one fabricated by the press erodes as well. For if, Kraus must presuppose, one had the capacity to experience a war as the soldier does, it would cease to be. When Kraus then writes of the press as the "ultima ratio of irresponsibility," he not only evokes Kierkegaard's related notions of the press's anonymity and the unaccountability it fosters; he also suggests that this institution has committed the doubly criminal deed of encouraging a criminal act and knowing it can do so with impunity (*F* 363, 28, 1912; *UW*, 450).

Not unrelatedly, Kraus adumbrates what we could call a theory of the mechanization or automatization of modernity, or what he sometimes abbreviates—as we saw in *The Last Days*—as "quantities." He claims:

> Since all of modern life has been subsumed under a quantity which is no longer measured but has always been attained—a quantity that finally will have no other recourse but to swallow itself—since the self-evident record leaves no more room for doubt and the painful completeness makes any further calculation unnecessary, the consequence is that, exhausted by this multiplicity, we no longer have use for the result. . . . But some day people might find out what a trifling matter such a world war was as compared to the intellectual self-mutilation (*geistige Selbstverstümmelung*) of mankind by means of its press and how at bottom it constituted only one of the press's emanations. (*F* 404, 10; *WG*, 14; *GT*, 77)

Kraus speaks once again of the "leveling," or the quantity of human existence that the war has made glaringly explicit, wherein the individual has been all but eliminated. But equally as disconcerting to Kraus is the erosion of a certain subjective disposition that he calls "doubt," brought about by the total mechanization of human life. Like imagination, doubt, for Kraus, is a potential source of resistance and thus serves, I would argue, a similar function to inwardness for Kierkegaard, since both imply a kind of reflection and thus a distancing from the surrounding ethos. The bleak Kierkegaardian prophecy that an abstract, indolent public would develop into a self-destructive monstrosity incapable of inward reflection seems thus to have found, in the war as Kraus views it, its fulfillment. For Kraus does not simply suggest that statistics render individual deaths meaningless ("we have no use for the result"). What also matters is that "the great quantity breaks down into individual fates which only the individuals perceive"; in other words, that there is an experiential gulf between, say, a newspaper reader/reporter and the death on the battlefield he reads/reports about—that individuals dying on the battlefield are the only ones experiencing their fates because their deaths are immediately rendered as numbers or serve as fodder for clichés (*F* 404, 10; *WG*, 14; *GT*, 77). For all of the talk of the "hero's death," Kraus asks who, indeed, actually experiences this phenomenon. Kraus's critique of his epoch's "intellectual self-mutilation" is motivated primarily by his horror at the collective inability to perceive pain and suffering on a grand scale. This, indeed, is the sine qua non of his ethical impulse. If Kierkegaard critiques the phenomena of chatter and anonymity in relation to the press and the public, Kraus spells out the implications of these phenomena during what he views as a political and humanitarian catastrophe.

If Kierkegaard relies frequently on irony to convey a philosophical critique of modernity, Kraus relies frequently on hyperbole and wordplay—but he nonetheless aims to achieve critical clarity. When he makes a distinction, for example, between "soul- and horse-power," he does so to suggest that the blind worship of technology in the name of progress precludes the development of inner life, and thus serves as a hindrance to progress. This thought is expressed more forcefully in the following statement: "The tyranny of necessity (*Lebensnotwendigkeit*) grants its slaves three kinds of freedom; opinion (*Meinung*) free from intellect (*Geist*), entertainment free from art, and debauchery (*Ausschweifung*) free from love. Thank God there are still goods that get stuck when freight is supposed to be constantly rolling" (*F* 404, 6; *WG*, 12; *GT*, 74). Kraus's use of notions such as *Geist* reveals a seemingly normative or anachronistic dimension to his critique of modernity, and there is no doubt that a certain cultural conservatism informs his views on these matters.[44] But this is only part of the story. For Kraus suggests that from the perspective of the consumer, freedom is tantamount to the immediate gratification of an impulse or desire, irrespective of the long-term damage it may incur to that individual or to the society of which he forms a part. "Opinion"—a key term in Kraus's lexical universe, which will be taken up by Benjamin—is essentially an expression masquerading as a thought and yet distinguished from the latter by virtue of its ability to be translated into other words and thus easily rephrased, rendering the form of its initial expression arbitrary. Entertainment, a by-product of art, has come to replace art entirely; and debauchery is merely the physical act of love, absent any emotion. For Kraus, however, these phenomena pass as substantive expressions of a culture that views itself as wholly liberated because it is (partially) liberated from the more explicit authoritarian strictures and structures of the past. This war has proven otherwise. Being a slave to market and machine, for Kraus, produces hardly more than the desire for the mere release from these conditions, and therein Kraus identifies a kind of negative freedom without articulating it as such.

The last line of the passage above also reveals a more structural dimension to Kraus's critique: only when goods get "stuck," that is, when the machine stops working, and, say, a genuine artwork is produced—or a war erupts—is the problem with the properly functioning machine itself made salient. The malfunctions that disrupt the system, in other words, are symptoms of the malfunctioning system. Without developing this point into a full-fledged critique of capitalism or technological progress, Kraus's aperçu conveys an awareness of the relationship between systematic malfunctioning and his epoch's impoverished conception of freedom. If Kierkegaard had argued that the modern age is blind to its internal contradictions, and that what this age gains in extensity it loses in intensity, Kraus similarly insists that in a world driven by efficiency, profit margins, and automation, the painless, laborless extraction of gratification from a cultural good is sufficient to convince such a world of the legitimacy of its congratulatory self-understanding. For both figures, a culture bent on expansion at all costs will eventually come to ruin. For Kraus, the repeated claim that the war is the expression of his age's "greatness" has already come into glaring conflict with the reality of this age becoming "small again" (*F* 404, 1; *WG*, 9; *GT*, 70). This war is, for him, the most violent expression of the desires and contradictions that inhere in the desire for profit, accumulation, and technological mastery over nature; it constitutes an extreme, though not a radical turning point. And it will continue to inflict, for Kraus, mental and bodily mutilation without resistance because it appears to fulfill a fantasy whose very realization, however, eludes the popular imagination.

As we have seen, Kraus and Kierkegaard share certain fundamental concerns with regard to the shortcomings of the modern, bourgeois public sphere, shortcomings they both view as self-destructive.[45] These have to do with insufficiently developed conceptions of the relationship between silence and speech, the private and the public, opinion and thought—all distinctly modern experiences that develop within the larger framework of liberalism and the subject's place within it. In the final sections of this chapter I aim to show, however, that Benjamin provides, vis-à-vis these related discourses, a context with which to best understand their implications. In his engagement with Charles Baudelaire, the press under capitalism, and Kraus in particular, Benjamin offers his own theory of the modern subject. His reflections help us not only better understand Kraus's project, but also bring to light his underexplored affinities to Kierkegaard, despite the irreconcilability of other aspects of their thought.

Benjamin on the Press

While much scholarship has been devoted to Benjamin's work on the new media of his era—film and photography, in particular—and the radical effects these media had on modern modes of perception, significantly less attention has been given to his scattered writings on journalism and the press: media that were not new in the way film and photography were, but had nonetheless assumed a new function in the era of commodity capitalism insofar as they had complicated the role of the author (and authority) in modernity.[46] It is, indeed, within this context that Benjamin's reflections on Kraus—the site of collision between Benjamin's interest in the bourgeois author, on the one hand, and his radical rethinking of authorship, on the other—are best illuminated.[47] A close reading of these pieces and their internal relationship brings into view, I argue, a provocative position in Benjamin regarding both the failure and the emancipatory potential of what Benjamin polemically calls the bourgeois press.

Benjamin is interested in both the sides—production and reception—in relation to the journalistic enterprise. In a short gloss from 1934, he notes that the newspaper is a scene of "literary confusion" and has bred in its readers a growing sense of "impatience," which has effectively become the reader's "state of mind."[48] Impatience, he writes, gives way to an insatiable longing for "nourishment," which the newspaper industry is eager to still—though only temporarily—for profit: "The fact that nothing binds the reader more tightly to his paper than his all-consuming impatience, his longing for daily nourishment, has long been exploited by publishers, who are constantly inaugurating new columns to address the reader's questions, opinions, and protests" (*GS* 2, 628–29; *SW* 2, 741). Benjamin thereby establishes a link between consumption and the desire to be informed: information is rapidly consumed, digested, and expelled, and the process begins anew the following day. Normatively speaking, this process, however, contains for Benjamin a latent dialectical moment: for as the reader becomes increasingly invested in the object of his consumption and the author both generates and panders to the reader's needs, the line between them disappears, and a new constellation of relations develops—one of the essential claims of "The Author as Producer," written a year earlier but not published during Benjamin's lifetime. What would such a press look like? In "The Author," Benjamin writes that "the decline of writing in the bourgeois press proves to be the formula for its revival in the press of *Soviet Russia*. For as writing gains in breadth what it loses in depth, the conventional distinction between author and public, which is upheld by the bourgeois press, begins in the Soviet press to disappear" (*GS* 2, 688; *SW* 2, 771).[49] Here, Benjamin's apparent ideal for a revived, revolutionary press is the Soviet model, even if the extent to which he was truly familiar with their press landscape remains unclear.[50] In "The Newspaper," this passage (re)appears almost verbatim, save for one crucial difference: what was earlier "the Soviet press" has become "a different [press]," leaving open-ended what form such a revolutionary press might take (*GS* 2, 629; *SW* 2, 741).[51] He offers a clue, however, in his cryptic conclusion: "And it is at the scene of the limitless debasement (*hemmungslosen Erniedrigung*) of the word—the newspaper, in short—that its salvation is being prepared" (*GS* 2, 629; *SW* 2, 742). The newspaper, Benjamin suggests in quasi-theological terms, has reached a nadir with respect to the quality of its language, which he identifies in this short piece as utterly debased. But it is precisely at this juncture that it has prepared itself for a radical transformation. Such a newspaper may, indeed, emerge from the very class that currently controls the means of production. Benjamin, that is, appears to have another press or another newspaper in mind distinct from the Soviet model, one that nonetheless has instantiated a radically new relationship between author, reader, and means of production, and has done so on the level of its language.

There is one more place to turn in Benjamin's oeuvre, however, that fills out his picture of the press, providing yet another vantage from which we can engage his reflections on Kraus. For if in "The Newspaper" and "The Author" Benjamin queries the relationship between the changing modes of production and reception in the realm of the press, in his essay "On Some Motifs in Baudelaire" (1939)—written several years later—his attention shifts to the relationship between the press and modern experience. Broadly speaking, Benjamin argues in this essay that Baudelaire constitutes one of the truly modern figures of literature who registered and parried modernity's "shocks" by reflecting on the sensorium of the modern subject. It is within the context of thinking through modern experience—including the phenomenological distinction he draws between *Erfahrung* (which has been described as the "means by which an individual relates to collective experience" accumulated over time) and *Erlebnis* (the phenomenon of lived, immediate experience)—that Benjamin turns, once again, to the role of the press.[52] He writes:

> If it were the intention of the press to have the reader assimilate the information (*zu eigen macht*) it supplies as part of his own experience (*Erfahrung*), it would not achieve its purpose. But its intention is just the opposite, and it is achieved: to isolate events from the realm in which they could affect the experience (*Erfahrung*) of the reader. The principles of journalistic information (newness, brevity, clarity, and, above all, lack of connection between the individual news items) contribute as much to this as the layout of the pages and the style of writing. (*Karl Kraus never tired of demonstrating the extent to which the linguistic habitus of newspapers paralyzes the imagination of their readers.*)[53] Another reason for the isolation of information from experience is that the former does not enter "tradition." Newspapers appear in large editions. Few readers can boast of having any information that another reader may need from them.—Historically, the various modes of communication have competed with one another. The replacement of the older relation by information, and of information by sensation, reflects the increasing atrophy of experience. (*GS* 1, 610–11; *SW* 4, 315–16)

For Benjamin, the newspaper has one goal: to mediate as much information about events to its readers in as efficient a way as possible. But what he furthermore claims is that there is an inverse relationship between the amount of information produced and the effect it has on our ability to experience the events being mediated. This must be the press's intention, Benjamin suggests, because if information were somehow wholly assimilated into the reader's experience, the entire apparatus would fall apart; the sheer excess of information would be unbearable. When Benjamin writes that journalistic information has come to replace traditional storytelling as the dominant mode of communication, his point is to foreground the loss that accompanied this ostensible gain: information is not embedded within a larger, social or cultural context apart from the widely circulated newspaper on which it is printed. The news presents itself as new every day. Benjamin's primary concern in this passage is thus with the press's role in the "atrophy of experience," which I take to be another term for "isolated experience," or *Erlebnis*. The press proves to be a particularly illuminating site for exploring the ascendancy of isolated experience in modernity, and the effects of this process on the modern subject. Benjamin finally suggests that not only has information replaced storytelling, but "sensation" has begun to replace information, a term that indicates the direction in which the bourgeois press tends as it succumbs to the pressure to entertain and be consumed. Echoes of Kierkegaard's notion of the press as a "sensate stimulation" and of Kraus's notion of the "unlimited promptness" of the press apparatus can be detected in the passage above. It is thus not surprising that Benjamin invokes Kraus in this very context.

Indeed, Kraus could be viewed on this reading as a successor to Baudelaire, whose primary accomplishment was his ability to capture the "shock experience" (*Chockerlebnis*) of modern life and render it an *Erfahrung*: "This is the nature of immediate experience (*Erlebnis*) that Baudelaire has given the weight of long experience (*Erfahrung*)," Benjamin concludes (*GS* 1, 652–53; *SW* 4, 343). Just as Baudelaire, in effect, quotes *Erlebnis* by turning it into a moment of modern consciousness, thereby providing his readers with the experience of this experience, so does Kraus, according to Benjamin, quote the language of modernity—the language of the press—in order to render the shocks that are frequently obscured more salient. In his own way, Benjamin's Kraus also transforms *Erlebnis* into *Erfahrung*.

Benjamin on Kraus

Beginning in the late 1920s, Benjamin composed a series of short writings on Kraus, most of which (with the exception of his review of Kraus's play, *The Unconquerable*) were integrated, in one way or another, into the labyrinthine essay he published in 1931 titled "Karl Kraus."[54] The height of his engagement with Kraus in the early 1930s thus coincided with his turn toward Marxism, rendering this essay what many consider a nexus of his Marxism and his earlier, quasi-theological speculations on language.[55] Benjamin published "Karl Kraus" in four sequential installments in the *Frankfurter Zeitung*—a bourgeois publication if there ever was one—and dedicated it to his friend, Gustav Glück.[56] The essay has not only challenged its interpreters since its publication, but also proved to be a riddle to Kraus himself, who was rarely befuddled.[57] Recent critics and readers of this essay—more often familiar with Benjamin than with Kraus—have tended to focus on Benjamin's ambivalence toward the satirist, the tripartite structure of the essay, and/or the dialectical relationship between the three personae he associates with Kraus: namely, "Cosmic Man," "Demon," and "Monster." Beatrice Hanssen, for example, argues that Kraus is an iteration of Benjamin's "destructive character," who provides a rejoinder to Marx's early humanism and whose "anarchic deployment of force" is "to be put at the service of divine justice."[58]

Paul Reitter is one of the few scholars who reads the essay with an equal investment in Kraus and his vexed relationship to journalism, specifically within the context of German Jewish modernity. Against this backdrop, Reitter shows how the enterprise of journalism constituted a central anxiety among assimilated German-speaking Jewry, given the common associations made between Jews and journalism by antisemites since the nineteenth century. What is important for Reitter, however, is that Benjamin identifies Kraus's work as the most revolutionary expression of German Jewish consciousness in the way that it transforms the practices of "mimicry" and "reproduction"—conventionally viewed by antisemites as Jewish vices—into its primary virtues. He also convincingly argues that Benjamin's own relationship to Jewish identity and theology was deeply intertwined with his thoughts on the press and its "debasement" of language—a sentiment we saw expressed in "The Newspaper." Yet for all its merits, Reitter's argument partially obscures the way in which Benjamin's treatment of Kraus also speaks to concerns that transcend this domain. For while Benjamin is certainly interested in the German-Jewish aspects of Kraus's work, he additionally treats Kraus as a figure through whom he can more fully articulate his own position on the relationship between the press, language, and authorship/authority under the conditions of commodity capitalism.[59]

For like Kierkegaard and Kraus before him, Benjamin probes the phenomenon of public opinion. In the opening section of his essay, "Cosmic Man" ("Allmensch"), he writes:

> The very term "public opinion" (*öffentliche Meinung*) outrages Kraus. Opinions are a private matter. The public has an interest only in judgments (*Urteile*). Either it is a judging public, or it is none. But it is precisely the purpose of the public opinion generated by the press to make the public incapable of judging, to insinuate into it the attitude of someone irresponsible, uninformed. (*GS* 2, 335; *SW* 2, 433)

Benjamin thus immediately takes issue with the very phrase "public opinion" insofar as it puts the conceptual cart before the actual horse. The public is a thing and opinions are things, but opinions, for Benjamin, are to be understood as private matters; "public opinion" thus conceals an ideological formation that needs to be further investigated. What was once for Kierkegaard a "public-private" sphere in which the line separating the private from the public had dissolved into a "private-public garrulousness" for Benjamin has become a paradoxical formulation that obscures the way the private domain—whose meaning has yet to be unfolded—has effectively privatized the public sphere. The distinction Benjamin draws between a judging public and none at all also echoes Kierkegaard's distinction between an abstract public and a concrete people, the former providing only the formal conditions for the development of the latter. We may further speculate whether Benjamin intentionally employs a Kantian register with his use of the term "judgments" (*Urteile*), implying that the press suppresses this most basic unit of thinking in the Kantian universe. That is, under the dominion of the press, public opinion has rendered inoperative the public's very ability to articulate a judgment of its own.[60] And if a public cannot articulate a judgment, it ceases to be, for Benjamin, a public at all; it becomes "irresponsible" and "uninformed." Benjamin thus effectively treats public opinion as a misnomer for what he perceives to be a generally uninformed public. By usurping the task of judgment from the individual, the press has generated an atmosphere in which the reader is absolved of the responsibility to think critically; and, as we learned from his Baudelaire essay, this is consistent with the press's implicit intention to isolate information from the reader's experience. This is precisely where he identifies Kraus's intervention: "*Die Fackel* [*The Torch*] need not trouble itself about public opinion, for the blood-steeped novelties of this 'newspaper' demand a passing of judgment (*Richtspruch*). And on nothing more impetuously, urgently, than on the press itself" (*GS* 2, 335; *SW* 2, 433). Kraus's journal, Benjamin suggests, distinguishes itself from the bourgeois press in its principled stand *against* public opinion: against both the demand that he speak on behalf of it, and against the newspapers that themselves claim to represent it.

Journalism, Benjamin continues in a key passage, is the "expression of the changed function of language in the world of high capitalism"; its propagation of the "empty phrase" (*die Phrase*)—an "abortion of technology" (*Ausgeburt der Technik*) that renders a thought "marketable" and thus exposes the arbitrary relationship between the phrase and the language used to express it—is Kraus's primary object of ridicule (*GS* 2, 336–37; *SW* 2, 435). We should pause at Benjamin's own phrasing, for if the empty phrase is an *abortion* of technology (*Technik* presumably equating both the press and the practice of journalism), his critique is not directed at technology as such, but at a form of language that is not equal to the experience of high industrialism.[61] The phrase becomes akin to the architectural ornament in the way that Kraus's friend, the Viennese architect Adolf Loos, once conceived of it: neither has value on its own, and yet both add value to the entity whence they emerge: the newspaper in the case of the former; a physical structure in the case of the latter.[62] Conceived otherwise, florid language put in the service of the news will always help sell the news. Ventriloquizing Kraus, Benjamin writes that capitalism has engendered a "changed life," but this life drags on in "unchanged forms," and among the more conspicuous of these forms is cant (*GS* 2, 336–37; *SW* 2, 435). The form of the phrase, that is, repeats itself daily as the world it claims to invoke radically changes—it thus fails to adequately mediate the vicissitudes of modern experience, and in that failure precludes novelty in thought and in experience.[63] The empty phrase is thus the salient feature of journalistic writing that betrays its anachronistic relation to modernity, its insufficiency vis-à-vis the press's own self-assigned task to keep its readers informed.

There is more to unpack, however, from Benjamin's argument. For when he speaks of public opinion—that which arises in virtue of the press's empty phrases—he speaks of its *commodity* function, the way it is in full accord with modern consciousness under the conditions of "high capitalism." He writes: "For opinion is false subjectivity that can be separated from the person and incorporated in the circulation of commodities" (*GS* 2, 343; *SW* 2, 439). Benjamin's negative assessment of opinion derives from his insistence that in its separation "from the person" it can only masquerade as genuine thought, which, for its part, naturally expresses itself as resistance to prevailing opinion. An opinion is an expression of anonymity insofar as it cannot be traced back to a source of authorship and inasmuch as it flows freely through the sphere of circulation. It can thus be conceived of as a commodity insofar as it conceals the social and economic relations informing its production: a newspaper, as the voice of public opinion, does not disclose the (private) interests it serves, which inform and determine its circulation among a broad readership. In other words, the subscribers of public opinion are alienated from the mode of its production. And as a commodity, finally, opinion becomes a fetish, or an object of "cultic worship" to which its subscribers willingly submit because it consistently supplies the appearance of the new.[64] Opinion exercises a high degree of authority over its subscribers even as it fails to represent their interests. I thus take Benjamin's point to be that its authority notwithstanding, opinion is not properly authored, which is why he calls it an expression of "false subjectivity." It is false because it cannot claim to be free of heteronomous restrictions: the newspaper whence it emerges and through which it is disseminated "is an instrument of power. It can derive its value only from the character of the power it serves" (*GS* 2, 344; *SW* 2, 440). In this sense, as a nonauthored form of expression, opinion relinquishes its claim to being a free expression of subjectivity; it expresses, instead, a nontransparent, private interest. In Habermasian terms, public opinion (falsely) presupposes a public sphere free of domination. And yet by making this claim, Benjamin also implies that a more genuine subjectivity may indeed be available; the commodity contains a utopian moment "locked" within it, a moment that can be activated (or reactivated).[65] Just as the empty phrase anticipates a redeemed form of language, public opinion betokens the possibility of a robust public sphere.[66]

After extensively quoting from Kraus's 1914 antiwar oration, "In these Great Times," Benjamin describes Kraus's language as "a silence turned inside out, a silence that catches the storm of events in its black folds and billows, its livid lining turned outward. . . . His silence is a dam before which the reflecting basin of his knowledge is constantly deepened" (*GS* 2, 338; *SW* 2, 436). We might first be able to identify resonances with Benjamin's description of Klee's *Angelus Novus* in the ninth thesis of the *Theses on the Philosophy of History*, the angel whose wings get caught in a storm that appears to *us* as progress but to *him* as an endless catastrophe.[67] Indeed, it would not be a stretch to make this connection given that Benjamin groups Klee and Kraus together as destructive messengers of a "more real humanism" in the last section of the essay, "Monster" (*GS* 2, 367; *SW* 2, 456). In the quote above, however, Benjamin also enters Kierkegaardian territory, conjuring up the image of an agitated silence turned outward as the gesture that stands in judgment over what he will elsewhere in the essay refer to as the chatter or gossip of the daily press and of the feuilleton in particular. Toward the end of the section entitled "Demon"—where Benjamin explicitly draws a comparison between Kraus and Baudelaire's attitudes toward journalism as a kind of "prostitution" of the mind—Benjamin writes: "Journalism is betrayal of the literary life, of mind, of the demon. Idle chatter (*Geschwätz*) is its true substance, and every feuilleton poses anew the insoluble question of the relationship between the forces of stupidity and malice, whose expression is gossip" (*GS* 2, 352; *SW* 2, 446). Kraus's "silence" and the press's "idle chatter" may be of the same medium—and Benjamin asserts that Kraus's own guilt is a function of his weddedness to this medium—but their antipodal relationship to language is what concerns Benjamin. Silence thus reveals itself as the red thread connecting the three central figures: for Kierkegaard, silence is the precondition for essential speech; for Kraus, it is an act of resistance against the compulsion to speak *immediately*; and for Benjamin, silence—Kraus's as an exemplary form thereof—is an interruption or a caesura that exposes the chatty core of journalism, capturing the formal gestures of the news and thereby producing news of a different order.

If for Benjamin the press fails to be assimilated into the reader's experience, Kraus's "silent" discourse is a reflection on this failure, or, structurally speaking, a self-reflective moment within the medium itself. In Kraus, the press becomes *conscious of itself*. His corrective thus embodies the kind of subjectivity and authority that the bourgeois press only gestures toward; he restores to journalism what it had betrayed insofar as he never offers opinions and cannot be separated from his position:

> The coincidence of personal and objective elements, not only in his opponents but above all in himself, is best demonstrated by the fact that [Kraus] never puts forward an opinion. . . . Kraus has never

> offered an argument that did not engage his whole person. Thus, he embodies the secret of authority: never to disappoint (*nie zu enttäuschen*). Authority has no other end than this: it dies or it disappoints. It is not in the least undermined by what others must avoid: its own despotism, injustice, inconsistency. (*GS* 2, 343; *SW* 2, 439)

Opinions detach themselves from their source (which is obscured from public view) and enter the sphere of circulation as commodities, whereas Kraus's language occupies a different domain altogether. His is the language of authority, which can only speak for itself. Such a language resists appropriation, and in this resistance it is only accountable to itself; it is not required to *represent* an opinion. Paradoxically, if other modes of discourse are undermined by "despotism, injustice, inconsistency," Kraus's language obtains authority precisely through its freedom to be inconsistent and even despotic in its judgments. Such a language therefore exercises a type of freedom denied to the bourgeois press because it is self-determining. To be sure, Benjamin does not champion Kraus as an authority on particular matters (apart, perhaps, from questions of language), as a lone soothsayer amidst a world of deception. His claim, rather, is of a more formal nature: it is that Kraus's authority is to be understood as a mode of discourse freed from the demands of the market and the need to appear (and appeal) as a commodity. In Kraus, the false subjectivity of opinion is dialectically transformed into genuine subjectivity, an expression of authority that Benjamin recognizes as "mercilessly binding, toward itself in the same degree as toward others." Such authority, he continues,

> never does enough to satisfy itself, to fulfill its responsibility toward itself; and . . . this sense of responsibility never allows [Kraus] to accept arguments derived from his private constitution or even from the limits of human capacity, but always only from the matter at hand (*aus der Sache*), however unjust it may be from a private point of view. (*GS* 2, 343; *SW* 2, 439)

Kraus's accountability—his willingness to forsake what might appear to be the more just perspective in favor of that which most accurately addresses the object of his critique—is what imbues his language with an objectivity otherwise unavailable to the press. When Benjamin writes that in Kraus, "personal" and "objective" elements coincide, he means that Kraus achieves a level of objectivity through recourse to an intensified subjectivity, universality via extreme particularity. Through Kraus, Benjamin thus articulates a nascent theory of authority, not to be confused with being right, or with occupying an official position of power (like the press).

For Benjamin, the bourgeois press thus amounts to a failed attempt to establish a boundary between the public and private spheres: the institution that, in 1789, was supposed to "inaugurate freedom" had devolved into a forum for the privatization of the public (*GS* 2, 356; *SW* 2, 448). Benjamin even quotes Kierkegaard from *A Literary Review* (without citing the source), suggesting that the philosopher had observed already in the nineteenth century how, through the newspaper, the distinction between public and private had dissolved into a "public-private prattle" (*GS* 2, 356; *SW* 2, 448). *The Torch*, Benjamin subsequently writes, has once and for all made a mockery of this distinction, for it conceives of the relationship between public and private in altogether different terms—there is no private interest to which the journal is beholden apart from Kraus's own. In multiple senses of the term, *The Torch* thus *owns* its discourse and its means of production.[68] Recalling "The Newspaper," Benjamin thus invokes an implicit parallel between his ideal of the Soviet press and *The Torch*: while the former entails the proletarian assumption of the means of production, the latter entails the self-overcoming of the bourgeoisie from within as part of a concerted effort to make transparent its inner contradictions. *The Torch* might be bourgeois prose, but it stands in a wholly different relationship to language than does the daily press, which remains, to an extent, unconscious of itself. If the bourgeois press disingenuously passes off what is private as public, *The Torch* embodies genuine publicity precisely by disavowing its public and their demands, which have been conditioned by the bourgeois press—that is, it embodies publicity by virtue of its genuine privacy. And by rendering the newspaper, as Benjamin writes, "quotable," Kraus consistently highlights the disjunctions the press aims to conceal (*GS* 2, 363; *SW* 2, 453). The author of authority, as it were, offers an alternative discourse to that of private-public opinion: "Authority and word against corruption and magic—these are the catchwords distributed in this struggle" (*GS* 2, 344; *SW* 2, 440). Like Haecker's, Benjamin's reference to the press as "magic" must be lifted from Kraus's repeated references to "black magic," which renders Kraus's phrase more Marxist: the illusory quality of the press is its fetish character, its tendency to conceal the conditions that inform its production.

How, finally, does *The Torch* accomplish such a feat? How does it momentarily bring the dialectic of privacy and publicity, subject and object, personal and historical to a standstill? On the one hand, Benjamin invokes—especially during the first section of this essay, "Cosmic Man"—his earlier reflections on the distinction between the nonreferential, prelapsarian "language of names" and the instrumental, "fallen" language of modernity, the language that only expresses itself as what Ilit Ferber has recently called "propositional communication."[69] Kraus's prose redeems the debased language of the press, fulfilling its hitherto suppressed potential. On the other hand, Benjamin identifies Kraus in the final section of his essay as a "Monster" (*Unmensch*), a figure who delivers modernity (momentarily) from its mythical entrapment—that is, from high capitalism's expression in the language of the press. Kraus does this through his use of quotation, which, as Benjamin argues, turns the words of others into "*corpus delicti*," the concrete evidence of a crime (*GS* 2, 349; *SW* 2, 443).

Benjamin thereby invokes yet another implicit analogy: this time between his earlier theory of "divine violence" and Krausian quotation as the genuinely anarchical gesture in his arsenal. In the "Critique of Violence," Benjamin writes, "If mythic violence is lawmaking, divine violence is law-destroying; if the former sets boundaries, the latter boundlessly destroys them; if mythic violence brings at once guilt and retribution, divine power only expiates" (*GS* 2, 197–98; *SW* 1, 249). While in this iteration Benjamin is ultimately concerned with the structural relationship between law and violence, let us note the similarity in his language when he describes the function of Krausian quotation:

> The fact . . . that there is no idealistic but only a materialistic deliverance from myth, and that at the origin of creation stands not purity but purification—all this did not leave its trace on Kraus's materialist humanism until very late. Only when despairing (*der Verzweifelnde*) did he discover in citation *the power not to preserve but to purify, to tear from context, to destroy*; the only power in which hope still resides that something might survive this age—because it was wrenched from it. (*GS* 2, 365; *SW* 2, 455)[70]

Moving from the first to the second passage, we could say that Kraus's quotations undermine the entire domain of journalistic language, not individual instantiations thereof. They expose its commodity, that is, its mythical character, if we understand the commodity as the reincarnation of myth in modernity in the spell that it casts over its beholders. The language of the press—reducible for Benjamin to opinion and the empty phrase—belongs to the sphere of circulation and cannot transcend its "law-preserving" function. Such language is, stated in different terms, barred from the dialectical moment of self-reflection. As *Unmensch*, Kraus is not a redeemer but a purifier or destroyer of such mythical contexts.[71] For through the destructive act of quotation, we could conclude that he enacts a form of Benjaminian divine violence in his attempt to atone for his age's transgressions by preserving their expression qua language in fossilized form.

Refusing to view Kraus as a creator, with all of that concept's ideological complications, Benjamin identifies Kraus (along with figures such as Klee, Scheerbart, Loos, and Brecht) as a figure who subtracts and destroys, who "wrenches" from his age its excesses and bequeaths them to posterity in the form of quotations—he is clearly thinking here of the Grumbler's predicament. But to again recall the Baudelaire essay and "The Newspaper," we could also conclude that Kraus renders the *Erlebnis* of modernity—for him, the endless repetition of the empty phrase that fails to keep pace with the "changed life"—into an *Erfahrung* befitting its time. *The Torch*, for Benjamin, is a *redeemed* newspaper, "a sheet full of war and pestilence, of cries of murder and pain, of danger from fire and flood—spreading everywhere the Latest

News (*die Neueste Zeitung*)" (*GS* 2, 334; *SW* 2, 433). Refusing to speak on behalf of public opinion, it speaks on behalf of the public, and it does so precisely when it appears to be speaking only for itself. Thus while Kierkegaard probed the problem of subjectivity and authority in an age of idle chatter, and Kraus explored the virtue of prolonged silence during a time of catastrophe, Benjamin, finally, teased out the political implications of a press critique in the language of dialectics.

Chapter 5

"Origin Is the Goal"

Adorno and Kraus

The first spring's rapture I recover
and live it now as it were then.
Oh all the birds are here again!
I see them. Through the room they hover.

—Kraus, "All the Birds Are Here Again" (1916)

In his essay "Taking on the Stigma of Inauthenticity: Adorno's Critique of Genuineness," Martin Jay points to a crucial distinction between the Frankfurt School philosopher's critical treatment of the philosophical notions of originality, genuineness, and authenticity (the latter two are commonly translated as *Eigentlichkeit* or *Authentizität*), and the more positive valence Adorno attaches to authenticity (often rendered *Echtheit*) when applied to the work of art. Generally associated with modern existentialism and the philosophical jargon through which this body of thought is often articulated, these terms, in one way or another, denote either immediacy or the retrieval of a lost, primordial unity—either way, they imply illusory modes of experience of which Adorno is highly suspicious. In part taking his cues from Walter Benjamin's notion of the nonauratic work of art, Adorno, Jay argues, would come to extol the virtues of the derivative over the original, the mimetic over the creative, and the ephemeral over the permanent; if anywhere, it is in conjunction with these categories that Adorno locates authenticity. Jay proceeds by conjecturing about the way Adorno's views on "inauthenticity"—invariably associated with the privileged categories mentioned above—are inseparable from what he calls his "performative practice." He writes that "many of Adorno's 'own' ideas betray precisely the kind of inauthenticity that he defended against jargon. Or, if one wants to rely on his critical use of the term, [this indebtedness] shows the nonauratic authenticity of the intellectual who knows himself not to be in full possession of his own ideas."[1] Even Adorno's most original insights, Jay argues, are best understood as the product of dialogue, imitation, and reformulation. These practices are, for Jay, indeed integral to Adorno's explicit contestation of philosophies grounded in the concepts of the origin, authenticity, and other related categories that amount to forms of what Adorno calls "identity thinking." A concept to be unfolded over the course of this chapter, identity thinking assimilates all particularity under the dominion of the philosophical concept without leaving a remainder; it presupposes that the "concept is rationally identical with the object."[2] Adorno's claim, broadly stated, is that identity thinking's hegemonic and quasi-colonial structure is as evident in the German Idealist tradition as it is in the political and ideological formations that dominated the twentieth century. His views on the notions of origin and authenticity—views that, as Jay and others have claimed, are embedded in the exposition of his own philosophy—thus obtain more significance when situated in relation to his critique of identity thinking.

These views also achieve greater clarity when we bring Kraus into the conversation. The relationship between Adorno and his primary interlocutors and collaborators—figures such as Benjamin, Siegfried Kracauer, and Max Horkheimer—is a well-documented aspect of his intellectual biography.[3] Significantly less critical attention, however, has been devoted to Adorno's relationship to Kraus, who, after Arnold Schönberg, was arguably the most influential presence in Adorno's life during his time in Vienna in the mid-1920s.[4] Kraus, I will argue, is one of Adorno's most important points of reference with regard to precisely those categories of thought and experience that Jay discusses in "Taking on the Stigma of Inauthenticity."[5] Yet despite important similarities in their respective readings, this is not the same Kraus that we encountered in Benjamin's work. Adorno's Kraus, rather, is more the lyric poet, aphorist, polemicist, and theorist of language than the "apocalyptic" satirist or the redeemer of journalism and critic of public opinion (though he is, to an extent, those things too). Kraus often makes appearances in Adorno's work when the latter arrives at a particular failure, aporia, or impasse within the various iterations of German Idealism that have emerged since Kant; at moments, that is, when identity thinking becomes most salient. For this reason, Kraus's role as a dialectician, or what I will call a *figure of nonidentity* in Adorno—a label that could as well be applied to other modernists such as Kafka, Beckett, and Benjamin—should not be underestimated if one wishes to obtain a more robust understanding of Adorno's critique of identity thinking and his philosophy of experience broadly conceived. Especially in the context of Adorno's treatment of Heideggerian ontology—the latest, and, for Adorno, most politically suspicious philosophy of origins—Kraus plays an important role. For it is at these junctures that Kraus is invoked as a necessary rejoinder to what Adorno refers to as the "jargon of authenticity" and its wide-ranging implications for the relationship between language and power.[6] Through Kraus, Adorno develops, finally, an inchoate notion of both exilic language and what I will call a metaphysics of exile. Adorno's dialogue with Kraus foregrounds a significant but overlooked point of contact between literature and philosophy in the twentieth century.

The most comprehensive study of this relationship to date is by Irina Djassemy, who presents a detailed and considered analysis of the "elective affinity" between the two figures, specifically regarding their respective writings on language (Adorno's *Sprachkritik* vs. Kraus's *Sprachsatiren*), the culture industry, "natural history," and the authoritarian personality.[7] Yet for all of its intellectual rigor and critical insight, Djassemy's work is more of a comparative study viewing Kraus and Adorno as thinkers who, in their own medium or mode of writing, arrived at similar conclusions and were bound to the "critical work of destruction."[8] By her own admission, Djassemy elides, ignores, or underplays the moments in Adorno's oeuvre in which he explicitly or implicitly mobilizes Kraus in order to articulate some of his central philosophical concerns—precisely the task of this final chapter. As she aptly points out in her introduction, Kraus does not appear in works by Adorno where one might most expect to find him, such as in his late essay "Opinion, Delusion, Society" (1963).[9] Given Kraus's own robust critique of opinion (as partially examined in chapter 4), this omission is almost shocking. By contrast, references to Kraus are littered throughout Adorno's more significant works, including his philosophical magnum opus, *Negative Dialectics* (1966). In light of this discrepancy, Djassemy aptly concludes that "the affinity between Kraus and Adorno must not be situated in the periphery, but rather at the center of Adorno's philosophy."[10]

What, however, would it mean to be situated "at the center" of Adorno's philosophy? What are the subtler ways in which Kraus's writing may have insinuated itself into Adorno's thought, methodology, and style? To address these questions, I will first reappraise some of Adorno's explicit writings on Kraus; next, I will turn to moments in his work where Kraus is invoked in order to assist Adorno in articulating a larger claim about originality or authenticity; finally, I will address the late text by Adorno in which Kraus's polemical style is most evident: *The Jargon of Authenticity*.

Kraus as Satirist, Polemicist, Immanent Critic

Divided into multiple sections of glosses, aphorisms, and short essays, *Minima Moralia: Reflections on a Damaged Life* bears, more explicitly than most of Adorno's works, the despairing imprint of exile.[11] "Juvenal's Error"—a section of the text named after the ancient Roman satirist, who, according to most accounts, spent a period of his life in exile—constitutes Adorno's most concise and critical engagement with the fate of irony and satire in the postwar American and European context.[12] Conflating the concepts of irony and satire (which, for the sake of taking Adorno at his word, I will also treat as apposite), Adorno initially suggests that these aesthetic modes have, historically, derived their authority from institutions of power, and have thus hitherto presumed a social consensus among their readers or viewers. Though such a consensus may have aligned with subversion at different moments in irony's history, today, Adorno observes,

> the medium of irony has itself come into contradiction with truth. Irony convicts its object by presenting it as what it purports to be; and without passing judgement, as if leaving a blank for the observing subject, measures it against its being-in-itself (*Ansichsein*). It shows up the negative by confronting the positive with its own claim to positivity. . . . In this, it presupposes the idea of the self-evident (*Selbstverständlichen*), originally of social resonance (*gesellschaftlichen Resonanz*). (*AS* 4, 239; *MM*, 210)

Irony, Adorno suggests, can no longer rely on "social resonance" or the "self-evident" to reveal the disjunction between what a given phenomenon is (to us as rational subjects) and what it claims to be, or between actuality and pretense. It has lost the power to critique ideology, for ideology and reality have overlapped to the point where identifying the distinction between the two has become impossible—or at least impossible to discern through irony or satire.[13]

To illustrate this point, Adorno invokes Aristophanes and Kraus, suggesting an affinity between the two in terms of their relationships to their respective historical periods (also possibly evincing his awareness of Kraus's specific relationship to the ancient Greek playwright). Aristophanean comedy, which Adorno cites as the historical origin and most salient iteration of irony, "relied on the mob it slandered" and derived its comic force by exposing how drastically the contemporary world had fallen from its erstwhile grandeur. Aristophanes thus put on display a "*laudatio temporis actii*," a praise of past times, times that were presumed to be bearers of a truth that had been abandoned (*AS* 4, 240; *MM*, 210). While over time, irony would come to represent the voice of the oppressed, even the modern irony that takes to task the values of the bourgeoisie has retained, for Adorno, something of its "authoritarian inheritance, its unrebellious malice," insofar as it presupposes a notion of the self-evident.[14] Satire has repressed this moment of its development, and Adorno wants to expose its limitations as a mode or genre as it rubs up against recent history and is forced to confront this historical residue—he clearly wants to preclude satire from occupying a place within the framework of a purer, less complicit, and more conceptually coherent notion of literary modernism.

The satirist Kraus has proven to be no exception. Adorno thus writes that Kraus entertained "no doubt concerning objective, immediate consciousness . . . no witticism . . . wavers over the decision who is decent and who a scoundrel, what is intelligence and what stupidity, what is language and what journalism (*Zeitung*)" (*AS* 4, 240; *MM*, 210). On the one hand, Adorno cautiously praises Kraus's "instantaneous grasp of the matter at hand"—akin to

Benjamin's privileging of Krausian authority over the language of the press—but on the other hand, he appears wary of such unflinching self-assurance in light of recent history. Kraus still relies on an audience to whom he can wink in the expectation of full accord on its part. Why, then, was Kraus so helpless (for Adorno) in the face of National Socialism?[15] In his most condemnatory statement, Adorno writes:

> The more emphatically . . . Kraus's prose posits its humanity as invariant, the more backward-looking it becomes. . . . That in the end his intransigence towards Hitler showed itself pliable towards Schuschnigg, attests not to want of courage but to the antinomy of satire. It needs something to hold on to, and the self-styled malcontent (*der Nörgler*) had to bow to its positivity. . . . All satire is blind to the forces liberated by decay. Which is why total decay has absorbed the forces of satire. (*AS* 4, 240; *MM*, 211)

Kraus's embrace of Austrian authoritarianism in the face of Hitler reveals, for Adorno, satire's internal "antinomy," which has forcefully been brought to light under the conditions of barbarity and "decay." This is, to be sure, an ill-informed conclusion, and suggests that Adorno was neither entirely aware of Kraus's full response to National Socialism, nor of Kraus's own reflections (primarily in *Third Walpurgis Night*) on how satire can continue on even after its impotence has been recognized. But Adorno's more theoretical point is that satire needs something to grasp on to; it needs social consensus and has thus manifested itself in Kraus's case as the embrace of the lesser of two evils. Satire is therefore compelled by its antinomian nature to become politically expedient for lack of viable alternatives; unable to conceive of anything beyond such alternatives, it necessarily succumbs to one of them (support for Austro-Fascism). Kraus's failure, for Adorno, is his total identification with his "medium," which is compromised by its authoritarian residues. Rather than point to particular texts or passages in Kraus (or Aristophanes), Adorno assigns culpability to the medium itself.

Without completely disavowing the ambivalent attitude he has toward Kraus, Adorno revises this bleak condemnation in the one essay he devoted exclusively to the satirist, "Morality and Criminality: On the Eleventh Volume of the Works of Karl Kraus," eventually published in the second volume of his *Notes to Literature* (1965). Taking as its point of departure Kraus's early polemics against the jurisdiction of sexual mores in Viennese society, the essay is named after Kraus's 1908 collection of essays, *Morals and Criminality*, and constitutes Adorno's most sustained treatment of Kraus.[16] The relevance of these essays, Adorno argues, has only increased in the context of postwar Germany.[17] Meticulously scrutinizing the verdicts of various court cases and the profit-oriented journalists who report on them, Kraus polemicizes against a legal system that intervenes in affairs concerning private morality, criminalizing certain behaviors (above all: homosexuality, prostitution, and divorce) and thus becoming the immorality it publicly condemns; such thoroughgoing hypocrisy then permits "immorality" to persist among the more protected members of society. An oft-cited passage from "The Friends of Children" has become the collection's metonymical seal, sufficiently capturing this double standard: "A morals trial (*Sittlichkeitsprozess*) is the systematic development of an individual indecency to a general one, against the murky background of which the proven guilt of the accused stands out in brilliant illumination."[18] Adorno identifies in this statement the words of an immanent critic who was "gradually forced to dialectics by the matter itself," who understands dialectics, that is, as a historical process through which self-ascription and actuality come into conflict with one another, and often in the most public of spaces (i.e., a "morals trial").[19] Kraus could thus be a dialectician without being an outspoken adherent of the tradition. To illustrate this claim, Adorno discusses how Kraus's defense of the moral superiority of the procuress of a brothel over the editor of a newspaper derives from the fact that the procuress never intervenes in affairs outside of her own domain and never claims to be aspiring to certain ideals in the work she carries out, whereas the editor—the "transmitter of opinions"—intervenes in domains beyond his own, and his condemnations of the work of the procuress are consistently belied by the sexual ads that appear in the back end of his newspaper (*AS* 11, 370; *NL* 2, 42). Kraus is thus able to merely discover hypocrisy without relying on the "common sense" at the heart of satire that Adorno had earlier criticized. This approach, indeed, represents a more felicitous formal possibility within Kraus's writing.

Adorno also wants to claim that Kraus ought not to be viewed as a moralist in the sense that a satirist is often thought to be. He does so by pointing to his Kantian-Socratic inheritance:

> Kraus does not confront society with morality—only its own morality. The medium in which this morality convicts itself is stupidity (*Dummheit*). For Kraus, the empirical proof of that stupidity is Kant's pure practical reason, following the Socratic teaching that sees virtue and insight as identical and culminates in the theorem that the moral law, the categorical imperative, is nothing but reason as such, freed of heteronomous restrictions. Kraus uses stupidity to demonstrate how little society has been able to realize in its members the concept of the autonomous and mature individual it presupposes. (*AS* 11, 378; *NL* 2, 49)

Inverting Kant's categorical imperative, Kraus relentlessly exposes the gap between the presupposed "autonomous" subject and the society that consistently fails to realize it. In a similar vein, Adorno identifies in Kraus the ethos of the "feudal knight" who would "will that the freedom of his own way of life be a general maxim," underscoring the autonomy of Kraus's judgment vis-à-vis the reigning morality (*AS* 11, 377; *NL* 2, 48).[20] If Kraus appears as conservative, Adorno implies, it is because his staunch individualism opposes reigning bourgeois morality and the exchange principle it embodies—unlike in *Minima Moralia*, however, Adorno guards against identifying an essentially restorative component to Kraus's polemical persona. And invoking yet another philosophical ancestor, Adorno writes that since Kierkegaard's campaign against Christianity, no individual "has so incisively safeguarded the interest of the whole against the whole" (*AS* 11, 372; *NL* 2, 44). That Kraus was always concerned with the whole of freedom explains why, for Adorno, he chooses to "take up the cause of the particular freedom of the most neglected (*verlassensten*) individuals" (*AS* 11, 376; *NL* 2, 48). Here, Adorno's Kraus most closely resembles Benjamin's, insofar as he identifies Kraus's Kierkegaardian inheritance while, at the same time, revealing the Jewish legacy of "litigiousness" that has become sublimated in him. Adorno thus conceives of Kraus as a disputatious lawyer who challenges a legal system such that the "injustice of the law becomes visible in the process."[21] While this aspect of Adorno's reading is less central to my argument (though not irrelevant), it is important to recognize that it is at this moment where Adorno begins to hint at what I would call the suppressed claims of the *nonidentical*, in this case, the marginalized, unassimilable individual not protected by a system of law that privileges abstract legality—and thus the abstract subject—over concrete justice. Kraus is a supreme defender, for Adorno, of the rights of that individual, and in so being, he exposes the failure of the system that claims to protect her.[22]

For the purposes of my larger argument, I want to draw attention to the moment Adorno discusses Kraus's *vis comica*. He argues that Kraus is at his most comically forceful when his language appears to go on what he calls "hiatus," when it seems to have escaped itself, as it were, and achieved an effect that goes beyond its discursive, argumentative content. To be sure, Adorno also invokes this "hiatus" in his essay on Hölderlin's late poetry, "Parataxis." In both essays, this term seems to indicate an omission—or an excess—of sorts that nonetheless appears necessary to the construction of the essay (Kraus) or poem (Hölderlin) and its truth content: "Only through the hiatus of form does the content (*Inhalt*) become substance (*Gehalt*)" (*AS* 11, 470; *NL* 2, 129). Adorno's reading of Hölderlin is part of his larger polemic against both Heidegger's misreading of the poet and, more circuitously, his entire philosophical method—a polemic that will resurface when Adorno pits Kraus against Heidegger. But returning to the essay at hand: when he cites a passage from Kraus's "Friends of Children," an essay that contains both a strong plea for the decriminalization of homosexuality and an assault against commercial and sexual blackmail, Adorno attempts to describe the hiatus at work.[23] The passage contains a quote from Kraus of a legal decision declaring that while the condemnation of homosexual relations is unwarranted, a man who had sexually abused underage boys is, indeed, deserving of censure. Kraus's punchline initiates the immediately subsequent paragraph: "But the fathers should not be the ones to turn him in" (*AS* 11, 383; *NL* 2, 54). In other words, in applying their double standards, those administering the law, for Kraus, do not possess the moral authority to decree such a punishment. Kraus is thus able to show how moral hypocrisy at the personal level reveals the corruption of the law in its general application. Yet for Adorno, it is in witty, pithy remarks such as this that Kraus's language is irreducible to a discursive argument. Through its joke-like structure and its interruptive force, Kraus's *Witz* is the vessel through which the hiatus in language becomes apparent, an albeit fleeting moment when language is nonidentical to itself.

Pursuing this thought further, Adorno invokes what he calls the "gestures" of the actor or the comedian, whose "mimic quality" has found refuge in Kraus's written word. In praise of Kraus's effective jokes (such as the one discussed above), Adorno somewhat cryptically writes that in them "language imitates the gestures of language the way the grimaces of the comedian imitate the face of the person he parodies. For all its rationality and its force, the thoroughgoing constructivism of Kraus's language is its translation back into gesture, into a medium that is *older than that of judgment*" (*AS* 11, 385; *NL* 2, 55).[24] The distinctively gestural quality in Kraus's prose—an idea Adorno is poaching from Benjamin's reading of Brecht and Kafka—evinces traces of an earlier, nonconceptual inheritance, which Adorno refers to as Kraus's "undomesticated mimetic impulse." I take this to be a Benjaminian reference to language's noncommunicative dimension, which resists conceptualization and inheres in language prior to its function qua "medium" of judgment.[25] Again, in mimicry Kraus's language is not entirely reducible to, or identical to, itself. For Adorno, this older, mimetic inheritance signifies the return of the repressed, and in so doing it enacts both a form of recollection and anticipation: "With Kraus," he continues, "immanent critique is always the revenge of the old on what it has turned into, standing in for something better *that does not yet exist*" (*AS* 11, 386; *NL* 2, 55).[26] If we can understand immanent critique in this context as the meeting point of the juridical and gestural aspects of Kraus's work, then for Adorno, the truth content of his work inheres in both its recollection of a relationship to nature not (yet) constituted by domination, and in its anticipation of a moment of reconciliation that has retained this memory, albeit in a transformed state—the not-yet-existing. This claim resonates with what Adorno elsewhere writes about mimesis in the work of art, which both contains a "trace of memory" and hints at conciliatory moment between "the individual and the collective."[27] In Kraus, the dialectic of memory and imagination, recollection and futurity is activated; his work counters identity thinking through the restless dynamism of its polemical style and its untamed mimetic impulse. It is this image of Kraus, I suggest, that both prefigures and is integrated into Adorno's more robust critique of origins, authenticity, and identity thinking as articulated in his later works. Kraus's development into a figure of nonidentity provides a model for negative dialectics in action.

Origins, Nonidentity, and Negative Dialectics

Adorno (like Benjamin) took particular interest in the semantic possibilities of Kraus's aphorism "origin is the goal," a phrase that has its provenance in two related poems written between 1910 and 1913: "The Dying Man" and "Two Runners."[28] The former takes the form of a dialogue between the eponymous man (possibly a soldier) and various interlocutors, both physical and metaphysical: his conscience, memory, the world, spirit, doubt, belief, a dog, a citizen, a prostitute, and God. The man appears to have lived an unfulfilled life, declaring at the outset of the poem that he has had enough and that "there will likely be nothing new to come."[29] Below I have reproduced only the last stanza, when "God" intones:

> Walking through the darkness, you knew of the light.
> Now you are there and standing in my sight.
> Looking behind, you sought the garden gate.
> You remained at the origin. Origin is the goal
> Refusing to drink from life's empty bowl,
> Now, man of God, you have not long to wait.[30]
>
> *Im Dunkel gehend, wußtest du ums Licht.*
> *Nun bist du da und siehst mir ins Gesicht.*
> *Sahst hinter dich und suchtest meinen Garten.*
> *Du bliebst am Ursprung. Ursprung ist das Ziel.*
> *Du, unverloren an das Lebensspiel,*
> *Nun mußt, mein Mensch, du länger nicht mehr warten.*

The second poem, "Two Runners," was written a few years earlier, but is thematically related to "The Dying Man." I have reproduced below the whole poem:

> Two runners run along the times,
> One brazen, one with fear in mind:
> who but of naught his own goal acquires;
> who comes of the origin en route expires.
> The one, who of naught his goal acquired,
> Makes way for the en route expired.
> And this one, ever fear in mind,
> Has reached the origin at all times.[31]

Zwei Läufer laufen zeitenlang,
der eine dreist, der andere bang.
Der von nirgendher sein Ziel erwirbt;
Der vom Ursprung kommt und am Wege stirbt.
Der von Nirgendher das Ziel erwarb
Macht Platz dem, der am Wege starb.
Und Dieser, den es ewig bangt,
Ist stets am Ursprung angelangt.[32]

Both poems foreground the relationship between "origin" and "goal," *Ursprung* and *Ziel*. In the first, it appears that the man whose death is approaching has remained faithful to some sort of inner essence all his life—his origin or source—and that this fidelity will be rewarded after a life of denial and deprivation. The poem thus seems to imply that the end of life—its actual end and its goal—amounts to a repetition of the moment whence it emerged, a moment, which, in the case of this man, always served as his guiding impulse. Edward Timms accordingly writes that "'The Man' [in the poem] testifies to the values of an inner world which are impossible to realize here and now," suggesting that the voice of God offers consolation only to the one "who has remained true to the inner source of his being ('der Ursprung')" (*AS* 1, 231).[33] The second, related poem evokes a race between a fearless runner who comes from nowhere and *appears* to win, and an anxious or fearful runner who comes from the "origin" and dies mid-race, but who, in a sense, is the true winner insofar as he never abandons this origin; origin, again, is the goal. This latter poem could be read as an allegory that pits the allure of a rootless modernity (the runner from "nowhere") and its corresponding phenomena—technology, the metropolis, publicity—against the truth of the "origin," connoting nature, the inner self, and essence. On this reading, one could easily identify a conservative strain in Kraus's thought, assuming that linking the origin to the goal bespeaks a desire for the restoration of some kind of virginal nature, a prelapsarian past, or the aesthetic and political values of a bygone age. In his thorough assessment of the various invocations of the origin in Kraus—including how it inspired Benjamin and Adorno to further philosophical speculation on the concept—John Pizer thus argues that "remaining at the origin for Kraus meant attaining the 'goal' of wisdom, of an extraordinary insight into and an understanding of human affairs. . . . Kraus felt a straying from *Ursprung* led to corrupt language usage, to immorality, rampant materialism, and even to war."[34]

Adorno invokes Kraus's aphorism at three distinct junctures in his work, and he discusses the ideological implications of philosophies of the origin throughout his oeuvre. Thus while it is only in *Negative Dialectics* where these two moments of Adorno's thought collide, it is worth briefly examining these other citations of the aphorism and his critiques of the origin prior to assessing their union. The aphorism first appears in Adorno's 1955 essay on the

American sociologist, Thorsten Veblen, and in rather negative light. Veblen's nostalgia for a kind of primal state, a "resurrection of the most ancient," Adorno critically writes, is comparable to Kraus's desire to return to the "origin" as expressed in his verse. Here, Adorno's point is not dissimilar from his critique of the foundations of satire we read earlier, which, for Adorno, invariably relied on erstwhile institutions of authority. Adorno thus points to the shared strand of conservative thought in these two figures, for whom origin and goal would be defined by their static relationship to one another, and modernity by its longing to return to its supposed origins.[35] Kraus's aphorism next appears in the section on "natural beauty" in Adorno's posthumously published *Aesthetic Theory* (1967).[36] In an extensive discussion of the irrational rationality that is smuggled into the work of art (too extensive to receive adequate treatment here), Adorno writes: "Quasi-rational tendencies in art—the outcome of subjectivization—such as the critical rejection of topoi, the complete internal organization of individual works progressively approximate, though not by imitation, something natural that has been veiled by the mastery of the omnipotent subject; if anywhere, then it is in art that 'origin is the goal.'"[37] Pizer sees little semantic difference between these two invocations of Kraus's aphorism, insofar as both imply the static "identity of origin and goal."[38] Yet upon closer inspection, it seems that Adorno actually invokes Kraus as a rejoinder to the vision of the artwork that would render its goal the mere retrieval of, or return to its origins in nature—something close to pure imitation. For Adorno, rather, the "goal" of the artwork would be to return to its "origin" only insofar as the work recalls not nature but natural beauty, an experience, Adorno suggests, that is "entirely distinct from the domination of nature."[39] The aphorism, in other words, suggests a more dialectical—and thus ambiguous—relationship between "art beauty" and natural beauty. For natural beauty recalls an experience of the freedom from the subjective domination of nature while, at the same time, seeking out this freedom in the "old unfreedom"—that is, the moment in which the desire for freedom first emerged—the wholly undifferentiated natural world.[40] Thus as the artwork has become more constructed and more rational over time, it has simultaneously taken on the appearance of something natural.[41] What Adorno reads into Kraus's verse is precisely, then, the *non*identical relation between origin (qua natural beauty) and goal (qua work of art). Viewed this way, Adorno harks back to the argument he had made in his essay on Kraus regarding the latter's "undomesticated" mimesis, or the gestural dimension of his work that evinces an earlier inheritance while simultaneously pointing to the not-yet-existent. What, then, do these readings and appropriations of Kraus's aphorism have to do with Adorno's more explicit treatment of philosophies of the origin?

The first of such treatments appears in a section of *Minima Moralia* titled "Gold Assay," in which Adorno poses a challenge to what he will eventually call the "jargon of authenticity" or "genuineness." These terms, he suggests, were being employed within various strains of contemporary existential philosophy and theology to dubious ends. For Adorno, such terms index appeals to what he calls the "isolated ego," which turns inward and away from the world—a notion of the self that somehow exists independent of the social. Thinking dialectically, he identifies this assertion as an "abstraction" that arises in reaction to what he calls modern, rootless "exchange society" and the alienation such a society entails. "Genuineness" (*Echtheit*), he writes, "is nothing other than a defiant and obstinate insistence on the monadological form which social oppression imposes on man" (*AS* 4, 175–76; *MM*, 154). Much like gold, the "I" becomes under these conditions a fetish, insofar as it is perceived as a spontaneous generator (or container) of intrinsic value rather than as an expression of a social relation. Adorno thus identifies authenticity as both an *illusory* phenomenon—inasmuch as it misrecognizes the relation between ego and world—and a *reactive* one, inasmuch as he perceives its invocation as a reaction to the suffering incurred by exchange society, a reaction, however, that fails to identify the true cause of suffering. What concerns me is when Adorno relates this insight to his critique of the origin. He writes:

> In [the concept of genuineness] dwells the notion of the supremacy of the original over the derived (*des Ursprungs übers Abgeleitete*). This notion, however, is always linked with social legitimism. All ruling strata claim to be the oldest settlers, autochthonous. The whole philosophy of inwardness, with its professed contempt for the world (*mit dem Anspruch der Weltverachtung*), is the last sublimation of the brutal, barbaric lore whereby he who was there first has the greatest rights; and the priority of the self is as untrue as that of all who feel at home where they live. (*AS* 4, 176; *MM*, 155)

Adorno's first move is to make a trans-epochal argument: namely, that the ruling strata of all types derive their legitimacy from their claim to being the first on the scene. They turn a historical contingency, that is, into a necessary element of their dominion: because we have been here longest, we rule. He then establishes a relationship between the "supremacy of origins" and what he calls the "philosophy of inwardness," with its appeals to authenticity. For Adorno, this philosophy has transformed ("sublimated") the ruler's claim to being the original into the contemporary notion of authenticity, a gesture that signifies removal from, and subsequent "contempt" for, the world. But notice how he calls this gesture *professed* contempt; in truth, he implies, it conceals silent complicity with the given world order and outward rejection of anything perceived to be a modification of this order, anything *un*original, indicated above as "the derived." Thus are the ruling strata, the historical conquerors—in whom the notion of the origin is firmly lodged—at one with the modern philosophers of inwardness, both of whom, it appears, have repressed the moment of their own consciousness that otherwise might enable them to perceive an affinity to those they deem to be the latecomers or the uprooted. When Adorno insists on the untruth of this sense of selfhood and of being at home with one's self, he thereby questions not only the notion of authenticity, but any claim to being at home in a world that remains fundamentally inhospitable—even to those who exercise dominion over it.

The second related passage comes from the introduction to Adorno's *Against Epistemology*—what he calls a "metacritique" of the phenomenology of Edmund Husserl—first drafted between 1934 and 1937 but later revised in the mid-1950s. Here, Adorno is even more explicit about the implications of philosophies that rely on the claim to origin or primacy. Amidst a lengthy discussion of totalitarian appeals to the elementary and the mythical, Adorno states:

> Fascism sought to actualize the philosophy of origins (*Ursprungsphilosophie*). *The oldest, what has existed the longest, should immediately and literally rule.* Hence the first's inclination to usurpation lurches glaringly into the light. Blood and earth (*Blut und Boden*), the original forces which the fascists concretized, and which in industrial society are entirely chimerical, became child's play even in Hitler's Germany. The identity of originality and lordship (*Ursprünglichkeit und Herrschaft*) came down to whoever had the power being presumably not just the first, but also the original.[42]

Here Adorno characterizes the most recent incarnation of a ruling stratum—the fascists—as the latest and most brutal expression of what he is now calling the philosophy of origins. But he goes even further in his attempt to expose this philosophy as a lie. The phrase *Blut und Boden* was bandied about in Nazi propaganda as a way to mobilize an entire nation against its "inner enemies"—primarily the Jews, but also other groups deemed to be foreign elements who had no rightful claim to the land. This is, Adorno suggests, a flagrant anachronism, an illusion or "chimera" in industrial society, when hardly any segment of the population can claim to have such an untainted, immediate relationship to the "soil" or to their own bloodline. Yet the appeal to this mythological sense of origin or rootedness succeeded, he implies, because it made the entire history of civilization disappear under its annunciation and imbued those to whom it was addressed with a sense of power. This, Adorno finally suggests, is what accounts for the ruling stratum's tendency to expropriate from, disenfranchise, or incur violence against any group deemed to be a latecomer and therefore undeserving of any status it has achieved. The rooted take vengeance on those they perceive to be the rootless, which is why Adorno will write in the *Jargon of Authenticity*—in yet a third iteration of this thought—that "the gesture of rooted genuineness is at one with the historical conquerors" (*AS* 6, 445; *JA*, 38–39).

The culminating iteration of this thought—both chronologically and philosophically—appears in *Negative Dialectics*, but it is only in this context where Kraus becomes once again explicitly relevant. Briefly and (all too) broadly stated: *Negative Dialectics* constitutes Adorno's most sustained critique of the regime of identity thinking in all of its incarnations: in German Idealism, the existentialisms of his own era, and the totalizing political regimes of the twentieth century. For Adorno, identity thinking is fearful of untamed and wildly differentiated nature—both inner and outer—and could be understood as the form of cognition that subsumes "sensuous particularity" under the dominion of the concept (e.g., taxonomy and its need to classify species, making identical in language things that are invariably different in empirical reality—or Kraus's critique of the journalistic cliché).[43] In annihilating or absorbing what does not correspond to the concept, identity thinking enacts a kind of violence against such particularity, whether we understand this as a suppressed moment of our own consciousness or as an empirical embodiment of otherness. The task of philosophy in the post-Auschwitz era is, as Adorno sees it, to think through what he calls "nonidentity," a manner of relating to or experiencing difference in the world (and in our own thought) that does not express itself as a form of domination. This is the charge of negative dialectics, or the method of nonidentity, which Adorno sees as a kind of "protest" lodged in our own consciousness against the rigidity of identity thinking. In contrast to positive dialectics, which results in stasis and reconciliation, Adorno's variant is wary of reconciliation, for to claim that such a moment has been achieved—has found a home, so to speak—would be to suppress the restless contradictions animating thought or experience (never strictly separated in Adorno) and thus to redound to identity thinking.

The chapter in which the final iteration of Adorno's origins critique (at least as it relates to the passages above) appears is devoted primarily to the possibility of thinking that neither "start[s] out from the concept" nor replaces the concept with another first principle, another origin.[44] The concept—which Adorno argues to be an archaic residue of our consciousness—cowers before the immediately unfamiliar and is compelled to place such unfamiliarity under its control. It thus turns the foreign into a projection of itself, an extension of its own subjectivity—all Objects become part of the Subject, or only obtain reality in their usefulness to the Subject (think: instrumental reason). Under this optic, what is other is then only a primitive version of the Subject yet to be assimilated; if it cannot be assimilated or incorporated, it is expelled. This is the crux of identity thinking and its consecration into origins-based philosophies. Thus, once again, Adorno turns to the significance of the origin as it has been traditionally conceived:

> The category of the root, the origin, is a category of dominion. It confirms that a man ranks first because he was there first; it confirms the

> autochthon against the newcomer, the settler against the migrant. The origin—seductive because it will not be appeased by the derivative, by ideology—is itself an ideological principle. Karl Kraus's line 'The origin is the goal' sounds conservative, but it also expresses something that was scarcely meant when the line was uttered: namely, that the concept 'origin' ought to be stripped of its static hauntings (*seines statischen Unwesens*).[45] Understood this way, the line does not mean that the goal had better make its way back to the origin, to the phantasm of 'good' nature; it means that nothing is original except the goal, that it is only from the goal that the origin will constitute itself. There is no origin save in ephemeral life (*Kein Ursprung außer im Leben des Ephemeren*). (*AS* 6, 158; *ND*, 155–56)

What binds all three of these passages is Adorno's emphasis on the origin as a suprahistorical category of legitimacy: it indexes a point so far back in time that can be invoked in order to impose its authority upon anything that seems foreign to it—or tries to escape its clutches—without ever reflecting on the arbitrariness of its own claim to legitimacy. Origin thus conceived is "ideological" insofar as it is tautological: I have authority because I was here first, and because I was here first, I have authority. The recourse to origin in the conventional sense conceals, for Adorno, an assertion of power, and, quite often, a reactive one at that. But only in *Negative Dialectics* does Adorno connect these mobile, migratory, and transient figures who are never at home in the world as it is—whose mobility is constitutive of their existence—to Kraus's aphorism, which Adorno claims to be reading against the grain and even against Kraus's conservative intentions.[46]

Accordingly, Adorno begins his reading by enacting his larger claim: this aphorism does not mean now what it once may have meant; this is what it means to quote something, a practice Kraus himself turned into an art form, as we saw in chapter 1. Deflating its seemingly conservative logic (whereby origin would equal goal), Adorno suggests that there is no return to the origin implied in this aphorism, no reversion back to what he calls "good" nature or the vision of a pristine paradise, where a wholly unmediated experience of, say, "blood and soil" awaits. Rather, for Adorno, the newcomer, the migrant, the exile, the refugee—all figures of "ephemerality" otherwise absorbed or sentenced to oblivion by the dominant visions of history and reason—are redeemed in the aphorism insofar as their sheer existence unsettles the claims of the ruling stratum and the settler. Pizer thus concludes that Adorno wants to liberate the goal of "subjectivist domination" and establish "an ephemeral *Ursprung* free of suprahistorical authoritarianism."[47] Hence Adorno's claim that Kraus unmoors origin from its "static hauntings," exposing this vision of origin as a reactionary fantasy. Adorno privileges movement over stasis, the exile over the native, not simply to reverse the hierarchy of these positions (and, I would add, not in an effort to conflate these distinct subject positions), but to ennoble the claims of suppressed or expelled particularity in their fleetingness. What Adorno identifies in Kraus's aphorism is thus more akin to a theory of originality, difference, or nonidentity, prior to its subsumption under a concept, absorption into a regime, or, the most immediate occasion for Adorno's thinking, extermination in a concentration camp.[48] What Adorno might have overlooked—if we think back to his critique of Kraus's satire—is that Kraus, in his own idiom, views identity thinking as informing the conditions of possibility not only for the rise of Nazism, but also for the inability to imagine what Nazism was capable of accomplishing. But what I take Adorno to be further claiming—and what invites comparison to his earlier discussions of Kraus—is that Kraus's aphorism betokens more the idea of *recollection* than *return*, similar but distinct categories. Interpreted in this way, the aphorism reminds us that the autochthon and the settler were, too, once migratory, that they suppressed (and thus forgot) a moment of their own history in order to establish their subsequent dominion. It recalls—and this requires reading Adorno at his most Freudian—those fleeting, migratory, and ultimately repressed moments of modern consciousness that are denied outlets in exchange society.

When Adorno thus concludes in an aphoristic follow-up to Kraus that "there is no origin save in ephemeral life," he means that the only legitimate invocation of origin is the recollection of the transience and instability of any proclaimed single moment of "origin-ness," the recollection of nonidentity.[49] For whereas conventional uses of the origin entail the illusion of return or restoration, *Ursprung* denotes a primal leap, a movement. Yet for Adorno, such a revelation is no occasion for total despair; it is, rather, an injunction to think the possibility of difference, the other, *originality*, or the nonidentical within the realm of experience from which it is otherwise excluded. As a committed dialectician, Adorno neither debunks the notion of the origin altogether nor dismisses it as an entirely irrational need. He provides, rather, a corrective to its conventional use: there is no pure return to the self, one's home (or homeland), or the childhood of humanity. These are distinctly modern fantasies that are reactivated in an atmosphere of insecurity, mobility, and uprootedness; they are symptoms of an "unreconciled" society, not the causes thereof. But because the most conspicuous embodiments of such phenomena (migrants, those deemed to be the foreigners within the imagined community, etc.) stir up fear and resentment among those who claim to occupy the origin, these fantasies are often deployed at their expense. The historical resonances pertaining to the perils of political and philosophical nativism—as well as the contemporary relevance of these sentiments—demonstrate the extent to which Adorno was thinking of the experience of exile in its relationship to the exigencies of philosophy.[50] With this perspective in mind, I will next turn to what I view as Adorno's crucial juxtaposition of Kraus and Heidegger.

Kraus contra Heidegger

In the chapter of *Negative Dialectics* titled "Immanent Critique of Ontology"—in which Adorno attempts to turn ontology's "own force against" itself—Adorno challenges Heidegger's central notion of Being, which Adorno presents as antinomical as it unfolds within Heidegger's philosophy (*AS* 6, 104; *ND*, 97). "The true philosophical task," Adorno states in an attempt at a corrective, "would be to conceive Being (*Sein*), yet Being resists any cogitative definition (*Denkbestimmung*). This makes the appeal to conceive it a hollow one" (*AS* 6, 105; *ND*, 98).[51] Adorno principally objects to the contradictions of Being in Heidegger's system, which force Heidegger into an opaque mysticism that allows nothing substantial to be said of Being while at the same time elevating it to the concept of all concepts, the sine qua non of thought.[52] As Gillian Rose has argued, for Adorno, if Being "is immediate, primeval and non-conceptual, it is meaningless; if it acquires a meaning, it is not immediate, primordial and non-conceptual, but is (equal to) its essence, and is thus a concept of reflection." In thus making the question of Being irreducible and granting it "ontological primacy," Heidegger is, for Adorno, guilty of redounding to yet another *Ursprungsphilosophie*, or "an absolute first."[53] Admittedly, Adorno presents, at times, a caricature of Heidegger that may not hold up to philosophical scrutiny, but my primary concern is with evaluating Adorno's critique on its own terms in order to understand its implications and how Kraus functions within it.[54] For his point is that while claiming to be historical, Being abstains from the empirical and thus amounts to an apology for the status quo. In so doing, Heidegger's thought participates in the very form of reification to which it ostensibly objects—recalling what Adorno earlier wrote about the merely "professed" contempt for the world expressed by the philosophers of inwardness.

Adorno's critique of Heidegger's notion of Being finds its most thorough articulation when the former turns to Heidegger's language. In discussing the "philosophical urge" to "express the inexpressible" (*AS* 6, 114; *ND*, 108), Adorno argues that Heidegger's language sidesteps the conceptual labor needed to even attempt to arrive at this paradoxical moment. He writes:

> The direct expression of the inexpressible is void; where the expression carried, as in great music, its seal was evanescence and transitoriness (*das Entgleitende und Vergängliche*), and it was attached to the process, not to an indicative 'That is it' (*Das ist es*).[55] Thoughts intended to think the inexpressible by abandoning thought falsify the inexpressible. They make of it what the thinker would least like it to be: the monstrosity (*Unding*) of a flatly abstract object. (*AS* 6, 116; *ND*, 110)

Adorno introduces the notion that Heidegger's thinking is devoid of process: the oracular enunciation of Being does not develop immanently from within language's inner dialectic. Secondly, he argues that by not subjecting language to this process, Heidegger betrays the "inexpressible"—what Adorno will later refer to as "transcendence"—by turning it into an abstract, static concept, an absurdity or "un-thing" (reminiscent of the *Unwesen* Adorno invoked in the context of his discussion of the origin). We can thus far identify an affinity between the inexpressible and Adorno's notion of origin if we draw our attention to how he characterizes the former by its "evanescence" and "transitoriness," precisely the qualities he ascribes to origin when conceived dialectically or as a property of nonidentity. For Adorno, Heidegger may have been on the right track in his thinking, but he abandoned this path when he sought to capture the immediate and the transcendent within a system of pure immanence—and indeed, the falsification of transcendence is a recurring motif in *Negative Dialectics* in relation to which Kraus plays no small role.

Adorno's even more polemical claim, however, is to next suggest that there is a dubious naïveté in Heidegger's fetishization and hypostatization of language's relationship to the thing, rendering such language oblivious to its internal dialectic. In the section titled "The Child's Question," he writes:

> The test of the power of language is that the expression and the thing (*Ausdruck und Sache*) will separate in *reflection.*[56] Language becomes a measure of truth only when we are conscious of the nonidentity of an expression with that which we mean. Heidegger refuses to engage in that reflection; he halts after the first step of language-philosophical dialectics. His thinking is repristinative also in its aim to restore the 'power of the name' (*Gewalt des Namens*) by a ritual of nomenclature (*Ritual des Nennens*). (*AS* 6, 117; *ND*, 111)

The "nonidentity of an expression with that which we mean" must be understood as a version of nonidentity thinking in the domain of language. Heidegger, it seems, wishes to employ a use of language that evinces the absence of reflection on the disjunction between expression and thing, a reflection that Adorno holds to be the more progressive, or more modernist enactment of philosophical language (if we understand Adorno's modernism at least in part to consist in his insistence on hypersensitivity to the relationship between expressed and expression).[57] This is most salient in Heidegger's use of the word-concept Being, on which, as suggested above, he apparently equivocates whether this is a mediated concept or an unmediated conjuring of our existential condition. Adorno calls such thinking "repristinative" because of its archaic religious overtones, and he claims that this thinking is "also" repristinative because earlier in the same section he had referred to Heidegger's "archaistic" thinking as akin to the phenomenon of "Mana [being] raised up under the name of Being" (*AS* 6, 112; *ND*, 106). Adorno's point is that Heidegger reveals himself through this use of language to be a traditional, quasi-religious thinker of origins. He thus writes: "He eludes criticism, but without letting go of the advantages of originality (*des Urpsrungs*): the origin is placed so far back that it will seem extratemporal and therefore omnipresent" (*AS* 6, 113; *ND*, 106). Heidegger is, in the end, an origins philosopher and an insufficiently modern thinker. This is revealed by the fact that he does not properly take into account the exposition of his philosophy of Being as he endeavors to articulate it.[58] And this failure amounts to linguistic regression, which is, for Adorno, a form of barbarism.

It is at this point in the argument that Adorno invokes Kraus. Let us thus consider the passage above (regarding the relationship between expression and thing) in light of the sentences that directly follow:

> Language is more than a sign only where it shows significative strength, where it most exactly and succinctly covers what is meant. It 'is' only insofar as it comes to be, in the constant confrontation of expression and thing—this was the premise Karl Kraus proceeded on, though himself probably leaning toward an ontological view of language. Heidegger's procedure, on the other hand, is a 'Teutonizing cabbalism' (*deutschtümelnde Kabbalistik*), in Scholem's phrase. (*AS* 6, 118; *ND*, 112)

Heidegger's theo-linguistic barbarism—and here Adorno borrows a line from Scholem that would have had serious implications in its allusion to an illicit appropriation of a Jewish tradition by a figure known for his ties to National Socialism[59]—is juxtaposed against Kraus's use of language. For unlike Heidegger, Kraus, we can infer, recognizes the tension between "expression and thing" and retains the dynamism that imbues it with what Adorno calls "significative power." Such a use of language understands that world always slips away from word and vice versa, and that language does not stand in a relation of possession or mastery over what it expresses, as seems to be the case in Heidegger. Adorno may even be channeling Kraus's own meditations on language at this juncture, specifically where Kraus speaks of what he calls "linguistic doubt," a discourse briefly addressed in chapter 4. In his essay "Language," Kraus writes that "linguistic doubt" is the strongest "safeguard imaginable in the realm of the moral," that it is the "father of thought" and the "grand moral offering (*große moralische Gabe*) that the human owes to language and up to today has spurned" (*F* 885, 2, 1932). Hesitation before the articulation of a thought in and through language—for Kraus, the ethical index of the speaker—could be thought of as the antipode to the "power of the name" and the "ritual of nomenclature" Adorno associates with Heidegger. While Kraus's vision of language may tend toward the ontological, still, under its optic, language does not naively *name* the way Heidegger's nominalism would have it. Contrary to its intentions, Heidegger's language thus serves as a cipher for linguistic reification in which word and thing are wholly exchangeable (language qua fetish) and for which Kraus's language is the antidote. The latter's has been banished from the very paradise where Heidegger's still problematically dwells, if we understand the act of reflection on linguistic nonidentity that Adorno ascribes to Kraus (and denies to Heidegger) as a function of having abandoned the paradise in which expression and expressed are perceived to be one.

Harking back to his earlier writings on the mimetic impulse in Kraus, Adorno juxtaposes Kraus's epigonal, derivative, dynamic, and imitative use of language with the nominalistic, "original," and pseudo-religious use of language in Heidegger. He thereby offers once again a critique of origins.[60] If the earlier discussion of Adorno's uptake of Kraus's aphorism hinted at his metaphysics of exile, the passages above point toward what I would call Adorno's exilic understanding of language—language, that is, without a home and abandoned to itself alone. This would help make sense of why Adorno consistently alludes to Heidegger's language as existing in a paradisiacal state, untouched by the vicissitudes of history and thus all too *at home* in an increasingly uninhabitable world. Kraus's language, by contrast, is a language in exile, bearing—as Adorno suggests in another reference to Kraus amidst a discussion of the aporetic structure of Kant's intelligible ego—the "stigmata" of a mutilated existence.[61] Though this concept is not fully fleshed out in Adorno's work, exile could be understood as a historical analog to nonidentity.

Several strains of Adorno's thinking with respect to this discourse are woven together in the closing chapter of *Negative Dialectics*, "Meditations on Metaphysics," in which he confronts the problem of metaphysics in a post-Auschwitz world. Whether in the form of Christian dogma, speculative philosophy, or more commonplace invocations of hope, all forms of metaphysical-transcendental thought have been forced, for Adorno, to acknowledge their impotence and the vanity of their attempts to extract "any kind of sense, however bleached (*ausgelaugter Sinn*), out of the victims' fate" (*AS* 6, 354; *ND*, 361). "It is why one who believes in God cannot believe in God"—this is the predicament of metaphysics, which paradoxically persists in its nonexistence lest it "recoil[s] into the mythus . . . the closed system of immanence." For any thinking that tries to move beyond this contradiction, "untruth threatens here and there" (*AS* 6, 394; *ND*, 401–2). Adorno thus places the antinomy of metaphysics on full display: on the one hand, all of its expressions are expressions of regression or barbarism in light of recent history; on the other hand, the metaphysical *need* still persists, and one cannot simply pretend that such a need has been adequately addressed. After a brief discussion of the end of *Faust II*, when Adorno questions whether Goethe's skepticism or ultimate submission to the doctrine of salvation prevails, Adorno invokes Kraus once again: "Any man who would nail down transcendence can rightly be charged—as by Karl Kraus, for instance—with lack of imagination (*Phantasielosigkeit*), anti-intellectualism (*Geistfeindschaft*), and thus a betrayal of transcendence" (*AS* 6, 392; *ND*, 400). In spite of his assaults against naive invocations of transcendence, Kraus, it seems, never relinquishes the need for some version of transcendence (of the merely existing) as inspiration for further thought. For Kraus "preferred to read transcendence longingly (*aus der Sehnsucht*) rather than to strike it out; and he was not a romantically liberal metaphoricist. Metaphysics cannot rise again . . . but it may originate only with the realization of what has been thought in its sign" (*AS* 6, 396; *ND*, 404).[62] In a summative reading, Adorno identifies the moment of longing in Kraus—for both something lost as well as something yet to be—as bound up with the fate of metaphysical experience in modernity, a longing for transcendence that is tinged with the realization of its absence. Whereas the mere talk of transcendence or meaning is, for Adorno, a symptom of the residual idealism that has become ethically unsustainable in the wake of Auschwitz, Adorno and Kraus's secularist, demystified vision of transcendence is both inconceivable and yet insisted upon in an altered form. To read transcendence longingly means to resist any form of metaphysics that could be unreflectively proclaimed under the regime of identity thinking: this was Heidegger's error, which, for Adorno, only brings the persistence of the ontological need to light. Heidegger is not, however, to be blamed alone; this failure is due to the failure of our concepts. Perhaps Adorno thereby provides a final reading of "origin is the goal": the goal, in this case, being the new way to think through, or meditate on metaphysics in the wake of its death—neither wholesale renunciation nor pure repetition.

Jargon and Journalistic Tone

> If the word "origin" had any meaning at all, then philosophy would be able to go beyond the opposition of mobility and fixity, of groundlessness and authenticity. It would then recognize these oppositions as elements of the same guilty whole.
>
> —Adorno, *The Jargon of Authenticity*

Despite the diminished role Kraus plays in *The Jargon of Authenticity*, his presence is arguably more detectable in this essay than anywhere else in Adorno's body of work. For it is in *Jargon*—initially intended as a chapter of *Negative Dialectics* until Adorno deemed that the matter warranted separate treatment altogether[63]—where Adorno is most attentive to the tone and affect of philosophical and public discourse. As a polemic (even a satire), it also reveals an Adorno who is stylistically indebted to Kraus. *Jargon* is essentially composed of three interrelated claims. The first is that the jargon of authenticity—that is, the language that permeates modern ontology, existentialism, and new theological trends in postwar West Germany—reinforces a dubious opposition between authenticity and inauthenticity, presupposing a subject that exists ontologically prior to its social and historical entanglements.[64] The second claim is that jargon contains the formal structure of religious or otherwise revelatory-metaphysical language, denuded, however, of the context that once imbued such language with a kind of transcendental meaning. Jargon creates around itself an "aura" of authority—or authenticity—that is implacable, and that has been elevated to the throne where a more explicit divinity once sat.[65] Adorno thus mentions a few examples of these word-concepts: "existential" (*existentiell*), "in the decision" (*in der Entscheidung*), "commission" (*Auftrag*), "appeal" (*Anruf*), "encounter" (*Begegnung*), "genuine dialogue" (*echtes Gespräch*), "statement" (*Aussage*), and "concern" (*Anliegen*), suggesting not that such words are inherently meaningless, but rather that they are oversaturated with meaning to the point where they have become meaningless (*AS* 6, 417; *JA*, 3). For Adorno, existential ontology thus "promises the satisfaction of concrete materiality, but remains stuck at a level of idealistic abstraction."[66] In this sense, it has become the new "German ideology," which is, to be sure, the subtitle of the essay (*Zur deutschen Ideologie*).

Finally, Adorno claims that in jargon's attempt to hermetically seal itself off from the reified discourse of modern society it ends up reproducing, and, in some instances, serving as a model for such discourse. As we know from this and other texts, Adorno identifies affinities between fascism and the top-down structure of American mass culture, both of which strove to create a false experience of totality. But what Adorno emphasizes to a greater degree in *Jargon* is the relationship between this particular use of language and fascist ideology, discourse, and practice. Peter Gordon has thus accurately pointed to the affinity between Adorno's text and Victor Klemperer's *LTI—Lingua Tertii Imperii* (1947), which assiduously scrutinizes the rhetoric of National Socialism in an attempt to expose how violence was already embedded into its language (similar to what Kraus accomplishes in *Third Walpurgis Night*).[67] Toward the beginning of the essay, Adorno writes:

> Prior to any consideration of particular content, [jargon] molds thought. . . . The authority of the absolute is overthrown by absolutized authority. Fascism was not simply a conspiracy . . . , it was something that came to life in the course of a powerful social development. Language provides it with a refuge. Within this refuge a smoldering evil (*das fortschwelende Unheil*) expresses itself as though it were salvation. (*AS* 6, 416; *JA*, 3)

The problem of jargon, for Adorno, is inseparable from the problem of identity thinking as such: it replaces language that is attuned to the object (the "particular content") with language that is preformed and applicable to any and all contexts. What thus links jargon and fascism—the latter understood, if we recall, as the historical concretization of the philosophy of origins—is not only the shared "subordination" they both demand from their respective audience (thus their social enactments), but also their shared internal structure, which entails suppression of the nonidentical moment within each phenomenon. Recalling the passage from *Minima Moralia* cited earlier, we can understand why Adorno would identify in both jargon and fascism a fetish character: each takes control of language or the social totality by fiat, presenting a unified front by concealing the "powerful social development" that inheres in their respective constitutions. If fascism found "refuge" in jargon, that is because it, too, expressed itself in salvific language, replete with (empty) promises of redemption, plenitude, and immediacy. Yet in further scrutinizing the use of the term "refuge" in the quote above, we can discern an even subtler, more dialectical claim: fascism, Adorno implies, is a rootless ideology, no more original than the modernity it rejects or the peoples it wishes to extinguish. Jargon, in a sense, may offer fascism a home, but one built on faulty foundations.

Adorno's specific critique of Heidegger—much of which is already stated or implied in *Negative Dialectics* and thus will not receive thorough treatment at this juncture—deserves, nonetheless, a brief word. As Max Beck and Nicholas Cooman have argued, for decades it was generally assumed that *Jargon* is primarily about Heidegger, that its author himself speaks a form of jargon, and that these two aspects of the text effectively disqualify Adorno's intended critique.[68] This perspective, however, misses the fundamental point of the essay precisely because it misreads its status as a polemic. Like Kraus's polemic against Heinrich Heine "and the consequences" a half a century earlier, Adorno's focus on Heidegger could be viewed as willfully exaggerated, to the point of misrepresentation. To explain: Adorno views Heidegger's ontology as containing a certain degree of culpability for what followed in its wake, since it is the most careful and sophisticated version of what Adorno calls a "disguised idealism"—but it remains an idealism nevertheless. This means that it remains unreflectively committed to certain ideological presuppositions that Adorno aims to bring to light. When Adorno addresses, for example, Heidegger's condemnation of "idle chatter" in *Being and Time*—a cultural phenomenon against which Kraus, too, polemicized—he does so in order to show how Heidegger views chatter as a fundamental feature of *Dasein* (existence) rather than as an expression of social unfreedom at this particular moment in human history. In effect, Adorno lays out the conflict between ontology and dialectics. When Adorno links Heidegger more explicitly to National Socialism—suggesting that Heidegger's language "clatters with weaponry" (*AS* 6, 481; *JA*, 83)—there are both philosophically *and* historically informed reasons for making this claim. The latter do not necessarily undermine the former, but they do relativize Adorno's position, which need not be wholly endorsed in order to understand the larger argument. Heidegger's language reveals for Adorno, most saliently, the ethical-political stakes of jargon, but it is not he alone who is at fault for its dissemination or its social effect. Adorno thus treats Heidegger not as the cause but as a symptom of what we could call—quoting Kraus on Heine's consequences—a pervasive "form of life" that extends well beyond the domain of philosophy.[69] For the polemicist Adorno (as for Kraus), sometimes a king needs to be dethroned in order for a more widespread phenomenon to be recognized in all of its implications.

More significant for my argument is thus the way Adorno's critique of origin-philosophies in *Negative Dialectics* finds in *Jargon* its correlate in his suspicion of the "original meaning" (*Ursinn*) that jargon consistently tries to excavate in the word-concepts it employs (*AS* 6, 418; *JA*, 5). In their respective searches for a first principle to which all subsequent developments return and are subordinate, both origin-philosophies and jargon disavow empirical history and suppress the potential for such thought or language to recognize their immanent nonidentical moments. For Adorno, such ur-meaning can only be surreptitiously mediated through jargon's *affective* dimension—hence, I claim, the argument's Krausian inflection.[70] For Adorno proposes that what jargon lacks in substance it compensates for in tone and in the effect it aims to achieve in its readers or listeners, the very effect to which it owes its success: "[Jargon] sees to it that what it wants is on the whole felt and accepted *through its mere delivery*, without regard to the content of the words used. *It takes under its own control the preconceptual, mimetic element in language*—for the sake of effect connotations (*Wirkungszusammenhänge*)" (*AS* 6, 418; *JA*, 5).[71] Jargon, we might say, is an accomplice to instrumental reason, or identity thinking.[72] By repressing language's mimetic moment—that nonstatic, spontaneous element of language that recalls its affinity to the natural world—jargon's rigid framework is an expression of pure indifference.

Kraus becomes relevant where Adorno invokes jargon's "effectual contexts."[73] Indeed, Kraus's essay "The Tone" from 1912 satirizes the reporting of sensational "events," or the "black magic" that turns facts into events in order to manufacture the desired effect in the reader. Its primary target of ridicule is, as the title suggests, the specific tone that informs journalistic discourse, even in its more ostensibly informative mode. Throughout the piece, Kraus both imitates this tone and provides commentary on examples culled from recent news stories in order to draw attention to this consistent feature. His piece opens:

> There is only one tone, and the congruence of paper (*Blatt*) and world must be demonstrable in every minute and in every line. The paper speaks like the world because the world speaks like the paper. But the paper also speaks like the family because the world speaks like the family, and the family like the world. There is only one tone, and that's the tone of those who are concerned (*besorgt*) because they are not yet provided for (*versorgt*). (*F* 357, 1, 1912; *UW*, 73)

What Kraus is concerned with above is the dimension of speech that carries over from the realm of public discourse (the newspaper) to the political sphere (the world), and, finally, to the private realm (the family), rendering the distinction between these domains irrelevant. This tone's homogenizing (or "leveling") function obscures the ideological prejudices smuggled into its articles. As a programmatic example of this phenomenon, Kraus identifies what he calls the "family sentiment" (*Familiengefühl*) that informs such headlines as "Her Own Child Thrown into the Danube" (*UW*, 73). Such a phrase, Kraus writes, suggests that a mother's murder of her *own* child is more morally reprehensible than the murder of another's child. But his larger point is that if we juxtapose this headline with a series of others—"One's Own Child Poisoned," "One's Own Business Neglected"—we can isolate a common denominator: the word "own" (*eigen*), indicating not only possession, but also the assumed identity between property and appropriation (*Eignung*, *geeignet*). The repeated use of this word indicates the "reflectionless" and "unnamed" assumptions of the propertied class, rooted in the ideology of the family.[74] Seemingly innocuous linguistic cues and prevailing morality reinforce each other. Much like jargon, tone coddles power and glosses over details that might actually serve to inform. "And since the tone is famously a ruminant (*bekanntlich ein Wiederkäuer*)," Kraus writes, "and leaves the fantasy nothing left to digest—indeed, starves the imagination completely—so must it busy itself with concerns that have proven themselves to be baseless. . . . Out of a fact it makes an event" (*UW*, 80). Kraus's use of the word "famously" serves both an imitative and argumentative function: it first demonstrates how this rather innocuous word is seamlessly inserted into descriptions of states of affairs which, Kraus mockingly suggests, everyone should already know about. But what is, or ought to be, obvious—*bekanntlich*—is Kraus's more fundamental claim, which is that journalistic tone serves as the great equalizer inasmuch as it turns the basest of mere facts into events. What Adorno thus calls jargon's "effectual contexts"—its tendency to evacuate language of any substantial content for the sake of producing a desired effect in its reader or listener—Kraus calls journalistic tone. Both figures are concerned with the pretense of immediacy upon which jargon and tone equally rely.

Without naming it as such, Kraus thus perceives in the press's tone—even, to be sure, as a medium of the written word—a form of perceptual coercion. In recognizing this tone prior to the widespread use of the radio or the phonograph, he furthermore anticipates in the language of the press what will become the distinguishing feature of the aural media that were to follow: namely, a uniform, pervasive sound. This is the tone that has informed and will continue to inform the norms of public discourse. It is a tone that has, indeed, become very much "at home" in the world:

> In the summer there are flies, and the flies feel everywhere at home (*zuhause*). We believe they're vermin. They don't know it. We ought not tell them. They have newspapers through which they only communicate where they are, and that they feel at home. The tone is the flies' only means of communication. Their humming (*Gesumme*) is everywhere. (*UW*, 75)

Humming, Kraus implies, is a white noise that is ubiquitous but only detectable when one consciously listens for it; nevertheless, it has an effect on our perceptual apparatus, on the way the message is received. Kraus thus strips journalistic language of its intended function as a vessel of information and reduces it to a noise that has become assimilated into the environment, but which has adverse effects on the public. As Burkhard Müller observes, the "obliteration of reason and reasoning in public discourse presents itself to Kraus as the regression to a mere affective surge."[75] The excess of affect becomes the substitute for, rather than a by-product, of public discourse. And as it appears in every context at home, the press asserts authority over its audience by limiting its ability to form an independent judgment regarding a set of facts or state of affairs. Kraus is thus ultimately concerned with the ways this institution exercises its power, with its consequences, and with the other modes of experience it necessarily suppresses in exercising its power.

Adorno, too, is clearly concerned with language that is too comfortable in its environs, if for understandably distinct reasons: his critique is thoroughly informed by the knowledge of fascism's actuality. He has witnessed how, as an idiom of power, jargon "strives to turn the bitterness of the indigenous, of the mute, into something like a metaphysical-moral verdict of annihilation against" those whom it excludes out of fear and resentment (*AS* 6, 445; *JA*, 38–39). The jargon of authenticity, Adorno concludes, is complicit with the "historical conquerors," much like for Kraus, journalistic tone is complicit with reigning ideology. Adorno's argument is, of course, more sociologically and philosophically constructed than Kraus's, since he views jargon's failure as its insufficient treatment of the interrelated concepts of origin and authenticity. Jargon is a symptom of a pathology that creates the oppositions of "mobility" and "fixity," "groundlessness" and "authenticity," in order to substantiate its hierarchy of ideals; and in its infelicitous attempt to overcome the rootless society it condemns it reifies these oppositions by claiming to occupy the root or the origin it presupposes. Jargon's own critique of subject-dominated, instrumental rationality—and the rootless world through which this rationality finds its expression—is, for Adorno, merely another instantiation of instrumental rationality.

While Adorno is thus leery of Kraus the satirist—whose medium fails in response to fascism—he extols Kraus's virtues as an immanent critic of the highest caliber. For in his critique of the identity thinking that has plagued German philosophy from Kant to the contemporary moment, Adorno invokes Kraus where aporias and impasses arise. And as a critic of conventional notions of the origin and all that this notion entails—the illusory experience of authenticity, the self-constituting ego, and rootedness in "blood and soil"—Adorno finds Kraus's aphorisms and lyrical poetry to be fitting, if unwitting, rejoinders; indeed, he elevates Kraus to a thinker of a different understanding of the origin altogether. Yet it is in *Jargon* where many of Adorno's Krausian positions on the relationship between language, history, and power come together. Recalling Martin Jay's reflections from the beginning of this chapter, it is thus worth considering the way Adorno related to Kraus through his own process of mimesis: integrating Kraus's polemical methodology into his own writing; focusing on specific examples of linguistic infractions in order to highlight a more general pathology that had taken shape in postwar Germany; and critiquing the affective dimension of a language that conceives of itself as restoring a harmonious, nominalistic relationship to the world. The most lasting expression of the dialogue between the satirist and the philosopher may have been the Krausian legacy that Adorno perpetuated through his own late work.

Coda

✦

"Shadows Cast Bodies"

Kraus and Posterity

In his recent translations of some of Kraus's most important essays—including those on Heinrich Heine and Johann Nestroy—the novelist Jonathan Franzen claims that Kraus's Habsburg Empire shares certain affinities with the America of the early twenty-first century. Franzen identifies these affinities in both the cultural wars of each respective moment and in the political precariousness of each empire, a precariousness consistently denied by those in power. One wonders whether Franzen has Hermann Broch's trenchant phrase for the Austro-Hungarian Empire in decline—the "gay apocalypse"[1]—in mind when he writes that America is yet "another weakened empire telling itself stories of its exceptionalism while it drifts toward apocalypse of some sort, fiscal or epidemiological, climactic-environmental or thermonuclear."[2] Both Broch and Franzen are clearly concerned with the role that self-deception and delusion play in the downfall of an empire. But Franzen's point is also that the cultural, political, and technological chasms separating these two historical moments notwithstanding, some of the central conflicts and contradictions invoked in Kraus's work have persisted, in one way or another, through to the present. In other words, Kraus's modernity is, to an extent, still our own.

How so? Fin de siècle Austria was home to the widest variety of print media the country has ever seen (before and since)—but it was all print media.[3] It would thus behoove us to first turn our critical gaze to the contemporary "mediascape" as a basis for comparison.[4] To invoke the term "mainstream media" today causes problems in view of the almost inconceivable number of publications, news websites, and media platforms that exist and are accessible to large segments of the population—or remain inaccessible due to paywalls and other restrictions. What *Die Neue Freie Presse* meant for public opinion in Austria is thus not the same as what the *New York Times* means for public opinion in contemporary America. Today, we can certainly speak not only of a proliferation, but also of a splintering of news media, such that what is still thought of as "mainstream" print media has less credibility, a more limited audience, and is more subject to criticism from both sides of the political spectrum than ever before. Yet significant differences between the two mediascapes notwithstanding, to speak of a qualitative break between these moments would be to deem the Krausian critiques of the print medium obsolete. My claim is that not only Kraus's, but also Kierkegaard's and Benjamin's insights into the relationship between journalistic discourse, "private-publicity," and political recklessness (discussed primarily in chapters 1 and 4) anticipate contemporary debates surrounding the media's social-political function precisely because these insights address the more inveterate contradictions within the "public sphere" in its continuous struggle to make good on its promises. Examples of these contradictions are sundry, but given that a more careful investigation of Kraus's contemporary relevance would require a separate study altogether, I will briefly address two relevant phenomena.

Social media networks—which, from one perspective, offer the ideal of participatory democracy and have shown glimpses of their ability to serve as sites of fomentation for emancipatory social movements—also function as platforms for the proliferation of hate speech and the dissemination of patently false information. Speaking precisely to this concern, the media theorist Geert Lovink argues that the era of Habermasian hope vis-à-vis social media's potential to usher in a truly robust public sphere has ended. Lovink thus enjoins his readers to develop a new set of critical tools and a new mode of self-reflexivity that respond to the reality of these networks and the problems they entail: surveillance, the concentration of power, social fragmentation, the commoditization of social life, echo chambers, detached engagement, information overload, etc.[5] Using by now familiar language, he warns his readers about something they have already intuited if they have been paying close attention: "Finally, automatic infantilization happens because Authority is nowhere in sight. Power exists, but remains invisible and unnameable."[6] From Lovink's perspective, it would appear that social media networks have thus introduced a set of problems unique to today's mediascape; in light of the present study, however, we could conclude that such networks have, rather, *amplified* problems that have existed long before their development.[7] For in effect, many of these problems are the result of social media having become "mainstream" despite the erstwhile potential of the form to challenge the top-down hierarchies of traditional media organs and thereby undermine their authority. Kraus, Kierkegaard, and Benjamin were clearly concerned with the media's role in the privatization of the public sphere and the publicization of the private sphere, a disruption that they viewed as an inevitable result of the drive to manufacture and maintain a particular type of reader or "subscriber." They, too, were concerned with questions of authorship and authority.

Yet for them, authority is not to be confused with objectivity, a notion with which they were, as modern thinkers, ready to part (at least when conceived of nondialectically). This brings us to a related, and perhaps more urgent issue that is addressed in Kraus's work: namely, the phenomenon and effect of "fake news" on the health and integrity of democracy, here understood as the blatant and intentional reporting of false information. Due to a conglomeration of factors—not least of which is the splintering of media discussed above—we are today faced with the serious threat of misinformation and the political effects that this entails. Kraus's anticipatory response to this phenomenon, I would submit, needs to be once again elucidated and qualified. For Kraus, because of the way subjectivity in journalistic language is either concealed or commodified—and because of the way power relations informing media organs are almost invariably concealed—there is an element of falsity or mendacity in every article, report, or feuilleton. From this perspective, the contemporary debate around fake news would presuppose a false dichotomy between the "real" and the "fake," even as it draws necessary attention to a phenomenon with serious consequences that Kraus could not have anticipated. But to extrapolate for a moment, the Krausian-inflected view on the contemporary phenomenon might be stated in the following way: there is a substantial difference between reporting on events that did and did not happen, and the rapidly increasing rise of the latter is a problem worth addressing; but this phenomenon should not obscure the fact that even ostensibly accurate, fair, or "mainstream" reportage embellishes, distorts, and creates realities through its use of particular words, phrases, and tones. While we cannot conflate these two versions of falsity, it is worth considering that there is, at the very least, *continuity* between the type of mendacity that Kraus was after and the type that is (rightly) being criticized today: the former, for Kraus, has created the conditions of possibility for our receptivity to the latter. What Kraus thus demands is attunement to the perspective and particularity, the visibility and audibility of any medium; for only through such attunement can critical and spontaneous—rather than manufactured—modes of thinking, speaking, imagining, and recollecting emerge. False news reports intended to sway public opinion and influence the political climate are, indeed, threats to the development of a more transparent and functional democracy, but treating them as the antipode of the "real" news merely reinforces the assumption of the inherent neutrality of the established media and its status as a purely positive force, however withering this assumption might be in light of recent attacks on its integrity.

Such attacks, indeed, merit critical attention. We must recognize—and this is where Kraus's views become potentially problematic—that the designation of traditional media networks as themselves purveyors of "fake news" hails from the far right, another increasingly more mainstream component of the social totality. It is thus worth drawing attention to what I view as a crucial difference between Kraus's polemics against the press and the reactionary assaults against the media circulating today, a difference best illustrated through recourse to Kraus's response to National Socialism. To briefly recall chapter 3: when Kraus declared that the Nazis—despite having disbanded the free press—had not actually abolished this institution but had, rather, incorporated it into their ideological apparatus, he was making two separate claims. The first and more obvious claim is that the right-wing press had given unsavory elements of society a voice and a platform to spread their insidious views. But more significantly, he was also claiming that the "free" press—an extension of liberal democratic culture—had already provided a model for how to package and sell incoherent and regressive ideas in a form and a style familiar to all. Kraus was referring to a technique and a context that had been successfully repurposed for illiberal ends; his more unsettling point was that the language and the ethos of the mass media of his day was, in part, responsible for creating the monstrosity of Nazism. He was thus making a more Adornian claim about the relationship between liberal frameworks (i.e., social democracy) and the reactionary moments that such frameworks contain and are thus incapable of suppressing. For Kraus, the potential for regressive ideas, factual distortions, or full-fledged mendacity to emerge within the press is as present as the potential for radical journalism. The Nazis thus abolished the press because they rightly viewed its more radical wing as a threat that needed to be quashed. At the same time, however, they were able to conceal their appropriation of the techniques of this institution, through which they were able to disseminate their ideas and gain political support. Ultimately, their decision to abolish the press was an illiberal act of censure declared in order to secure their power; Kraus's critique, by contrast, queries the relationship between political systems and their concomitant institutions, exposing the way, speaking in structural terms, that content (i.e., reactionary impulses that are given platforms to voice their grievances) can take over form (i.e., the way a democracy can, through democratic means, morph into fascism). Kraus points, in other words, to one of the ways in which liberalism fails to comprehend itself, even if he appears unreceptive to the way in which elements of the media can actually serve as a check on power and thereby fulfill one of its stated functions. The "media," for Kraus, can indeed provoke those in power to desire its abolishment, even if it cannot deny the role it plays in bringing about the state of affairs that now renders its function dangerous.

I want to conclude by suggesting that Kraus's work does not contain a comprehensive vision of modernity. Neither did Kraus fully anticipate the present moment and the issues invoked above, since the notion of anticipation presupposes that his moment has come to a definitive end, that historical epochs are defined exclusively by wars and the reconstitution of states, borders, and ideologies. Kraus was attuned, rather, to the sights and sounds of modern experience that have not entirely faded into oblivion. To recall the Grumbler's words from *The Last Days*, Kraus claimed to see and hear what others could not, and he sought to make such sights and sounds more visible and audible. His attempts to slay the gods of the modern world—the press, war profiteering, "techno-romanticism," ethnonationalism, and political extremism—while also ensuring that the gods of old remained dead, were always couched as warnings, and as warnings, they were always untimely. They came too late insofar as they could not even hope to prevent the impending catastrophes they intuited; they came too early, insofar as their implications may still have yet to find a more receptive audience. The primary charge of this study was to further explicate, translate, and situate Kraus's insights within both a literary tradition and a broader critique of the discourse (and discourses) of modernity. Kraus's work and its resounding echoes in some of the seminal thinkers before and after his time speak to the forces, movements, and institutions—even the progressive among those—that wittingly or unwittingly contributed to the most violent and jolting experiences of the twentieth century. If his work seems distant to us, perhaps that is because we are still not reading and listening closely enough.

NOTES

Introduction

1. *F* 1, 1, 1899. Though there are limitations to the comparison of the Austrian newspaper landscape of the early twentieth century and the contemporary U.S. context, a similar motto might be identified in the *New York Times* of today: "All the News That's Fit to Print!"

2. The Austrian novelist and critic Hermann Broch—an avid reader and admirer of Kraus—provides a cultural-intellectual history of the downfall of the Austro-Hungarian Empire and the role Kraus's journal played in providing a corrective to what Broch perceived to be an ethically vacuous political unit that relied on "kitsch." See Hermann Broch, *Hugo von Hofmannsthal and His Time: The European Imagination, 1860–1920*, trans. Michael P. Steinberg (Chicago: University of Chicago Press, 1984), 166–83.

3. For more on the early years of *Die Fackel*, see *AS* 1, 3–59. For more on Kraus's complicated relationship to Viennese modernism, see Nike Wagner, *Geist und Geschlecht: Karl Kraus und die Erotik der Wiener Moderne* (Frankfurt am Main: Suhrkamp Verlag, 1982), 7–66.

4. For a brief recapitulation of the public discourse on journalism and its discontents in the nineteenth- and early twentieth-century German context—including Kraus's role within it—see Paul Reitter, *The Anti-Journalist: Karl Kraus and Jewish Self-Fashioning in Fin-de-Siècle Europe* (Chicago: University of Chicago Press, 2008), 1–30.

5. See *A*, 381. Translated in *Half-Truths and One-and-a-Half-Truths: Selected Aphorisms*, trans. Harry Zohn (Chicago: University of Chicago Press, 1990), 82.

6. For more on Kraus's polemic against Harden, see Reitter, *Anti-Journalist*, 87–91, and Andreas Stuhlmann, *"Die Literatur—das sind wir und unsere Feinde": Literarische Polemik bei Heinrich Heine und Karl Kraus* (Würzbug: Königshausen and Neumann, 2008), 157–224.

7. Harden's original German: "Eine Schicksalsstunde ruft die zwistlos gesammelte Kraft deutscher Menschheit herbei"; and Kraus's translation: "Die Stunde der Entscheidung verlangt ein einiges Deutschland." *F* 307, 47, 1910; *LL*, 24.

8. The Frankfurt School theorist Herbert Marcuse would later spell out the implications of Kraus's long-standing polemic against the mainstream press, concluding that, for Kraus, "crimes against language, which appear in the style of the newspaper, pertain to its political style. Syntax, grammar, and vocabulary become moral and political acts." See Marcuse, *One-Dimensional Man: Studies in the Ideology of Advanced Industrial Society* (Boston: Beacon Press, 1991), 196.

9. "Im Anfang war die Presse / und dann erschien die Welt." See *G*, 412.

10. As Stephanie Harris argues, the term "*medium* does not merely delimit a particular technology of communication but serves as the historical *a priori* of

the organization of perception itself." See Stephanie Harris, *Mediating Modernity: German Literature and the "New" Media, 1895–1930* (University Park: Penn State University Press, 2009), 4.

11. Several important studies have been devoted almost exclusively to Kraus's vexed relationship to the press. See, for example, Burkhard Müller, *Karl Kraus: Mimesis und Kritik des Mediums* (Stuttgart: Metzler, 1994); Helmut Arntzen, *Karl Kraus und die Presse* (Munich: W. Fink, 1975).

12. For a recent analysis of what could be perceived as Kraus's "violent" modernism as reflected in the work of Benjamin and Canetti, see Kai Evers, *Violent Modernists: The Aesthetics of Destruction in Twentieth-Century German Literature* (Evanston, Ill.: Northwestern University Press, 2013), 156–207.

13. Other artists, writers, and intellectuals could certainly be included in the impressive list of modernists and modern thinkers influenced by Kraus, in one way or another. Their numbers include Brecht, Kafka, Schönberg, and Wittgenstein, to name just a few notable figures.

14. "Der Fortschritt macht Menschenhaut aus Portemonnaies." *F* 287, 11, 1909; *A*, 279; *GT*, 56. On this aphorism—initially embedded in Kraus's essay "The Discovery of the North Pole"—Roberto Calasso writes that Kraus "would never have wished to describe that dialectic [of Enlightenment]. And if we have reason to be grateful to Theodor Adorno for having done so, we recognize at the same time that the implications of Kraus's metaphors continue to multiply beyond the point where Adorno's involved explication begins to rest on its oars." See Calasso, *Forty-Nine Steps*, 189.

15. Within the Anglophone world, Edward Timms has provided by far the most thorough and comprehensive intellectual biography of Kraus to date. Without his efforts, subsequent scholarship would be unthinkable. I include him as part of this general trend only to suggest that his two-volume biography is still a work of detailed *history*, with less of an emphasis on Kraus as a viable *thinker* of modernity (though nods to Kraus's relationship to other theorists and writers are by no means absent in his work). I rely on Timms heavily in my analysis.

16. As suggested above, one of these notable exceptions is Müller's *Karl Kraus*, which, broadly stated, treats Kraus as an early media critic whose "mimetic" inclinations (i.e., his sophisticated employment of quotation in glosses, essays, and literary works) anticipated many of the theoretical questions and critiques that began to be generated only with the introduction of forms of mass media that developed subsequent to the newspaper (radio, television, and, most recently, the internet).

17. See Reitter's brief response essay to Timms, "Edward Timms's '*Die letzten Tage der Menschheit* as a German-Jewish Tragicomedy and the Challenge to Translators': A Response," in *Nexus: Essays in German Jewish Studies*, ed. William Collins Donahue and Martha B. Helfer (Rochester, N.Y.: Camden House, 2017), 3:65–69; and Leo Lensing's essay, "Kraus the Mouse?," in the same volume, 71–95.

18. Daniel Bowles, *The Ends of Satire: The Legacies of Satire in Postwar German Writing* (Berlin: De Gruyter, 2015), 3; for a broad introduction to the history of the reception of satire in the German and European tradition, along with speculations regarding the "semiotics of satire," see 3–9.

19. Even today, a cultural-theoretical bias against satire and the laughter it aims to elicit persists in scholarly circles. In her excellent work on the particular mode of "comic irony" to be identified in works by Franz Kafka, Robert Walser, and Joseph Roth, Erica Weitzmann, for example, relegates satire—and specifically, Krausian satire—to an inferior mode of the comic because of its claims to authoritative judgment and thus its ultimate seriousness. See Weitzmann, *Irony's Antics: Walser, Kafka, Roth and the German Comic Tradition* (Evanston, Ill.: Northwestern University Press, 2015), 173–77.

20. See G. W. F. Hegel, *Vorlesungen über die Ästhetik I*, in *Werke* (Frankfurt: Suhrkamp, 1986), 14:122. The one notable exception (within idealist aesthetics) to this view on satire is Friedrich Schiller. In his treatise *Über naïve und sentimentalische Dichtung* (1795), Schiller argues that satire is one of the three examples of the sentimental, and thus has a decidedly modern bent to its expression. "A poet is satirical," he writes, "when he takes as his subject the distance from nature and the contradiction between reality and the ideal (in their effect on the spirit both come to the same thing). However, he can accomplish this seriously and with emotion as well as jokingly and with merriment, according to whether he lingers in the area of the will or in the area of the understanding." See Schiller, *Sämtliche Werke, Band 5: Erzählungen, Theoretische Schriften* (Munich: Carl Hanser Verlag, 2007), 711; translated by Helen Watanabe-O'Kelly as *On the Naïve and Sentimental in Literature* (Manchester: Carcanet New Press, 1981), 43.

21. See Georg Lukács, *Essays über Realismus* (Neuwied: Luchterhand, 1971), 83.

22. Ibid, 87.

23. Ibid., 100. For a reading of Lukács's concept of "holy hatred" (or "holy hate") in the context of John Heartfield's photomontages, see Sabine Kriebel, *Revolutionary Beauty: The Radical Photomontages of John Heartfield* (Berkeley: University of California Press, 2014), 179–87. Kriebel writes: "What is it that prevents such lampoons from becoming coarse and fleeting surface amusement, laughing away social injustices that warrant action, not mirth? For Georg Lukács in 1932, it was the driving moral force penetrating social satire, its 'holy hate' (*heiliger Hass*)" (182). For a recent reading of Lukács's correlation of hate and satire, see Jakob Norberg, "Anticapitalist Affect: George Lukács on Satire in Hate," *New German Critique* 45, no. 3 (135) (2018): 155–74.

24. For more recent theoretical approaches to satire in primarily the Anglophone world, see Fredric Bogel, *The Difference Satire Makes: Rhetoric and Reading from Jonson to Byron* (Ithaca, N.Y.: Cornell University Press, 2001); Jonathan Greenberg, *Modernism, Satire, and the Novel* (Cambridge: Cambridge University Press, 2011); and Charles Knight, *The Literature of Satire* (Cambridge: Cambridge University Press, 2004).

25. For a recent analysis of pathos in modernist literature, including its function in Kraus, see Rainer Dachselt, *Pathos: Tradition und Aktualität einer vergessenen Kategorie der Poetik* (Heidelberg: Winter, 2003), 245–98.

26. For an excellent essay on the paradoxes of Kraus's satire, specifically the way it is always implicated in the object it ridicules, despite its intentions to the contrary, see Jakob Norberg, "Creative Destruction: Karl Kraus and the Paradox of Satire," in *Seminar: A Journal of Germanic Studies* 49, no. 1 (2013): 38–51.

27. *F* 349, 23, 1912; *UW*, 243. Jonathan Franzen's translation from *The Kraus Project* (New York: Farrar, Straus and Giroux, 2013), 253–61. This essay—recently translated and annotated by Franzen, Paul Reitter, and Daniel Kehlmann—is often read in conjunction with Kraus's more notorious polemic against Heinrich Heine, "Heine and the Consequences," written two years prior. Much scholarly literature has been devoted to Kraus's relationship to Heine, but it should suffice at this point to suggest that Kraus was highly suspicious of Heine's widespread popularity, thinking him to be not only an inferior satirist, but also partially responsible for the development of the particular style of the feuilleton. I will briefly return to this larger discourse in the final chapter on Kraus and Adorno.

28. In this sense, Kraus comes close to what Henri Bergson writes about laughter as a corrective to what he calls "mechanical inelasticity" in his treatise on the subject. The primary and fundamental difference between Kraus and Bergson, however, is that whereas for Bergson laughter is decidedly absent of feeling and pathos, Kraus demands that pathos be incorporated into his understanding of genuine laughter—these are not unrelated faculties. For more on Bergson's theory, see "Laughter," in *Comedy*, ed. Wylie Sypher (Baltimore: Johns Hopkins University Press, 1956), 61–190.

29. *F* 405, 20, 1915; *WG*, 23–24.

30. Ibid. Maximilian Häusler has shown that the "concept of the *Blutlache* characterizes thereby not only a puddle of blood, but can also be understood as a neologism for the combination of suffering and laughter, of war and comedy." See Häusler, *Die Ethik des satirischen Schreibens: Karl Kraus, Hermann Broch und Robert Musil* (Heidelberg: Winter, 2015), 26.

31. Kai Evers, accordingly, understands Benjamin's turn to the satirist Kraus—as opposed to the storyteller Kraus—as the new communicator of experience during and after the war. See Evers, *Violent Modernists*, 172. I will return to this point in chapter 4.

32. This is what I take Elias Canetti to mean when he writes that the "world war entered *The Last Days of Mankind* completely, unsparingly, discomfortingly, without embellishment, without reduction, and above all and most important, without habituation." See Elias Canetti, *Die Stimmen von Marrakesch: Aufzeichnungen nach einer Reise / Das Gewissen der Worte: Essays* (Munich: Carl Hanser Verlag, 1995), 237; here quoted from *The Conscience of Words*, trans. Joachim Neugroschel (New York: Farrar, Straus and Giroux, 1984), 217. For more on Canetti's long process of disavowing Kraus (from Canetti's own perspective), see *Conscience of Words*, 28–39, and for a recent, critical-theoretical account of the relationship between Kraus and Canetti vis-à-vis the question of satire, see Evers, *Violent Modernists*, 156–207.

33. For Benjamin's cannibal reference, see *GS* 2, 355; *SW* 2, 448.

34. See *GS* 1, 10–13; *SW* 1, 255–59. For a thorough reading of Benjamin's notion of "translatability," see Samuel Weber, *Benjamin's -abilities* (Cambridge, Mass.: Harvard University Press, 2010), 53–94.

35. David Hollinger, "The Knower and the Artificer," *American Quarterly* 39, no. 1 (Spring 1987): 50.

Chapter 1

An earlier version of this chapter, titled "Beyond Repetition: Karl Kraus's 'Absolute Satire,'" was first published in *German Studies Review* 36, no. 3 (2013): 515–36. Copyright © 2013 by The German Studies Association. Reprinted with permission by Johns Hopkins University Press.

1. Jan Mieszkowski, *Watching War* (Palo Alto, Calif.: Stanford University Press, 2012), 148–49.

2. Kraus began in a fury to work on *The Last Days* in the summer of 1915 at Janowitz Castle, the Bohemian estate of his intimate friend and lover, Baroness Sidonie Nádherny. As Kraus explains, "Parts of this work, whose essence came about during the summers between 1915 and 1917, were first written down in 1919." Beginning a year after the war itself began, Kraus essentially followed the war through to its end, adding and revising along the way. The complete, *unabridged text* was first published in 1920 and 1921; the first book edition appeared in 1922. For a while, the play bore the subtitle "An Anxiety Dream" (*Ein Angsttraum*)—it was not until the play's first draft was completed in May 1918 that Kraus officially called his semifinished work a "Tragedy." For a recapitulation of the history of the work's publication, see Christian Wagenknecht in *LTM*, 775–89.

3. In reference to the theatrical inconceivability of the drama, Calasso writes that "perhaps only Ernst Lubitsch could have filmed it properly"; see *Forty-Nine Steps*, 107. Timms has done a thorough job of dispelling the "myth" of the drama's unperformability, pointing to historical performances and readings and to its inherent need to be performed rather than read. See *AS* 1, 380–87. However, its performance history is separate from its self-declaration, and I would argue that there is value to be gained in thinking through the implications of writing a play for which there is no intended audience.

4. Peter Szondi, *Theory of the Modern Drama*, trans. Michael Hays (Minneapolis: University of Minnesota Press, 1987), 84.

5. For a brief discussion of the Schiller reference, see Timms and Bridgham in *LDM*, 632–63.

6. Charles Knight writes that Kraus's drama is only the "host form for the satiric parasite." I disagree and argue that there is a more necessary relationship between satire and the form it assumes in *The Last Days*, since Knight's claim overlooks the very theatricality of the war being dramatized, and thus the play's mimetic dimension. See Knight, *Literature of Satire*, 255.

7. Alenka Zupančič, *The Odd One In: On Comedy* (Cambridge, Mass.: MIT Press, 2008), 175.

8. Irina Djassemy thus argues that *The Last Days* dispenses with the conventional notion of the tragic hero, since neither the Grumbler—whose role is still more that of a commentator than an actual plot-driving character in the play—nor humanity, which does not constitute a proper subject—would qualify. See Irina Djassemy, *Die verfolgende Unschuld: Zur Geschichte des autoritären Charakters in der Darstellung von Karl Kraus* (Vienna: Böhlau, 2011), 115.

9. Kraus is probably thinking here of one of his major cultural icons, the German-born French (and Jewish) composer Jacques Offenbach, whose operettas Kraus often recited during his public readings. For more on Kraus's Offenbach

performances, see Edward Timms, "Karl Kraus's Adaptations of Offenbach: The Quest for the Other Sphere," *Austrian Studies* 13 (2005): 91–108.

10. Words like *Zeitdinge* recall one of Benjamin's insights regarding the aesthetics of the Baroque *Trauerspiel*; namely, its predilection for arabesque neologisms, which often expressed a "desire for new pathos." See *GS* 1, 236; Walter Benjamin, *The Origin of German Tragic Drama*, trans. John Osborne (New York: Verso, 2009), 49. Not to be pursued in this context—but perhaps worthy of exploration—is whether we can potentially view Kraus's drama as a modern *Trauerspiel*.

11. Broch, *Hugo von Hofmannsthal and His Time*, 181–83.

12. For more on the reading of *The Last Days* as a documentary play, see *AS* 1, 374, and Timothy Youker, "The Sound of Deeds: Karl Kraus and Acoustic Quotation," *Theatre Journal* 63, no. 1 (2011): 86. For a discussion of the cinematic elements in the play, see Leo Lensing, "'Kinodramatisch': Cinema in Karl Kraus' *Die Fackel* and *Die letzten Tage der Menschheit*," *German Quarterly* 55, no. 4 (1982): 480–98.

13. See Marjorie Perloff, *Edge of Irony: Modernism in the Shadow of the Habsburg Empire* (Chicago: University of Chicago Press, 2016), 20–22. Perloff's emphasis on the drama's modernism will be important to consider in my analysis of the Grumbler, if we can preliminarily understand as endemic to modernism the questioning of the work's own premises, of its own authoritative voice. For a longer discussion of Kraus's "mediated war," see ibid., 19–40.

14. Wilhelm Hindemith, *Die Tragödie des Nörglers* (Frankfurt: P. Lang, 1985), 103.

15. For more on the theme of the apocalyptic in Kraus and its relationship to communicative language, see Jakob Norberg, "The Black Book: Karl Kraus's Etiquette," in *Modern Austrian Literature* 40, no. 2 (2007): 45–64.

16. Kurt Krolop, *Sprachsatire als Zeitsatire* (Berlin: Akademie-Verlag, 1987), 65.

17. Calasso, *Forty-Nine Steps*, 99. Following Timms, Calasso suggests that Büchner's *Dantons Tod*, about a sixth of which consists of actual quotations, could be considered "political" in the same sense as *The Last Days* and thus its closest theatrical precursor. For a thorough textual analysis of the relationship between Kraus and Büchner, see Reiner Niehoff, *Die Herrschaft des Textes: Zitattechnik als Sprachkritik in Georg Büchners Drama* Dantons Tod *unter Berücksichtigung* Der Letzten Tage der Menschheit *von Karl Kraus* (Tübingen: Niemeyer, 1991).

18. This is from Kraus's gloss, "The Plagiarism" (*Das Plagiat*), in which Kraus responds to the accusation that he had lifted lines from the Gospel of John and from *Hamlet* and inserted them into various satirical poems without properly citing them. See *F* 572, 61–62, 1921.

19. Kraus always confers this authority on himself, since for him it is a "plagiarism of the suitable subject (*an der tauglichen Sache*)." See *F* 800, 2, 1929.

20. Kraus uses the word *Einschöpfung*. See, for example, *F* 572, 62, 1921.

21. See Hindemith, *Die Tragödie des Nörglers*, 62.

22. For a theoretical engagement with the poetics of citation and Benjamin's in particular (who is inspired by Kraus), see Marjorie Perloff, *Unoriginal Genius: Poetry by Other Means in the New Century* (Chicago: University of Chicago Press, 201), 24–49.

23. To be sure, Kraus's attacks on Schalek (which prompted her brother to challenge Kraus to a duel) contain some problematic assumptions about womanhood and femininity. As Timms writes, Schalek represented to Kraus the transition from "woman into journalist into feuilletonist into war correspondent," with each role functioning as a betrayal of a certain conception of "womanliness that Kraus sought to uphold." See *AS* 1, 328–29.

24. Kraus did actually defend Schalek on one account: that she, unlike many other war correspondents, actually had the courage to visit the front in person. To read a montage of Schalek quotations as they appeared in *The Torch*, see *F* 406, 17–19, 1915.

25. See Youker, "Sound of Deeds," 89.

26. The German is "Bin ich der verantworthliche Redakteur vom Weltkrieg?"

27. Benedikt was a prime target of Kraus's satire between 1908 and 1920, when he was in power, but the editor-proprietor appears in *The Torch* as early as 1899, the journal's founding year. For more on Kraus's notorious relationship to Benedikt—including the antisemitic undertones that inform many of his portrayals of the press mogul—see *AS* 1, 144–46; *AS* 2, 87–89; and Reitter, *Anti-Journalist*, 86–88.

28. It is worth noting that Bertolt Brecht's character "Mother Courage" is accused in his eponymous play by the Chaplain of being a "hyena of the battlefield" for desiring war—not peace—because of the profits that she reaps from it. It is hard to determine how widespread of a trope this was during the interwar period, but it is likely that Brecht borrowed the trope from Kraus. See Brecht, *Werke, Große kommentierte Berliner und Frankfurter Ausgabe*, ed. Werner Hecht et al. (Berlin: Aufbau and Suhrkamp, 1988–2000), vol. 6, 65; *Collected Plays: Five*, trans. John Willett (London: Methuen Drama, 2005), 165–66.

29. This is also the Exhortation whose republication in 1931 served as the occasion for Kurt Tucholsky's polemic, *Der bewachte Kriegsschauplatz*, in which he famously called soldiers "murderers." See Kurt Tucholsky, *Gesamtausgabe, Band 14: Texte 1931*, ed. Sabina Becker (Hamburg: Rowohlt, 1998), 348.

30. Erich Heller has written that Kraus's "single word" is "precise through its infinite ambiguity," and by this he means that each possible connotation of a word is concrete and that, combined, these connotations exhaust the meaning of the word. "Dictate" both means to voice aloud such that one's words are written, but also contains political implications. See Erich Heller, *The Disinherited Mind: Essays in Modern German Literature and Thought* (New York: Barnes and Noble, 1971), 239.

31. A similar scene—one of many—can be found in a wartime issue of *Die Fackel*, the only difference being that in the journal, Kraus places the quotations next to one another in two adjacent columns, the first under the title "Benedikt's Prayer," the second under the title "Benedikt's Dictation." See *F* 406, 1, 1919.

32. For a thorough analysis of Kraus's "dialogic" satire and its relationship to his authorial voice, see António Ribeiro, "Satirical Discourse and Intertextuality: The Dialogic Construction of Satirical Authority in *Die Fackel*," in *Oxford German Studies* 45, no. 4 (2016): 444–58.

33. Perloff, *Edge of Irony*, 19.

34. For a historical account of the Siege of Przemysl, see Graydon Tunstall, *Written in Blood: The Battles for Fortress Przemysl in WWI* (Bloomington: Indiana University Press, 2016).

35. Helmut Qualtinger, the Austrian actor and cabaret performer, recorded his readings of several scenes from *The Last Days*—including this one. See *Qualtinger liest Karl Kraus*, performed by Helmut Qualtinger (Preiser, 1999), CD.

36. The enjoinment not to forget will be important to recall for Adorno's uptake of Kraus in chapter 4.

37. Krolop, *Sprachsatire*, 66.

38. For an explanation of the difficulties encountered in translating Kraus—especially when it came to translating local Viennese dialects and inflections—see *LDM*, 591–97.

39. See Arntzen, "Einige Dialogstrukturen in Karl Kraus' Drama," in *Sprachspiel und Bedeutung: Festschrift für Franz Hundsnurscher zum 65. Geburtstag*, ed. Franz Hundsnurscher (Tübingen: Niemeyer, 2000), 434.

40. Bogel, *Difference Satire Makes*, 68.

41. Hindemith refuses to see the Grumbler's monologues as "one-sided" or as a "static commentary" on the work as a whole, instead identifying him as a central moment of the work and the only figure in the drama who undergoes a development. For his sake alone is the work entitled a tragedy. See Hindemith, *Die Tragödie des Nörglers*, 133–34.

42. "In the figure of the 'Grumbler' the author himself begins to speak, the Fackel-Kraus, who takes the language and speaking (*Sprache und Sprechende*) of his time at its word." See Karl Riha, *Kritik, Satire, Parodie: Gesammelte Aufsätze zu den Dunkelmännerbriefen, zu Lesage, Lichtenberg, Klassiker-Parodie, Daumier, Herwegh, Kurnberger, Holz, Kraus, Heinrich Mann, Tucholsky, Hausmann, Brecht, Valentin, Schwitters, Hitler-Parodie und Henscheid* (Opladen: Westdeutscher Verlag, 1992), 138. Timms also has made clear that the Grumbler is not to be confused with Kraus himself, but is, first and foremost, a character in a play. See *AS* 1, 388–91.

43. For Arntzen, this marks the fundamental distinction between the ironist and the satirist: the ironist hovers above the reality he has invented and merely plays with it, while the satirist suffers from that which he satirizes and yet continues to shape reality in his art. For more on this conceptual distinction, see Helmut Arntzen, *Literatur im Zeitalter der Information: Aufsätze, Essays, Glossen* (Frankfurt: Athenäum Verlag, 1971), 168.

44. Hindemith aptly characterizes the Optimist as "the bad, unsuccessful mediation of the opposition of phrase and word. . . . Hardly satirized, he represents both the healthy common sense that there cannot be, and one who, precisely because of this, wants with obstinacy and blinkered earnestness to be what he cannot be: a source of reconciliation and reason." See Hindemith, *Die Tragödie des Nörglers*, 59–60.

45. Perloff, *Edge of Irony*, 36.

46. For more on Kraus's use of *Heldentod* in his wartime writings, see *AS* 1, 279.

47. I am referring to Robert Musil's unfinished modernist novel, *The Man without Qualities* (1930–1943).

48. Enzo Traverso has argued that, with rare exception, there were very few even among the intellectual class of Europe that predicted a world war to be Europe's fate, convinced as most were by the doctrine of progress and its ability to prevent barbarity from overtaking this most "civilized" continent in the world. See Enzo Traverso, "European Intellectuals and the First World War: Trauma and New Cleavages," in *Cataclysm 1914: World War I and the Making of Modern World Politics*, ed. Alex Anievas (Leiden: Brill, 2015), 201–15.

49. For more on this general discourse, see *AS* 1, 397–402.

50. Though this is a much larger discourse and ultimately the subject of another study altogether, Kraus and Sigmund Freud overlapped to a degree with respect to their positions on the war, despite Kraus's outspoken resistance to psychoanalysis more generally (or at least the way in which it was being popularized in Vienna). In his short essay from 1915, "Thoughts for the Times on War and Death," Freud writes of the profound "disillusionment" (*Enttäuschung*) of the war as well as the "altered attitude towards death" that it has engendered. In different ways, both he and Kraus were invested in the *un*reason that underlay this historical catastrophe. See Sigmund Freud, *Gesammelte Werke, Band X: Werke aus den Jahren 1913–1917* (Berlin: Fischer, 1969), 324–55; here quoted from *The Standard Edition of the Complete Psychological Works of Sigmund Freud*, vol. 14, trans. James Strachey (London: Hogarth Press, 1981), 275–300. For more on the relationship between Kraus and Freud, see Leo Lensing's review of the psychoanalyst Franz Wittels's autobiography, "'Freud and the Child Woman' or 'The Kraus Affair?' A Textual 'Reconstruction' of Franz Wittels's Psychoanalytic Autobiography," *German Quarterly* 69, no. 3 (1996): 322–32; and Thomas Szasz, *Anti-Freud: Karl Kraus's Criticism of Psychoanalysis and Psychiatry* (Syracuse, N.Y.: Syracuse University Press, 1990). Szasz's text is a highly tendentious defense of Kraus's criticisms of psychoanalysis.

51. For a thorough discussion of the loaded phrase translated by Timms and Bridgham as "innocent instigators"—*verfolgende Unschuld*—and its relationship to Kraus's untheorized yet robust notion of the "authoritarian character," see Djassemy, *Die verfolgende Unschuld*, 11–34.

52. For a more historical account of Austria's specific role in the outbreak of the war and its place in the Europe of pre-1914 more broadly, see Geoffrey Wawro, *A Mad Catastrophe: The Outbreak of World War I and the Collapse of the Habsburg Empire* (New York: Basic Books, 2014), 15–49.

53. Kraus quotes this phrase throughout his wartime writings in *The Torch*, but Timms has shown that Kraus was repeatedly misquoting the original line from the Kaiser's Proclamation, which was, "Ich habe alles geprüft und erwogen," or, "I have examined and weighed everything in the balance." According to Timms, Kraus was steeped at the time in Shakespeare's *King Lear* and may have had the line "Ripeness is everything"—in German, "Reifsein ist alles"—in mind when he misquoted the Kaiser. Either way, it was Kraus's memory/imagination that would supplant the actual line, at least in this work of literature. For more on this, see *AS* 1, 342–46.

54. The stylistic repetition of the "Z" sound in the original German ("in Szenen der zerfallenden Menschheit zerfällt") betrays another resemblance to Büchner. Krolop has specifically written on Büchner's potential influence on Kraus's

wartime writings and on *The Last Days* in terms of their language-oriented approach to ideology critique. See Krolop, *Sprachsatire*, 125.

55. Calasso writes that "Kraus does not want to remove himself from guilt; he is not seeking a paradise of origins nor one of postrevolution, and his inflexible immobility has a strength that criticism leaves intact." Calasso, *Forty-Nine Steps*, 224. He thereby appears to be distinguishing Krausian satire from more general criticism by the former's admission of complicity in the object of his critique. Lensing similarly claims that "by equating this 'fundamental sound of the times' with the 'echo of his bloody insanity,' [the Grumbler] points to his own inescapable complicity in the war. Kraus's monstrous drama remains as ambiguous as it is bold and scathing." See Lensing, "War and the Press," in *A New History of German Literature*, ed. David Wellbery and Judith Ryan (Cambridge, Mass.: Harvard University Press, 2005), 717. Lensing's translation of *Grundton* as "fundamental note" is, however, too literal.

56. In referring to the witnesses of the Shoah, Giorgio Agamben draws attention to one of the Latin roots of the word "witness"—*superstes*—which designates "a person who has lived through something, who has experienced an event from beginning to end and can therefore bear witness to it." See Giorgio Agamben, *Remnants of Auschwitz: The Witness and the Archive*, trans. Daniel Heller-Roazen (New York: Zone Books, 2002), 17.

57. Calasso confirms the Grumbler's prescience by writing, "Before Nazism existed, even only as a name, Kraus wrote the most precise description of Nazism to appear in the German language." See Calasso, *Forty-Nine Steps*, 106.

58. A decade after the war had ended, Kraus was still conceiving of his writing as a form of warfare and thus of living in a time of war. In 1929 he gave a speech entitled "In the Thirtieth Year of War," which likely alluded to or commemorated three events: the thirtieth anniversary of *The Torch*, the war that Kraus had been waging during the journal's entire span of existence, and the actual Thirty Years War. See *F* 800, 1, 1929.

59. Commenting on this particular scene, Djassemy writes: "Battisti's hangman becomes, in this way, the prototype of the meaningless (*begriffslosen*), tautological, and self-stylized 'autochthonous' (*Bodenständigen*) man unhampered by scruples of conscience. He grooms himself as an object and treats others just the same." Djassemy, *Die verfolgende Unschuld*, 165. For a historical account of this and related photos, see *AS* 1, 331–33. For more on the images used in this drama, see Anton Holzer, *Die letzten Tage der Menschheit: Der Erste Weltkrieg in Bildern. Mit Texten von Karl Kraus* (Darmstadt: Primus, 2014).

60. The stage direction reads: "Viennese wine-tavern music (*Heurigenmusik*), feverishly distorted. The execution of Battisti. Laughing soldiers surround the corpse. The curious stretch their necks. The jolly executioner with his hands above the dead man's head," followed by the appearance of "the Austrian face." See *LTM*, 723; *LDM*, 549.

61. Roland Barthes writes that the primary effect of the photograph as such "is not to restore what has been abolished (by time, by distance), but to attest that what I see has indeed existed." See Roland Barthes, *Camera Lucida: Reflections on Photography*, trans. Richard Howard (New York: Hill and Wang, 2010), 82. For more on Kraus's use of photography in the play and elsewhere in *The Torch*,

see Leo Lensing, "'Photographischer Alpdruck' oder politische Photomontage? Karl Kraus, Kurt Tucholsky und die satirischen Möglichleiten der Photographie," in *Karl Kraus et son temps*, ed. Gilbert Krebs and Gerald Stieg (Paris: Presses Sorbonne Nouvelle, 2018), 173–88.

62. This tactic recalls Brecht's use of ironic captions and poetic commentary in his *War Primer*, which he wrote during World War II and published in 1955. This text contains photos collected between 1939 and 1945, all of which index the brutality of war and its complicity with the interests of capital. One image contains the editorial caption "The Germans were 'kind' to this Frenchman. They blindfolded him before he was shot," to which Brecht adds this poem: "And so we put him up against a wall: / A mother's son, a man like we had been / And shot him dead. And then to show you all / What came of him, we photographed the scene." See Brecht, *Kriegsfibel* (Berlin: Eulenspiegel Verlag, 1994), 12–13; quoted here from *War Primer*, trans. John Willett (New York: Verso, 2017), 12–13.

63. For a thorough glossary and index of the important historical figures, events, and names that appear in the drama, see *LDM*, 601–45.

Chapter 2

This chapter's first epigraph is a slightly modified version of the translation by Albert Bloch—Kraus's first officially approved English translator—and is excerpted from the foreword to a collection of poems by Kraus that Bloch translated during the 1920s. Bloch, an American-born artist, journalist, and caricaturist who had lived in Germany from 1909 to 1921, composed these translations upon his return to the United States while he was working as a professor of art and art history at the University of Kansas. See Albert Bloch, *Karl Kraus: Poems* (Boston: Four Seas, 1930), 16–17. For more on Bloch's life, work, and relationship to Kraus, see Frank Baron and Jon Blumb, eds., *Albert Bloch and the Blue Rider* (Lawrence: Jayhawk Ink / University of Kansas, 2014); see also Werner Mohr, *Albert Bloch: Caricaturist, Social Critic, and Translator of Karl Kraus* (Riverside, Calif.: Ariadne Press, 2003). With regard to the second epigraph, Emil Schinck's nineteenth-century translation of *The Birds* is the version Kraus relied on for his own adaptation.

1. For a brief history of Kraus's invocations of Aristophanes's in *The Torch*, see Friedrich Pfäfflin and Eva Dambacher, eds., *Marbacher Kataloge 52: Karl Kraus* (Marbach: Deutsche Schillergesellschaft, 1999), 61–70; *D*, 360–62.

2. For a more comprehensive introduction to both Old Comedy and *The Birds* in particular, see Jeffrey Henderson, *Aristophanes: The Birds* (Newburyport, Mass.: Focus, 1999), 1–20.

3. A writer, dramaturge, and later film director who fled Vienna for the United States, Viertel was also a great admirer of Kraus, whom he met in 1905. Viertel was later indebted to Kraus for the financial support the latter provided to help save Viertel's theater ensemble in Berlin, "Die Truppe." Grateful that Kraus dedicated his play to him, Viertel hoped to direct and stage *Cloudcuckooland*, but these plans never came to fruition. For more on this moment, see Friedrich Pfäfflin and Eva Dambacher, eds., *Marbacher Kataloge 52: Karl Kraus*, 68–69. For more on Viertel's reflections on Kraus, see Viertel, *Karl Kraus: Ein Charakter und die Zeit* (Dresden: Rudolf Kaemmerer Verlag, 1921). For a recent and thorough

discussion of Viertel's relationship to Kraus, see Katharina Prager, *Berthold Viertel: Eine Biographie der Wiener Moderne* (Vienna: Böhlau, 2018), 268–90.

4. Kraus himself even called it a "sublimation of 'The Last Days of Mankind' into an airier region." See *F* 800, 64, 1929; here as quoted by Heinrich Fischer in *D*, 361.

5. Heinrich Fischer writes that Kraus gave readings in front of workers from 1919 to 1924 on both the *Republikfeiern* and on May Day. Quoted by Franz Mautner, "Über Karl Kraus' Komödie 'Wolkenkuckucksheim,'" in *Austriaca: Beiträge zur österreichischen Literatur. Festschrift für Heinz Politzer zum 65. Geburtstag*, ed. Winfried Kudszus and Hinrich Seeba (Tübingen: Niemeyer, 1975), 322. Kraus, as many critics have observed, was a convert to democratic republicanism, even if he was among the republic's most persistent critics and maintained a strained and ultimately doomed relationship with its most representative party, the Social Democrats. As Alfred Pfabigan wrote: "In a certain sense we can characterize Kraus as *the* writer (*Schriftsteller*) of the First Republic. Not as its poet laureate but as the writer who co-created (*mitschuf*) the Republic through his journalistic practice during the World War, supported it during its early years (*Freizeit*), and was, indeed, organically bound to it. At the same time, he reproduced within himself its contradictions, such that in the end, he stood on the side of its destroyers" (emphasis added). See Alfred Pfabigan, *Karl Kraus und der Sozialismus: Eine politische Biographie* (Vienna: Europaverlag, 1976), 194. For longer discussions of Kraus's complex relationship to Austrian social democracy, see ibid., 192–219, and *AS* 2, 249–347.

6. "Republican festival drama" is Timms's translation of "republikanisches Weihefestspiel." The cultural context surrounding this play is also worth noting: Kraus was responding to the Salzburg Festival and to Max Reinhardt's production of Hugo von Hofmannsthal's adaptation of Calderón, a religious allegory that in no way engaged with the social realities of postwar Austria. Kraus's play would certainly pose a challenge to the "theo-centrism" of Hofmannsthal, and its secular impulse is indeed crucial for its interpretation. For more on this episode—including how Kraus's critique of the church qua theater was entangled in his antisemitism—and on *Cloudcuckooland*'s publication and transmission history, see *AS* 2, 281–84.

7. Kraus actually composed a parody of the Austrian "Volkshymne" ("People's Hymn") in 1920. Its first stanza reads as follows: "May God keep, may God protect / our country from the emperor! / Powerful without his support / secure without his slapping hand! / Unshielded by his crown / we stand against this enemy: / Never more shall the Habsburg Throne / Be tied to Austria's destiny! (*Gott behalte, Gott beschütze / vor dem Kaiser unser Land! / Mächtig ohne seine Stütze / sicher ohne seine Hand! / Ungeschirmt von seiner Krone / stehn wir gegen diesen Feind: / Nimmer sei mit Habsburgs Throne / Österreichs Geschick vereint*)." See *F* 554, 59, 1920; *G*, 337. In a letter written to Gershom Scholem in the same year, Walter Benjamin writes that Kraus's national anthem—along with both his public letter defending the revolutionary Rosa Luxemburg against the accusations of a wealthy estate owner and his essay "Bread and Lies"—"unquestionably shows [Kraus] to be on his way to becoming a great politician. . . . It is as if the demonic and deeper side of his nature has died off, petrified, and as if his torso

and its eloquent head now had an unshakeable marble pedestal from which to talk down." The "demonic" in Kraus will resurface in Benjamin's essay on Kraus a decade later. See Walter Benjamin, *Gesammelte Briefe, Band II: 1919–1924* (Frankfurt am Main: Suhrkamp, 1996), 120; quoted here from Walter Benjamin, *The Correspondence of Walter Benjamin, 1910–1940*, ed. Gershom Scholem and Theodor W. Adorno, trans. Manfred R. Jacobson and Evelyn M. Jacobson (Chicago: University of Chicago Press, 2012), 171.

8. Mautner, "Über Karl Kraus' Komödie 'Wolkenkuckucksheim,'" 325.

9. Ibid., 322.

10. Bernhard Greiner, "*Polos* und *Polis*: Aristophanes's *Vögel* und deren Bearbeitung durch Goethe, Kraus und Peter Hacks," in *Ancient Comedy and Reception: Essays in Honor of Jeffrey Henderson*, ed. S. Douglas Olson (Berlin: De Gruyter, 2013), 629–726.This largely negative assessment accords with Hans Weigel's brief reading of the play, in which he calls it one of Kraus's four "unsuccessful stage works." See Hans Weigel, *Karl Kraus oder die Macht der Ohnmacht*: *Versuch eines Motivenberichts zur Erhellung eines vielfachen Lebenswerks* (Vienna: F. Molden, 1968), 219.

11. While Aristophanes was not a major literary figure for Kraus, the playwright is invoked in *The Torch*'s very first issue, in the context of Kraus's criticism that every time a humorist of even middling talent emerges in Vienna, he is referred to as a "Viennese Aristophanes." See *F* 1, 18, 1899. The one exception to this rule Kraus granted was Johann Nestroy—and perhaps himself.

12. For more on Heine's relationship to Aristophanes—including his defense of the Greek poet as part of a larger polemic against the Romantics—see David Pugh, "Heine's Aristophanes Complex and the Ambivalence of 'Deutschland: Ein Wintermärchen,'" *Modern Language Review* 99, no. 3 (2004): 665–80.

13. The play was allegedly composed in a matter of a weeks during the summer of 1923. See Mautner, "Über Karl Kraus' Komödie 'Wolkenkuckucksheim,'" 326.

14. The German names are rough translations of the Greek original.

15. For a thorough discussion of the transitional period from the end of the war to the early years of the First Republic, including the anxiety that surrounded its formation, see Anson Rabinbach, *The Crisis of Austrian Socialism*: *From Red Vienna to Civil War, 1927–1934* (Chicago: University of Chicago Press, 1983), 18–31.

16. Each of these birds has its own symbolic meaning; *Weihe* ambiguously refers to the Catholic sacraments and to an extinct bird of prey, the Eyles's harrier.

17. In his provocative reading of Aristophanes's *The Birds*, Leo Strauss points out that "Peistetaerus" is actually a combination of these two meanings, which is not without significance in terms of his character. See Leo Strauss, *Socrates and Aristophanes* (Chicago: University of Chicago Press, 1996), 160.

18. "Alleweil lustig, fesch und munter, / denn der Weaner geht net unter" was a popular folk song, which would have been familiar to Kraus's readers and audience. Its content obviously speaks to the self-aggrandizement and ostensible immortality of the Athenian / Viennese that is here being parodied. See Mautner, "Über Karl Kraus' Komödie 'Wolkenkuckucksheim,'" 316.

19. "Wenn ihr Häuser baut und Mauern zieht, / dann hat die Menschheit ausgesungen ihr Lied. / Dann ist der Mensch gegen euch eine Laus. / Und mit den Göttern ist's aus, denn die hungert ihr aus!"

20. “Und seid ihr einmal Herr, so seid ihr nicht mehr Knecht; / dann zieht sich Zeus zurück vor dem grünen Specht. / Man hat doch schließlich heut sein Selbstbestimmungsrecht!”

21. Karl Renner, the Austrian socialist who led the first government of German-Austria and then the First Austrian Republic in 1919 and 1920, was a major theorist and proponent of the *Selbstbestimmungsrecht*. This term would become an important foundation for all subsequent international law. See Karl Renner, *Das Selbstbestimmungsrecht der Nationen in besonderer Anwendung auf Oesterreich* (Leipzig: F. Deuticke, 1918).

22. “. . . wenn eine Kette reißt, / und der Gefangne wird zum Kerkermeister. / Denn oft im Völkerleben soll es glücken, / den einstigen Tyrannen zu bedrücken.”

23. Adler was an instrumental figure in the political and intellectual development of the Austrian Socialist Party. For a recent reading of Adler’s role within the intellectual current of Austro-Marxism—and the larger context of both “red” and “black” Vienna—see Janek Wasserman, *Black Vienna: The Radical Right in the Red City, 1918–1938* (Ithaca, N.Y.: Cornell University Press, 2014), 47–73.

24. In Greek mythology, Prokne (alternatively, Procne) begged the gods to turn her into a bird so she could escape the rage of her husband King Tereus, who pursued her with vengeance after she had killed their son and served him as a meal to Tereus. The gods granted her wish and she was turned into a swallow.

25. Albert Bloch’s translation in *Karl Kraus*, 40. Bloch was an admirer of this play and translated several of its verses in his collection of Kraus’s poems.

26. “Alle Vögel sind schon da” (*D*, 127)—the title of the subheading of this chapter—refers to a famous German children’s song about the approaching spring; its invocations in the play’s first act would have been highly recognizable to Kraus’s audience. While the phrase adds to the play’s fantastical, fairytale-like quality, it also, I would contend, suggests that something is in the air: a rebirth of sorts, perhaps a revolution.

27. A *Dompfaff* is a bullfinch, but Kraus is clearly punning with this word, which also contains within it an allusion to a priest or a cleric (*Pfaffe*).

28. For more on Kraus’s relationship to Seipel, whom Kraus ultimately respected neither as a politician nor as a prelate, see *AS* 2, 273–76.

29. For more on Kraus’s attacks against the extortionary practices of press moguls—specifically on his assault against Imre Bekessy—see *AS* 2, 306–11.

30. Kraus is parodying the Expressionists with this figure. Franz Werfel—whom Kraus had parodied in his earlier play, *Literature, or We’ll See about That* (1921)—is most certainly the referent for the next visitor, the “Friend of the World” (*Weltfreund*), who poetizes pathetically and unintelligibly about the new bird city. For more on this parody, see Mautner, “Über Karl Kraus’ Komödie ‘Wolkenkuckucksheim,’” 318.

31. “Ich bin dem Verständnis der Sache entfernt; / das Idiom, das er spricht, hab ich niemals gelernt.”

32. Compare Kraus: “die Botschaft hören sie, es fehlt der Glaube” to Goethe’s Faust: “Die Botschaft hör ich wohl, allein mir fehlt der Glaube.” See *GF*, l. 765.

33. In *The Last Days*, Kraus plays with the notion of a *Verteidigungskrieg*—a defensive war—by implanting it in the mouth of a belligerent drunkard, whose slurring makes the word sound like *Verteilungskrieg*, or “war of repartition.”

Timms renders this wordplay as the distinction between "a lowly whore of self-potence" and a "holy war of self-defence." See *LTM*, 71; *LDM*, 49.

34. "Die Menschensitte wird hier eingepflanzt: / wie dort gelebt, getötet und getanzt!"

35. The phrase "einrückend gemacht" shows up numerous times throughout *The Last Days* and Kraus's wartime writings in *The Torch*. In one scene, the Grumbler and the Optimist are in conversation and the former tries to explain to his interlocutor the paradox of being "compulsorily enlisted": "Properly speaking, they've been compulsorily enlisted (*einrückend gemachte*). The present participle 'enlisting' would indicate that they're doing it of their own free will, that's why it has to be a past participle. So they are compulsorily enlisted (*einrückend Gemachte*). Soon they'll be in the front line (*werden sie einrückend gemacht sein*)." See *LTM*, 253; *LDM*, 187.

36. "Wir opfern uns für solchen Heldenwahn. / Blickt euch nur um und seht das Elend an!"

37. Calasso writes that these words—"Dort bilden sich ja Gruppen," which John Shepley (Calasso's translator) renders as "Clusters form"—are among the most frightening words in *The Last Days*, since they "discreetly accompany us in the stage directions from the very first page, the second line to be exact. They swell like poisonous clouds for hundreds of pages and strike us at the end, when their unique significance is finally revealed in scene 4, 29, where they are spoken by the Faultfinder [the Grumbler] to designate the throng of bystanders who want to have their picture taken alongside the corpse of the hanged Battisti, while the jovial hangman looks on. Groups are not an expression of democratic spontaneity. Their origin is much older. Groups form around a corpse." See Calasso, *Forty-Nine Steps*, 98.

38. Kraus perceived a revolution from the far left as one of the three dangers threatening the new republic (the other two being the press and human idiocy), but this scene seems to confirm that at least at this historical juncture, his attention was more (justifiably) preoccupied with the potential alliance between right-wing clericalism and burgeoning fascism. For more on Kraus's relationship to the communists and the Austrian *Arbeiterbewegung*, see Pfabigan, *Karl Kraus und der Sozialismus*, 220–54.

39. Emphasis added. The second of the two stanzas quoted is Timms's translation. See *AS* 2, 284–85.

40. Kraus, it should be noted, warned of the dangers of the swastika as early as 1921—well before most intellectuals perceived it to be a legitimate threat. In an essay entitled "Christmas Gifts," he writes that in Germany the "swastika looms high above the ruins of the world conflagration (*über den Trümmern des Weltbrands*)." *F* 557, 59, 1921.

41. *AS* 2, 286. For a brief analysis of Kraus's response to the persistence of clericalism in Austria—and specifically Kraus's critique of one of its most celebrated exponents, the historian and author Richard Kralik—see Wasserman, *Black Vienna*, 16–18.

42. See Mautner, "Über Karl Kraus' Komödie 'Wolkenkuckucksheim,'" 320.

43. This is a slight modification of Wilma Iggers's translation from *Karl Kraus: A Viennese Critic of the Twentieth Century* (The Hague: Martinus

Nijhoff, 1967), 141. The original German: ". . . in einer Republik sind die Menschen zunächst so schlecht und so dumm, wie sie sind, aber von keiner Schranke gehindert, den Zustand zu heben. Die monarchische Macht muß, um zu bestehen, die Menschen dümmer und schlechter machen, als sie sind." *F* 501, 18, 1919.

44. Canetti once compared the two satirists, claiming that Kraus was "the greatest German satirist, the only one in the literature of this language whom one has the right to name next to Aristophanes, Juvenal, Quevedo, Swift, and Gogol." Canetti, *Conscience of Words*, 216.

45. In a sense, this makes Wiedehopf the most Kraus-like figure if we consider the full evolution of Kraus's politics from the beginning of the war to the early years of the First Republic. Having once been a supporter of the monarchy and the monarchical idea, he became a committed—if, as discussed earlier, hesitant—convert to republicanism, and also its most scathing critic.

46. Albert Bloch's translation in *Karl Kraus*, 97.

47. Timms's translation. *AS* 2, 286. The original German: "Wir sind erwacht. Behüten wir das Glück. / Wir träumten Macht! Wir leben Republik!"

48. Albert Bloch's translation in *Karl Kraus*, 98. The original German: "Der Mensch ist fort. Die Luft ist rein!"

49. During one of their exchanges, the Optimist claims: "You don't give up, do you! No wonder you'll be denounced one day as a bird fouling its own nest," and the Grumbler interrupts (as is his wont) "—and tearing it to bits instead of building a new one, I know. That accusation would certainly kill one bird with two stones. How unjust when he's actually fulfilling the moral precept of cleaning his own backyard. This dirty world accuses whoever clears away its dirt of being the one who brought it. My patriotism—unlike that of the patriots—could not bear to leave the job to an enemy satirist. . . . The testimony of someone who has breathed the same air as those he satirizes cannot be refuted." *LTM*, 508–9; *LDM*, 383–84.

Chapter 3

An earlier version of this chapter, titled "'Wo ungesetz gesetzlich überwaltet': Karl Kraus's Reading of National Socialism," was published in *Oxford German Studies* 46, no. 1 (2017): 75–91. Reprinted with permission by Taylor & Francis.

1. On the early successes of the Social Democratic Party in Austria, see Rabinbach, *Crisis of Austrian Socialism*, 18–40.

2. The so-called Kraus-Bekessy affair played a significant role in Kraus's departure from this particular sphere of politics. Though I will briefly discuss this "affair" in chapter 4, it should suffice to suggest for now that it involved a longstanding dispute between Kraus and a corrupt press mogul, Imre Bekessy—the editor of the major tabloid *Die Stunde*—and ultimately resulted in Bekessy's effective expulsion from Vienna.

3. For this reason, Kraus became a source of controversy among the hardline communists, with some factions claiming him as an enforcer of the status quo and some as a true revolutionary. See *AS* 2, 256–57.

4. For various accounts of Kraus's prominent role during the aftermath of July 15, including his public demand that the Viennese police chief, Johann Schober, "step down," see Stefan Jonsson, *Crowds and Democracy: The Idea and*

Image of the Masses from Revolution to Fascism (New York: Columbia University Press, 2013), 33–37; Elias Canetti, *Die Fackel im Ohr: Lebensgeschichte 1921–1931* (Frankfurt: Fischer Verlag, 2005), 231–37; *AS* 2, 332–39.

5. Elias Canetti, *The Torch in My Ear*, trans. Joachim Neugroschel (New York: Farrar, Straus and Giroux, 198), 246.

6. Timms's translation of "Der Hort der Republik." *AS* 2, 337.

7. See also *SG*, 293.

8. Jonsson, *Crowds and Democracy*, 37.

9. See Werner Anzenberger, *Absage an die Demokratie: Karl Kraus und der Bruch der österreichischen Verfassung 1933/34* (Graz: Leyker Verlag, 1997), 119. Anzenberger gives a thorough account of Kraus's slow departure from the sphere of democratic politics. On Kraus's deteriorating relationship with the social democrats, the *Arbeiterbewegung*, and the communists, see also Pfabigan, *Karl Kraus und der Sozialismus*, 311–36.

10. This infamous decision led to the disillusionment of many of his most ardent supporters, including Bertolt Brecht and Elias Canetti. In response to Kraus's final poem, "One Shall Not Ask," which declared an expiration of the "word" as Hitler came to power (*F* 888, 4, 1933), Brecht wrote a poem entitled "On the Meaning of the Ten-line Poem in the 888th Number of *The Torch* (October 1933)." In it, he refers to Kraus as "the eloquent one" (*der Beredte*), who was, however, only able to produce a "small message" (*kleine Botschaft*) in response to the rise of the Third Reich. Brecht took Kraus's poem as a vow of silence. See Bertolt Brecht, *Die Gedichte in einem Band* (Frankfurt: Suhrkamp, 2007), 501–3. For more on Kraus's endorsement of Dollfuss and the feeling of betrayal it unleashed in his most ardent readers and supporters, see *AS* 2, 472–81. For a thorough account of the origins and history of fascism in Austria, see Michael Mann, *Fascists* (Cambridge: Cambridge University Press, 2004), 207–36.

11. Timms's translation of "Hüben und Drüben." *AS* 2, 459.

12. For a reading of Kraus's final polemic against (primarily) his socialist and communist readers, now mostly living and writing in exile, see Gerald Stieg, "Ein verfrühter Nachruf auf Karl Kraus und seine Folgen," in *Österreichische Satire (1933–2000): Exil—Remigration—Assimilation*, ed. Jeanne Benay, Alfred Pfabigan, and Anne Saint Sauveur (Bern: Peter Lang, 2003), 3–12.

13. This allusion to Luther would have had immediate resonance with Kraus's audience. On Kraus's rhetorical strategy, Brigitte Stocker writes, "This Luther allusion . . . functions as a topos of reckless courage (*draufgängerischen Unerschrockenheit*) in the face of real danger. A fulminant beginning to the speech: even when a world full of swastiklers threatens to swallow us, the social democrats, whole, 'we will remain, in spite of this, what we have always been.'" Brigitte Stocker, *Rhetorik eines Protagonisten gegen die Zeit: Karl Kraus als Redner in den Vorlesungen, 1919 bis 1932* (Vienna: Lit Verlag, 2013), 109. For more on the history of Kraus's use of Luther's *Kirchenlied*, see ibid., 108–10.

14. Heinrich Fischer, who published the first completed version of this text (with the original title *Die Dritte Walpurgisnacht*) with Kösel Verlag in 1952, reported Kraus's concerns about this book falling into the hands of the minister of propaganda, Joseph Goebbels, who could, Kraus allegedly told Fischer, "out of rage have fifty Jews from Königsberg brought to the coffins (*Stehsärge*) of a concentration camp." Kraus apparently responded: "How could I take responsibility

for this?" See Heinrich Fischer's "Anmerkungen" in *Die Dritte Walpurgisnacht* (Munich: Kösel, 1952), 308.

15. For more on the notion of the caesura as it was conceived of by German and German-Jewish thinkers, see Anson Rabinbach, *In the Shadow of Catastrophe: German Intellectuals between Apocalypse and Enlightenment* (Berkeley: University of California Press, 2001), 5.

16. The most comprehensive readings of the Goethe references in *Third Walpurgis Night* are to be found in Jochen Stremmel, *'Dritte Walpurgnisnacht': Über einen Text von Karl Kraus* (Bonn: Bouvier, 1982), and Krolop, *Sprachsatire als Zeitsatire*, 210–51.

17. In this sense, I agree with Stocker's statement that "Kraus's relationship to politics does not end in 1932, but rather enters into a new phase." Stocker, *Rhetorik eines Protagonisten*, 18.

18. Stremmel comments, for example, how greed and lust play significant roles as "dominating instinctual drives" in both Goethe's and Kraus's visions of society, and indeed in many sections of *Walpurgis* Kraus focuses on the way sexual politics or economic envy informed much of Nazi antisemitism. Stremmel, *'Dritte Walpurgisnacht,'* 130.

19. For an illuminating discussion of how Kraus negotiates the relationship between word (*Wort*) and deed (*Tat*)—and the "Nazi perversion of the Faustian concept of the deed (*Tatbegriffs*)"—in his eulogy for Adolf Loos, his last poem, and *Walpurgis*, see Anne Peiter, *Komik und Gewalt: Zur literarischen Verarbeitung der beiden Weltkriege und der Shoah* (Cologne: Böhlau, 2007), 146–47.

20. Christian Wagenknecht offers a thorough history of the transmission of this text, including which sections were published in *The Torch* and thus available to a contemporary audience. *DW*, 331–43.

21. It may be, as Timms has provocatively suggested, that the "nichts" in this phrase is to be read as a cipher for the nihilism Kraus associated with the Nazi movement: quite literally, "nothing" or "nothingness" would come to mind in connection to Hitler. See *AS* 2, 496.

22. "Wäre in solchem Motto nicht alles enthalten, mit Zögern und Angehen, Schweigen und Sagen dazu? Aber das deutscheste Ereignis—dem der Superlativ ziemt—ist wunderbarer Weise Zug um Zug im deutschesten Gedicht präformiert. Und was würde aus dieser Fülle von Motiven." *F* 890, 81, 1934; *HD*, 272.

23. Irina Djassemy has similarly argued: "The representational form (*Darstellungsform*) of *Third Walpurgis Night* supports its critical content on every level." See Djassemy, *Die verfolgende Unschuld*, 256.

24. According to David Constantine, Goethe later identified this scene as having been modeled after the court of Maximilian I, which would suggest that multiple historical moments are being imbricated and alluded to in this act. See DC, lxxx.

25. "Wenn's fieberhaft durchaus im Staate wütet, / Und Übel sich in Übeln überbrutet." *GF*, ll. 4780–81.

26. DC, 8.

27. *DW*, 10; *GF*, ll. 4782–86.

28. The first part of this quotation is my translation; the last two lines are Constantine's. DC, 9.

29. *DW*, 299; *GF*, ll. 4793–94; DC, 9.

30. Simon Ganahl, "'Natur! Natur!' Die 'Zweite Revolution' in der 'Dritten Walpurgisnacht' von Karl Kraus," *Weimarer Beiträge: Zeitschrift für Literaturwissenschaft, Ästhetik und Kulturwissenschaften* 3 (2011): 325.

31. Emphasis added. See Hannah Arendt, *Origins of Totalitarianism* (New York: Harcourt, Brace, Jovanovich, 1973), 326.

32. Kraus will elsewhere be more explicit about this claim about Nazism: "It is, however, its very essence never to be what it seems, and to embrace all antitheses in such a way that it has a stronger effect in its denial than in what it denies (*daß es sich verleugnend stärker wirkt als mit dem, was es verleugnet*)." *DW*, 273.

33. Ganahl, "Natur! Natur!," 333.

34. For a longer discussion of the term *Faustnaturen* in Kraus's text and other related references to the "Faustian" in general, see Krolop, *Sprachsatire*, 217–30. In the passage above, this loaded, polysemic concept might be referring to the idea of *acting* before thinking ("In the beginning was the deed")—the violent deed being associated with the vagaries of an indifferent, violent nature.

35. DC, xliii.

36. DC, 9.

37. *DW*, 299; *GF*, ll. 4812–26.

38. DC, 10.

39. *DW*, 299–300; *GF*, ll. 4827–30.

40. *DW*, 214; translated by Harry Zohn in *GT*, 113.

41. DC, 202.

42. *DW*, 304; *GF*, ll. 10511–15.

43. For an interesting reading of the history of the *Schopf* or hair braid and its status as a signifier of Jewish identity, see Jay Geller, *The Other Jewish Question: Identifying the Jew and Making Sense of Modernity* (New York: Fordham University Press, 2011), 50–87.

44. Kraus quotes a report of an old communist subjected to physical torture by a group of Nazis who stuck the old man's recently wounded hand into a sack of salt and began laughing at his wailing (*Jammergeschrei*)—thereby literalizing the metaphor "to rub salt in the wound." *DW*, 140.

45. As Ganahl writes, this scene seems to have anticipated "an appropriate image of unrestrained nature . . . as it was introduced in Germany." See Ganahl, "Natur! Natur!," 334.

46. See *GF*, ll. 8458–87; DC, 131–32.

47. *GF*, l. 7856; DC, 110.

48. For a brief discussion on the implications of this ancient/modern debate for Goethe, see DC, xxxiv–xxxv; and R. H. Stephenson, "The Diachronic Solidity of Goethe's Faust," in *A Companion to Goethe's Faust: Parts I and II*, ed. Paul Bishop (Rochester, N.Y.: Camden House, 2001), 260–61. For a discussion of both Goethe and Kraus vis-à-vis this discourse, see Ganahl, "Natur! Natur!," 334–37.

49. "Nicht näher! drohend-mächtige Runde, / Du richtest uns und Land und Meer zugrunde!" See *DW*, 10; *GF*, ll. 7918–19; DC, 112.

50. In order to help with distinguishing his voice from that of another author (or newspaper report—as in this particular example), the non-Kraus speaker's

text will often be printed in a smaller font. At other times, there are no visual cues to distinguish between Kraus's monologue and the other voices he incorporates into it.

51. Citing from Heidegger's Rectoral Address of 1933, Kraus satirizes the philosopher's "blue mist" (*blaue Dunst*), claiming that it has very easily been "coordinated" (*gleichgeschaltet*) to the "brown mist" of National Socialist jargon—that they are both, in a sense, speaking the same language. Heidegger's speech addresses both what *Geist* is and is not, and Kraus rightly points to the unsettling substance of his appeals to the forces of "blood and earth." In Heidegger (and Gottfried Benn), Kraus argues, we can identify the "training school" for the "Hitler thought" (*Hitler-Gedanken*). *DW*, 71–72.

52. "Hast du, o Thales, je in einer Nacht, / Solch einen Berg aus Schlamm hervorgebracht?" *DW*, 75; *GF*, ll. 7859–60; DC, 111.

53. Ganahl argues that like Goethe, Kraus, too, ultimately affirms Thales's position given his recitation of Homunculus's harmonious transformation into fire prior to entering the sea, but I am less certain that this can be considered Kraus's final word on the matter. See "Natur! Natur!," 337.

54. DC, 111.

55. *GF*, ll. 7861–64.

56. For a longer discussion of Goebbels's function in Kraus's text—and his parallel to Mephisto in Goethe's poem—see *AS* 2, 523–28.

57. *AS* 2, 527. Timms's translation.

58. Timms's decision to translate *Asphaltschriftum* as "rootless intellectuals" is an interesting choice in terms of the unsettling sentiment Kraus is expressing: Jews, deemed rootless by the Nazis, are henceforth no longer able to be journalists.

59. "Am Ende hängen wir doch ab / Von Kreaturen, die wir machten." *DW*, 305; *GF*, ll. 7003–4; DC, 82.

60. I will revisit this issue in chapter 5 in conjunction with Adorno.

61. Djassemy reads this passage as an example of what she calls Kraus's "Jewish humanism" and places Kraus subsequently in a tradition of thought that includes Adorno, Horkheimer, and Rosa Luxemburg. Irina Djassemy, *Der "Productivgehalt kritischer Zerstörerarbeit": Kulturkritik bei Karl Kraus und Theodor W. Adorno* (Würzburg: Königshausen and Neumann, 2002), 381–82.

62. DC, 201.

63. *DW*, 327; *GF*, ll. 10469–72.

64. For more on the issue of "cultural inheritance" in this text, see Krolop, *Sprachsatire*, 229–30.

65. The murder of Philemon and Baucis for the sake of creating space for Faust's empire contains an analogue to the Nazi destruction of Jewish-owned property, but, as Joachim Stremmel observed, it would be false to conclude that Faust represents anything unambiguously *symbolic* in Kraus's text. Stremmel writes: "However, just as Kraus is not capable of discussing the problematic of the Faust-figure as a problem of the 'German soul' or the 'German essence,' so is he at the same time able to escape the danger of mythologizing National Socialism." Stremmel, *'Dritte Walpurgisnacht'* 140. While this is not the proper place to launch into a full-fledged discussion of *Faust*'s appropriation by the

National Socialists or fascist ideologues in the early decades of the twentieth century, it should suffice to suggest that Kraus is certainly challenging the crude appropriation of Goethe's *Faust* to support "Aryan" or German supremacy. For recent work on this vexed discourse, see Inez Hedges, *Framing Faust: Twentieth Century Cultural Struggles* (Carbondale: Southern Illinois University Press: 2009), 44–71.

66. In specific reference to this part of Kraus's text, Werner Kraft wrote: "Language in Kraus is always scrupulously absolute, aiming at shifting content, and searching for a *stance*" (emphasis added). Werner Kraft, '"Es war einmal ein Mann . . .': Über die *Dritte Walpurgisnacht* von Karl Kraus," in *Merkur: Deutsche Zeitschrift für europäisches Denken* 10, no. 22 (1968): 927.

67. For Nancy, the "Nazi myth" represents the fundamental myth of modernity, while literature operates according to the logic of "interruption," upending the very foundations upon which myth rests. In this way, modern literature might be said to struggle against its own constitution (as myth) in its very struggle against the myths that dominate modernity. See Jean-Luc Nancy, *The Inoperative Community*, trans. Peter Connor (Minneapolis: University of Minnesota Press, 1991), 46–48.

68. At the end of his last major broadside, "Wichtiges von Wichten," Kraus accordingly writes, in reference to the fundamental difference between Austria's and Germany's authoritarian regimes: "A little dictatorship; not to be compared to the event through which extortion (*Erpressung*) became world-political and which the men and boys of freedom (*Männer und Buben der Freiheit*) call 'fascism,' hoping in vain that something relating to this jaguar occurs to the satirist as if he were a typical shmuck (*Trottel*)." See *F*, 917, 112, 1936; *HD*, 377.

69. Arendt, *Origins of Totalitarianism*, 308–9.

70. Ibid.

Chapter 4

Kraus cites or refers to Balzac multiple times throughout *The Torch*, most prominently in a piece entitled "The Press" from 1926, which contains three passages from three different authorities speaking or writing on the dangers of the press, the other two being Wilhelm Liebknecht and the pope. In this short piece, Kraus quotes the longer version of the passage in *Lost Illusions* from which I have excerpted. For more, see *F* 717, 3–5, 1926; *SG*, 111–13.

1. Jurgen Habermas, *The Structural Transformations of the Bourgeois Public Sphere: An Inquiry into a Category of Bourgeois Society*, 6th ed., trans. Thomas Burger (Cambridge, Mass.: MIT Press, 1991), 185.

2. Ibid., 183.

3. Ibid., 184.

4. Though Weber's argument is embedded in a more comprehensive argument about the modern state and the legitimate use of coercive power, his remarks on the position of the journalist in society are not insignificant. See Max Weber, *The Vocation Lectures*, trans. Rodney Livingstone (London: Hackett, 2004), 55. Though not included in this section, Weber's claim about the journalist/demagogue/lawyer is curiously similar the argument he (and others) have made about the figure of "the Jew" in modern society.

5. Worthy of its own study, for example, would be Ferdinand Tönnies's views of the press in light of his systematic critique of the notion of "public opinion." Tönnies was skeptical of what he called the "capitalist press," and particularly of its influence in the United States, citing the contemporary American sociologist Lester Ward, who scoffed at the notion of an "independent press." For Tönnies, this was a paradoxical concept. For more on his critique of public opinion, see Ferdinand Tönnies, *Ferdinand Tönnies on Public Opinion: Selections and Analyses*, ed. and trans. Hanno Hardt and Slavko Splichal (Lanham, Md.: Rowman and Littlefield, 2000), 96–103.

6. For a comprehensive account of their relationship, see Gerald Stieg, *Der Brenner und Die Fackel: Ein Beitrag zur Wirkungsgeschichte von Karl Kraus* (Salzburg: O. Müller, 1976), 153–201. For a more recent account of Haecker's position on satire during the interwar period—along with a discussion of his shifting relationship to both Kraus and Kierkegaard—see Helena Tomko, "The Reluctant Satirist: Theodor Haecker and the Dizzying Swindle of Nazism," *Oxford German Studies* 46, no. 1 (2017): 42–57.

7. For Kierkegaard's most intensive explanation of his notion of "subjective truth," see Søren Kierkegaard, *Concluding Unscientific Postscript to Philosophical Fragments*, ed. Howard V. Hong and Edna H. Hong (Princeton, N.J.: Princeton University Press, 1992), 189–251.

8. The second half of Kierkegaard's dissertation (1841) addresses, accordingly, Socratic irony and Socrates's world-historical role qua ironist as the ethical legitimacy of the ancient Greek world was faltering. See Søren Kierkegaard, *The Concept of Irony, with Continual Reference to Socrates / Notes of Schelling's Berlin Lectures, Vol. 2*, ed. Howard V. Hong and Edna H. Hong (Princeton, N.J.: Princeton University Press, 1992), 7–218.

9. As one scholar has put it, religious truths for Kierkegaard "require subjective *self-understanding* as a condition for [their] understanding," and "affirmations of faith" cannot be "secured without *inward* compliance." See John Whittaker, "Kierkegaard on the Concept of Authority," *International Journal for the Philosophy of Religion* 46 (1999): 99 (emphasis added). For more on the concept of authority in Kierkegaard, see Søren Kierkegaard, *The Book on Adler*, ed. Howard V. Hong and Edna H. Hong (Princeton, N.J.: Princeton University Press, 2009), vii–xix, and the collection, *Anthropology and Authority: Essays on Søren Kierkegaard*, ed. Paul Houe, Gordon Marino, and Sven Hakon Rossel (Amsterdam: Brill Rodopi, 2000).

10. For a historical account of the so-called *Corsair* affair, see Søren Kierkegaard, *The* Corsair Affair *and Articles Related to the Writings*, ed. Howard V. Hong and Edna H. Hong (Princeton, N.J.: Princeton University Press, 2009), vii–xxxviii. For a critical interpretation, see Alastair Hannay, *Kierkegaard: A Biography* (Cambridge: Cambridge University Press, 2003), 351–53.

11. For a thorough reading of Kierkegaard's "review" in its intellectual, historical, and biographical context, see Hannay, *Kierkegaard*, 317–31. For a philosophical exploration of both the problem of nihilism in Kierkegaard and where *A Literary Review* and its notion of "leveling" fit into Kierkegaard's larger project, see Jane Rubin and Hubert Dreyfus, "You Can't Get Something for Nothing: Kierkegaard and Heidegger on How Not to Overcome Nihilism," *Inquiry* 30, no. 1–2 (1987): 33–46.

12. In reference to the historical irony that Kierkegaard wrote these words a mere two years before revolutions swept through Europe, Walter Kaufmann writes in an introduction to this text that Kierkegaard was essentially speaking to the "deeper trends" in society: "Of course, one could consider extenuating circumstances. After all, [Kierkegaard] might well have perceived the deeper trends even if he did not foresee the future; and a good deal of what he said about the present age in 1846 might still be true of the second half of the twentieth century. Some historians might even argue that the revolutions of 1848 were peculiar in some ways and lacked the profundity of the French Revolution. If our author was right in spite of apparent evidence to the contrary, then it is not he that deserves to be well hung but rather his interpreters." See *The Present Age*, trans. Alexander Dru (New York: Harper Perennial, 1962), 21.

13. As Sophie Wennerscheid writes of the revolutionary age, "For Kierkegaard, what makes a subject a subject in the strict sense is the capability and the vital will for decision making." Sophie Wennerscheid, "The Passage of Negativity, or From Self-Renunciation to Revolution? Kierkegaard and Žižek on the Politics of the Impassioned Individual," in *Kierkegaard and Political Theory: Religion, Aesthetics, Politics and the Intervention of the Single Individual*, ed. Armen Avanessian and Sophie Wennerscheid (Chicago: University of Chicago Press, 2015), 150.

14. Hannay, *Kierkegaard*, 331.

15. Curiously, Hannay spends hardly any time discussing Kierkegaard's actual critique of the press, despite the fact that it constitutes a significant portion of this review.

16. Emphasis added.

17. See Peter Fenves, *"Chatter": Language and History in Kierkegaard* (Palo Alto, Calif.: Stanford University Press, 1993), 17 and 244. For a broad overview of his reading of this discourse in Kierkegaard, see ibid., 1–18.

18. Kierkegaard's point also prefigures an aspect of Carl Schmitt's critique of the privatization of the public sphere as articulated in *Römischer Katholizismus und politische Form* (1923). For a reading of Schmitt's take on the press and public opinion, see Kirk Wetters, *The Opinion System: Impasses of the Public Sphere from Hobbes to Habermas* (New York: Fordham University Press, 2008), 3.

19. The philanderer thus exists in what Kierkegaard, in another context, calls the "aesthetic" stage of life, suspended in a realm of infinite possibility in his refusal to act, decide, or make commitments. For a recent account of Kierkegaard's notion of the aesthetic stage vis-à-vis the ethical and the religious—as well as its articulations in different forms of literature—see Eric Ziolkowski, *The Literary Kierkegaard* (Evanston, Ill.: Northwestern University Press, 2011), 87–182.

20. *KW* XIV, 106. Quoted by Haecker as an epigraph to his essay "The War and the Leaders of Spirit" ("Der Krieg und die Führer des Geistes") published in 1915. Theodor Haecker, *Werke III: Satire und Polemik: Der Geist des Menschen und die Wahrheit* (Munich: Kösel, 1961), 71.

21. Haecker was initially a contributor to Ludwig von Ficker's *Torch*-inspired, Innsbruck-based journal, *Der Brenner*. After his conversion to Catholicism in 1921, however, he became more involved with the Catholic periodical *Hochland*. For more on the relationship between Kraus and Ficker, see Stieg, *Der Brenner und Die Fackel*, 29–91.

22. See Theodor Haecker, *Philosophie der Innerlichkeit* (Munich: Schreiber, 1913), 58.

23. Ibid., 59 (emphasis added).

24. Tomko astutely argues that even prior to his conversion to Catholicism, Haecker expresses ambivalence toward Kraus as a cosmopolitan satirist. She writes: "Haecker seems already to fear that satire might ensnare the soul in its own derisive practices—that the prejudices it enlists might consume any good it is capable of accomplishing." Tomko, "Reluctant Satirist," 48.

25. Stieg accordingly writes: "Kraus's name does not appear in this afterword, and yet it is precisely in this text that complete 'harmony of style and intuition (*Anschauung*)' is achieved. Kierkegaard's critique of liberalism from 1846 proves itself, finally today, to be fully valid. One could interpret this critique, point for point, to have anticipated Kraus." Stieg, *Der Brenner und Die Fackel*, 156 (my translation).

26. Haecker, *Werke III*, 50.

27. For an explanation of the ways in which Haecker was influenced by Kraus as satirist and polemicist, see Stieg, *Der Brenner und Die Fackel*, 191–201.

28. See Theodor Haecker, *Werke I: Essays* (Munich: Kösel, 1961), 377. On the question of satire and its role within this larger discourse, Haecker had much to say, even if his position on the subject matter would significantly alter after his conversion to Catholicism. For although he turned to "humor" as a more noble and "Christian" stage of existence and attendant mode of writing, he remained fundamentally committed to Kraus as a satirist and an ethical force in modernity. As Tomko argues, Haecker would, indeed, revert back to satire during his "inner emigration" when the Nazis were in power, conceiving of it as the only possible mode of resistance to the "swindle of Nazism." See Tomko, "Reluctant Satirist," 52–56.

29. Kraus's collection of essays, *The Destruction of the World through Black Magic* (*Untergang der Welt durch schwarze Magic*), was originally published in 1922 and contains a number of essays originally composed for *The Torch* between 1908 and 1915, including his famous essays on Heinrich Heine and Johann Nestroy. The titular essay of this collection addresses the perils of modern journalistic writing and foreshadows some of Kraus's wartime pieces.

30. Haecker, *Werke I*, 371. As Stieg writes, Haecker was ultimately interested in replacing the "ideal conceptual system of satire" with Catholicism, and despite his abiding respect for Kraus, he was not able to offer anything more than a prayer for the satirist's soul. Stieg, *Der Brenner und Die Fackel*, 173.

31. Stieg writes: "Kraus is, for Haecker, at first an ethical and then later a theological problem that Haecker—as a satirist—would also like to clarify for himself. Haecker for Kraus was probably hardly more than a faithful adept, perhaps an interesting mediator in the case of Kierkegaard. Kraus remained, however, silent about Haecker's real concern. For Kraus was never ready to become a *sacrificium satirae*. . . . Haecker and *Die Brenner*, however, wanted nothing more than this from Kraus." Stieg, *Der Brenner und Die Fackel*, 201.

32. Quoted in Joachim Grage, "Karl Kraus: 'The Miracle of Unison'—Criticism of the Press and Experiences of Isolation," in *Kierkegaard's Influence on Literature, Criticism, and Art, Tome 1: The Germanophone World*, ed. Jon Stewart

(Abingdon, U.K.: Routledge, 2013), 159. The quotations originally come from Kierkegaard's journals.

33. See *F* 418, 1, 1916; *WG*, 32. The phrase "the shooting guns and the blood that runs" is Grage's translation; apart from that phrase, the translation is my own. See Grage, "Miracle of Unison," 160.

34. "Hinaus aus Wien mit dem Schuft!" *F* 691, 122, 1925. As Timms points out, this slogan combines multiple registers and is more complex than its apparent simplicity would initially convey: "Hinaus" had been commonly associated with the antisemitic slogan "Hinaus mit den Juden!"; "aus Wien" speaks to the political impetus of the campaign; and "mit dem Schuft" has an undeniably literary quality. See *AS* 2, 325–26.

35. For a thorough account of the Kraus-Bekessy affair, see *AS* 2, 302–27. Kraus eventually wrote a satirical play about this affair and his role in it, entitled *The Unconquerable* (*Die Unüberwindlichen*), which premiered in Berlin in 1928. In its printed version, the play opens with an epigraph from Kierkegaard that was surely mediated to Kraus via Haecker's translation. The quote reads: "A single person can neither help nor save an epoch; he can only express that it's foundering (*Ein einziger Mensch kann einer Zeit nicht helfen oder sie retten, er kann nur ausdrücken, daß sie untergeht*)". See *D*, 225. *The Unconquerable* is the only work of Kraus's that Benjamin officially reviewed (1929). See *GS* 4, 552–54. Kraus additionally quotes the Kierkegaard passage in a short gloss titled "Kierkegaard's Words" (*SG*, 344).

36. Timms's translation. *AS* 2, 325.

37. In his contemporary review of Haecker's book on Kierkegaard, the Catholic theologian Carl Dallago (part of the *Brenner* circle), indeed, places Kraus in a tradition that includes Socrates (in his relationship to Athens) and Kierkegaard (in his relationship to Copenhagen). For Dallago, the *vis comica* often emerges "where more devilment (*Unfug*) reigns." Carl Dallago, *Ueber eine Schrift: Søren Kierkegaard und die Philosophie der Innerlichkeit* (Innsbruck: Brenner-Verlag, 1914), 40–41.

38. As Stieg has pointed out, Kierkegaard is a radical Christian whereas Kraus is a "radical idealistic ethicist." Stieg, *Der Brenner und Die Fackel*, 164. Effectively repeating the claim that Haecker had made in his initial comparison of the two figures, Grage concludes that Kraus and Kierkegaard belong to a shared tradition of "productive subjective thinkers," for whom truth always means subjective truth. Grage, "Miracle of Unison," 165. Both of these points are valid and need to be taken into consideration in any comparative analysis, but my argument is that there is more to explore in terms of the deeper affinities between the two figures.

39. See *Kierkegaard's Journals and Notebooks*, vol. 4, ed. Niels Jørgen Cappelørn, Alastair Hannay, David Kangas, Bruce H. Kirmmse, George Pattison, Joel D. S. Rasmussen, Vanessa Rumble, and K. Brian Søderquist (Princeton, N.J.: Princeton University Press, 2011), 150.

40. In the initial iteration of this essay in *The Torch*, Kraus uses the term *Einbildungskraft*, whereas in the published version of *The Destruction of the World through Black Magic* (1922) he changed the word to *Vorstellungskraft*, also the word used in the Kösel edition published in 1960. The semantic difference

between the two in this context does not appear to be of great significance, but the philosophical prehistories of each concept would lead me to believe that *Vorstellungskraft* contains both the elements of fantasy and imagination, while *Einbildungskraft* is associated with imagination alone.

41. Kraus's assertions about the power of the press may, indeed, have been overstated, but, as Timms has argued, the early part of the twentieth century in Central Europe was a period of "intense imperial rivalries, backed by highly trained forces and sophisticated armaments industries. Given the precarious situation, it was possible at moments of crisis for journalists to tip the balance between war and peace." See Edward Timms, "Karl Kraus and the Transformation of the Public Sphere," in *Changing Perceptions of the Public Sphere*, ed. Christian J. Emden and David Midgley (New York: Berghahn Books, 2012), 170.

42. Timms criticizes Kraus for his naïveté in ignoring the relationship between the state and the press and thereby focusing too narrowly on the latter, as if it operated as an entirely independent agent. But this argument overlooks key moments in the text in which Kraus exaggerates—and even brackets out—certain key political features of the war in order to make a more informed claim about the function of the press. See *AS* 1, 282.

43. Kraus's near obsession with the biblical-Goethean relationship between words and deeds—a motif throughout *Third Walpurgis Night*—reveals itself in this speech as well.

44. An electronic search within the online version of *The Torch* reveals that Kraus uses the word *Geist* over 1,500 times throughout the journal's existence. It would be safe to conclude that this word assumed different valences in Kraus depending on the context, but that in the case above, it is meant to indicate thought in its most individualized, robust form—the very opposite of opinion (*Meinung*).

45. Kraus repeatedly referred to the "opinion-press" (*Meinungspresse*)—including in the essay from 1912 (*F* 363, 5, 1912; *UW*, 464)—and used the phrase "public sphere" (*Öffentlichkeit*) nearly 600 times over the course of *The Torch*'s existence. See Timms, "Karl Kraus and the Transformation of the Public Sphere," 164.

46. For a recent reading of Benjamin's treatment of storytelling within the context of film, montage, and photography, see Patrizia McBride, *The Chatter of the Visible: Montage and Narrative in Weimar Germany* (Ann Arbor: University of Michigan Press, 2016), 62–82.

47. A recent collection of English translations of Benjamin's writings on film and media contains a chapter devoted to these texts along with a short introduction on their place in Benjamin's oeuvre. See Walter Benjamin, *The Work of Art in the Age of Its Technological Reproducibility, and Other Writings on Media*, ed. Michael W. Jennings, Brigid Doherty, and Thomas Y. Levin (Cambridge, Mass.: Harvard University Press, 2008), 343–52.

48. This text was initially published in *Der öffentliche Dienst*, a Zurich-based periodical, and was composed roughly around the time Benjamin left Paris for a trip to Denmark to visit Brecht. See *SW* 2, 742 and 854.

49. Emphasis added.

50. Even in Benjamin's observations about Moscow, there is hardly any discussion of the Soviet press, and the little that Benjamin has to say about the

press is rather negative. He writes: "Bolshevism has abolished private life. The bureaucracy, political activity, the press are so powerful that no time remains for interests that do not converge with them." *GS* 4, 327; *SW* 2, 30.

51. It is not entirely clear whether or to what end this omission was intentional; what matters is that Benjamin did not presume that the Soviet model was the only possible model for how the press could be revived. For a brief introduction to Benjamin's engagement with Soviet culture and his time in Moscow in 1926–27, see Susan Buck-Morss, *The Dialectics of Seeing: Walter Benjamin and the Arcades Project* (Cambridge, Mass.: MIT Press, 1991), 27–32.

52. David Ferris, in his reading of Benjamin's "The Storyteller" (1936), elucidates the distinction between these terms as follows: "Here, experience is not confined to what an individual encounters in the present, but rather it has both an individual and a collective aspect. It is the means by which an individual relates to collective experience. The German word Benjamin uses confirms this: *Erfahrung*. Unlike another word for experience, *Erlebnis*, which refers to experience as something lived or witnessed, *Erfahrung* emphasizes the sense of a wisdom drawn and communicated from experience." See David Ferris, *The Cambridge Introduction to Walter Benjamin* (Cambridge: Cambridge University Press, 2008), 111.

53. Emphasis added.

54. These texts consist of a fragment entitled "Karl Kraus" (*GS* 2, 624–25; *SW* 2, 194–95); a gloss entitled "Monument to a Warrior" in *One-Way Street* (*GS* 4, 121; *SW* 1, 469); a review of a Kraus performance of Jacques Offenbach entitled "Karl Kraus Reads Offenbach" (*GS* 4, 515–17; *GS* 2, 110–12); and finally, a review of *The Unconquerable* (*GS* 4, 552–54), the satirical play Kraus wrote in response to his involvement with Bekessy and *Die Stunde*. For a detailed account of the place of these shorter pieces vis-à-vis Benjamin's more sustained study of Kraus, see Christian Schulte, *Ursprung ist das Ziel: Walter Benjamin über Karl Kraus* (Würzburg: Königshausen and Neumann, 2003), 45–55. Benjamin and Gershom Scholem had also been corresponding about Kraus since 1920 (at the latest), when Benjamin wrote to Scholem about how impressed he was by Kraus's polemic against the "shameless" attack on Rosa Luxemburg. See *Correspondence of Walter Benjamin: 1910–1940*, 171.

55. Quoting from Scholem and Benjamin's correspondences, Rabinbach writes about how Scholem was increasingly frustrated with Benjamin's Marxism, which he saw in its most confused form in the Kraus essay. Rabinbach writes: "Scholem's frustration and disappointment with Benjamin's Marxism, and his antipathy toward Brecht, his antipode, is evident from the tone of his missives. . . . Adopting the self-assumed role of an 'old theologian,' Scholem accused Benjamin of confusing religion and politics and of 'engaging in a singularly intensive kind of self-deception.' Benjamin's essay on Karl Kraus, the Viennese moralist, he said, exhibited 'an astonishing incompatibility and unconnectedness between [his] real and [his] pretended modes of thought,'" Quoted in Gershom Scholem, ed., *The Correspondence of Walter Benjamin and Gershom Scholem, 1932–1940*, trans. Gary Smith and Andre LeFevere (Cambridge, Mass.: Harvard University Press, 1992), xxiii. For a recent theoretical exploration of how Benjamin links (and separates) Marx and Kraus vis-à-vis their relationship to Shakespeare's *Timon*

of Athens, see Julia Ng, "Each Thing a Thief: Walter Benjamin on the Agency of Objects," *Philosophy and Rhetoric* 44, no. 4 (2011): 382–402.

56. For a brief account of the historical circumstances surrounding this publication, see Howard Eiland and Michael Jennings, *Walter Benjamin: A Critical Life* (Cambridge, Mass.: Harvard University Press, 2014), 350–51.

57. Kraus's response: "All that I really understand of this work—which is certainly well meant and also, it would seem, well thought out—is that it is about me, and that the author appears to know a good many things about me that I myself was previously ignorant of, things that I now don't clearly recognize; and I can only express the hope that other readers will understand it better than I do. (Perhaps it is psychoanalysis)." *F* 852, 27, 1931. Benjamin was deeply offended (if unsurprised) by Kraus's response, and swore to Scholem that he would never write about Kraus again. For more on this, see Eiland and Jennings, *Critical Life*, 353–54. This turned out to be a false promise: Kraus shows up again in Benjamin's Baudelaire essay in 1939 (to be discussed) and briefly in his correspondences with Scholem regarding Kraus's death. See Scholem, *Correspondence of Walter Benjamin and Gershom Scholem*, 194–98.

58. Beatrice Hanssen, *Walter Benjamin's Other History: Of Stones, Animals, Human Beings, and Angels* (Berkeley: University of California Press, 2000), 114–26. To date, several important studies exist on the Benjamin/Kraus relationship. See Sigrid Weigel, *Walter Benjamin: Die Kreatur, das Heilige, die Bilder* (Berlin: Fischer Verlag, 2008), 27–56; Bettina Menke, "Das Nach-Leben im Zitat. Benjamins Gedächtnis der Texte," in *Gedächtniskunst: Raum—Bild—Schrift Studien zur Mnemotechnik*, ed. Anselm Haverkamp and Renate Lachmann (Frankfurt: Suhrkamp, 1991), 74–110; Manfred Voigt, "'Die Mater der Gerechtigkeit.' Zur Kritik des Zitat-Begriffs bei Walter Benjamin," in *Antike und Moderne: Zu Walter Benjamins "Passagen,"* ed. Norbert Bolz and Richard Faber (Würzburg: Königshausen and Neumann, 1986), 97–115; Schulte, *Ursprung ist das Ziel*; and Christopher Thornhill, *Walter Benjamin and Karl Kraus: Problems of a 'Wahlverwandschaft'* (Stuttgart: H.-D. Heinz, 1996).

59. In the paralipomena to his essay, Benjamin provides the metaphor of a fortress to express his relationship to Kraus. He writes: "Comparison of fortresses (*Festungsvergleich*). I enter the glacis of the fortress that Kraus built and I say: this point must be retained. But the shape of the fortress that I'm sketching does not correspond with the shape of his fortress; it overlaps with it on a thousand points. That is my relationship (*Verhältnis*) to Kraus. {My Kraus essay characterizes the place where I stand and do not participate (*und nicht mitmache*).}" *GS* 2, 1093. In other words, Benjamin claims to overlap with Kraus on countless points but nonetheless remains ambivalent toward him.

60. With this passage—and especially evident in the use of the word "judgments"—Benjamin might also be invoking Kant's distinction between public and private reason that he articulates in his essay *What Is Enlightenment?* (1784). In the context above, Benjamin could be suggesting that the press is yet another self-incurred form of "tutelage" that prevents reason from realizing its fullest capacity.

61. In her analysis of the conceptual difference between *Technik* and *Technologie* in Adorno's aesthetic theory, Miriam Hansen argues that Adorno and

Benjamin are united in their agreement that modern art must prove itself equal to high industrialism; in other words, that it must incorporate the artistic techniques made available by modern technology. See Miriam Hansen, *Cinema and Experience: Sigfried Kracauer, Walter Benjamin, and Theodor W. Adorno* (Berkeley: University of California Press, 2011), 210–18.

62. Benjamin writes: "The hack journalist is, in his heart, at one with the ornamentalist, as one who blurred the boundary between journalism and literature." *GS* 2, 336; *SW* 2, 434.

63. A more fleshed-out version of this notion is what we will encounter again in Adorno's understanding of identity thinking, to be explored in chapter 5.

64. I take this from Graeme Gilloch's discussion of commodity fetishism in Benjamin's *Arcades Project*. Graeme Gilloch, *Walter Benjamin: Critical Constellations* (Cambridge: Polity, 2002), 122.

65. Graeme Gilloch, *Myth and Metropolis: Walter Benjamin and the City* (Cambridge: Polity, 1997), 122.

66. As Katrin Trüstedt has argued, Kraus is concerned not with "public opinion" but with "the publicity (*Öffentlichkeit*) of law." See Katrin Trüstedt, "Fluch des Verfahrens: Karl Kraus und der 'Fall Kerr,'" *Modern Language Notes* 131, no. 3 (2016): 714.

67. Robert Lehman has recently offered a Kantian reading of this famous figure that sheds some light on the way Benjamin may have been thinking of its relation to Kraus. He writes that the angel represented could be understood as a form of "intellectual intuition" and thus the "possessor of a non-mediated experience": "Benjamin is quite clear in the ninth thesis that we do not share the angel's vision; indeed, he dedicates much of the thesis to distinguishing what we see—'a chain of events,' 'progress,'—from what the angel sees—'one single catastrophe,' 'this storm.'" Could Kraus be seeing this same storm? See Robert Lehman, *Modernism Impossible: T.S. Elliott, Walter Benjamin, and the Critique of Historical Reason* (Palo Alto, Calif.: Stanford University Press, 2016), 183.

68. Kraus was adamant about retaining editorial independence throughout his writing career. Enjoying a modest income inherited from his father and actually making a profit, he was able to subsist without commercial advertising, which distinguished his journal not only from the mainstream press but also from other small magazines. Benjamin was clearly aware of the material independence of *The Torch*, though his concerns extended beyond this biographical fact. For more on the material conditions surrounding the production of *The Torch*, see Edward Timms, "From the Habsburg Empire to the Holocaust: *Die Fackel* (1899–1936) and *Der Brenner* (1910–54)," in *The Oxford Critical and Cultural History of Modernist Magazines*, vol. 3, *Europe (1880–1940)*, ed. Peter Brooker, Sascha Bru, Andrew Thacker, and Christian Weikop (Oxford: Oxford University Press, 2013), 1014–19.

69. See *GS* 2, 148; *SW* 1, 64–66 and Ilit Ferber, *Philosophy and Melancholy: Benjamin's Early Reflections on Theater and Language* (Palo Alto, Calif.: Stanford University Press, 2013), 129.

70. Echoes of Haecker can be detected in Benjamin's reference to Kraus as a "despairing" figure, though this descriptor assumes a more positive valence in Benjamin. For a recent comparative analysis of Haecker and Benjamin as readers

of Kraus, see Helene Tomko, "Word Creatures: Theodor Haecker and Walter Benjamin between *Geschwätz* and Pure Language in the Late Weimar Republic," *New German Critique* 45, no. 1 (133) (2018): 23–47.

71. For a reading of some of the unsettling implications of Benjamin's fascination with destruction in Kraus and other contemporaries, see Hanssen, *Walter Benjamin's Other History*, 121–26.

Chapter 5

The translation in the epigraph is from Albert Bloch, *Karl Kraus*, 42.

1. See Martin Jay, "Taking on the Stigma of Inauthenticity: Adorno's Critique of Genuineness," *New German Critique* 33, no. 1 (97) (2006): 30.

2. Gillian Rose, *The Melancholy Science: An Introduction to the Thought of Theodor W. Adorno* (New York: Verso, 2014), 44.

3. See, for example, Martin Jay, *Adorno* (Cambridge, Mass.: Harvard University Press, 1994), 24–55.

4. For more on Adorno's time in Vienna, see Stefan Müller-Doohm, *Adorno: A Biography*, trans. Rodney Livingstone (London: Polity, 2009), 82–94.

5. It is symptomatic of the way Kraus has been largely ignored by many scholars by the fact that his name does not appear once in Jay's essay.

6. As Fredric Jameson writes, Kraus's "expressive syntax" provides, for Adorno, a paradigm in which "the actual machinery of sentence structure is itself pressed into service . . . and mobilized to convey meaning far beyond its immediate content as mere communication and denotation." Fredric Jameson, *Late Marxism: Adorno or the Persistence of the Dialectic* (New York: Verso, 2007), 64.

7. Djassemy, *Der "Productivgehalt kritischer Zerstörerarbeit."* Djassemy also pursues this relationship once again through the lens of Adorno's "authoritarian character" in Djassemy, *Die verfolgende Unschuld*.

8. This is a phrase coined by Kraus, but, for Djassemy, applicable to both figures. See Djassemy, *Productivgehalt kritischer Zerstörerarbeit*, 7.

9. In this essay ("Meinung Wahn Gesellschaft"), Adorno starts with the ostensibly self-evident claim that the free expression of opinion constitutes the cornerstone of democratic society, only to undermine the presuppositions that would substantiate this claim. Because, the argument continues, individual consciousness is repressed in modern society, freedom of expression is not free in any robust sense and it would be delusional to think otherwise. Adorno thus renders opinion not opposed to, but synonymous with the pathological delusion of an increasingly irrational and regressive society. See *AS* 10, 573–94; translated in Theodor W. Adorno, *Critical Models: Inventions and Catchwords*, trans. Henry W. Pickford (New York: Columbia University Press, 1998), 105–22.

10. Djassemy, *Productivgehalt*, 11.

11. Adorno composed the majority of this text between 1944 and 1947 while living in Californian exile; he completed it in 1949. For an astute commentary on the entirety of *Minima Moralia*, see Alexander García Duttmann, *So ist es: Ein philosophischer Kommentar zu Adornos "Minima Moralia"* (Frankfurt: Suhrkamp, 2004). For a thorough treatment of the impact of exile on Adorno's writing, see Katja Garloff, "Essay, Exile, Efficacy: Adorno's Literary Criticism," *Monatshefte* 94, no. 1 (2002): 80–95.

12. For more on the disputed evidence regarding Juvenal's exile, see William S. Anderson, *Essays on Roman Satire* (Princeton, N.J.: Princeton University Press, 2014), 7–10.

13. Adorno may at this juncture be convicting the entire enterprise of immanent critique of impotence under the current social and political conditions. Gillian Rose has argued that for Adorno both methods or "mediums" (irony and immanent critique) seek to measure the truth content of a given claim or a state of affairs against nothing but its own standards. Rose, *Melancholy Science*, 21–24. Jay makes a similar claim, citing these passages in particular to suggest that Adorno had "registered his fear that the method of immanent ideology critique, the comparison of ideologies with their alleged realization . . . , was itself losing the capacity to provide a truly critical leverage on the world." Jay, *Adorno*, 43.

14. As we will later encounter, Adorno is usually opposed to seeking out the truth of historical phenomena in their ostensible origins, so this inquiry marks something of an inconsistency or deviation from his normal method.

15. While Adorno may have had access to the last issues of *The Torch*—and thus would have been privy to some of Kraus's final words on the Nazi regime—he wrote this text seven years prior to the publication of *Third Walpurgis Night*.

16. Kraus first published the essay "Morals and Criminality" ("Sittlichkeit und Criminalität") in 1902 (*F* 115, 1–24), and he produced the rest of the essays that would ultimately comprise the collection over the next few years. This collection was published in 1908 and was dedicated to Kraus's friend, Ludwig Ritter von Janikowski. Adorno is responding in his essay of the same name to Heinrich Fischer's republication of Kraus's volume in 1963. For more on the publication and reception history of this volume, see *SK*, 347–57.

17. Adorno's interest in this aspect of Kraus's work is also foregrounded in his essay "Sexual Taboos and Modern Law" (1963), which considers the relationship between sexuality, law, and repression in society. At the beginning of the essay, Adorno brings Kraus and Freud together and identifies them as peerless authorities on this matter. See *AS* 10, 533–54; Adorno, *Critical Models*, 71–88.

18. For the quote in its original context, see *F* 187, 2, 1985; *SK*, 176; as quoted by Adorno: *AS* 11, 368; *NL* 2, 41.

19. *AS* 11, 368; *NL* 2, 41.

20. This claim resonates slightly with Benjamin's reading of Kraus's "tact." Benjamin writes: "For tact is not . . . the gift of allotting to each, on consideration of all relationships, what is socially befitting. On the contrary, tact is the capacity to treat social relationships . . . as natural, even paradisal relationships, and so not only to approach the king as if he had been born with the crown on his brow, but the lackey like an Adam in livery. Hebel possessed this *noblesse* in his priestly bearing; Kraus in armor." There would appear to be an affinity between "noblesse" and the "feudal" disposition of which Adorno writes. See *GS* 2, 339; *SW* 2, 436–37.

21. The entire quote reads as follows: "Kraus incorporates juristic thought so rigorously into his casuistry that the injustice of the law becomes visible in the process; the legacy of the persecuted and litigious Jews has become sublimated (*vergeistigt*) in him in this form, and through this sublimation the disputatiousness has broken through its walls at the same time." See *AS* 11, 371; *NL* 2, 43.

22. The most thorough engagement with Kraus as a legal mind—specifically in the context of his polemics against the Austrian penal code—is Reinhard Merkel, *Strafrecht und Satire im Werk von Karl Kraus* (Frankfurt: Suhrkamp, 1998).

23. In "Friends of Children," Kraus favorably cites Freud's condemnation of the sentencing of a man for homosexual behavior as opposed to pederasty, which is a justifiably punishable crime. For more on this particular essay, see Carl Hill, *The Soul of Wit: Joke Theory from Grimm to Freud* (Lincoln: University of Nebraska Press, 1993), 208–10.

24. Emphasis added. Ulrich Plass argues that Adorno's treatment of Heinrich Heine—an essay to which I will return at the end of this chapter—must be seen in conjunction with Adorno's essay on Kraus, which he views as centering on the question of mimesis or the mimetic moment. For Plass, Adorno treats Kraus as a "wound" in much the same way that he treats Heine, since both figures belong essentially to the same cultural-historical matrix. Bringing Adorno together with Benjamin, Plass writes: "As an heir to the bloody legacy of the persecution of the Jews, Kraus is also wounded himself, and his disputatious legal rhetoric and his destructive polemics are, in the final analysis, self-destructive attempts at bringing about a cathartic 'second innocence' (Adorno) or 'justice' (Benjamin): to heal the wound by re-opening it." See Ulrich Plass, *Language and History in Theodor W. Adorno's* Notes to Literature (Abingdon, U.K.: Routledge, 2012), 129. This is a compelling reading, but I view Adorno's position as more dialectical: for Adorno, Kraus's disputatiousness is also what makes his polemics authoritative and peerless in their insights into the matter at hand. Adorno's essay on Kraus is also, as I contend throughout this chapter, as much a commentary on Kraus's work and significance as it is a reflection on his own style and method.

25. Mimesis is a fraught and complicated discourse in Adorno. A good place to begin is Tom Huhn, "Introduction: Thoughts beside Themselves," in *The Cambridge Companion to Adorno*, ed. Tom Huhn (Cambridge: Cambridge University Press, 2004), 1–18. In it, Huhn focuses on how mimesis or the mimetic impulse gets "objectified" in the artwork, which, in turn, "embodies" this impulse. If the work objectifies without reifying or expresses "without expressing something" (13), then it is a proper artwork—and this could be applied to Kraus's self-reflective, gestural prose as well.

26. Emphasis added.

27. The whole sentence reads: "The trace of memory in mimesis, which every artwork seeks, is simultaneously always the anticipation of a condition beyond the diremption of the individual and the collective," or, as I understand it, beyond the given, reified state of social relations both integrated into the work and against which the work stands in relief. See *AS* 7, 198; quoted here in Theodor W. Adorno, *Aesthetic Theory*, trans. Robert Hullot-Kentor (Minneapolis: University of Minnesota Press, 1998), 131.

28. Kraus's aphorism serves as the epigraph to Benjamin's Fourteenth Thesis in "On the Concept of History," the thesis that introduces his notion of "now-time" (*Jetztzeit*) and the revolutionary explosion of historical time. See *GS* 1, 701; *SW* 4, 395.

29. "Und neues wird wohl nicht mehr geben." *F* 381, 74, 1913; *G*, 66.

30. *F* 381, 76, 1913; *G*, 66–68. Mine is a slight modification of Timms's translation. *AS* 1, 265.

31. Brigitte Stocker and Peter Winslow, trans., "Two Runners," *a bit of pitch* (blog), n.d., http://www.abitofpitch.com/187-Two_runners#endnote_1.
32. "Zwei Läufer," *F* 300, 32, 1910; *G*, 12.
33. For Timms's discussion of the context in which this poem first appears, see *AS* 1, 231–32.
34. John Pizer, "'Ursprung ist das Ziel': Karl Kraus's Concept of Origin," *Modern Austrian Literature* 27, no. 1 (1994): 18. In this article, Pizer offers a thorough account of Kraus's poems, the various reformulations of the line in question throughout his oeuvre, the importance of the concept of origin for Kraus's poetics, and a recapitulation of the twentieth-century reception of Kraus's concept of origin.
35. *AS* 10, 89; Theodor W. Adorno, *Prisms*, trans. Shierry Weber Nicholson and Samuel Weber (Cambridge, Mass.: MIT Press, 1983), 88. As Robert Hullot-Kentor writes, Adorno invokes the aphorism in this context in order to expose the "archaic intention of Veblen's technocracy." See Robert Hullot-Kentor, *Things beyond Resemblance: Collected Essays on Theodor W. Adorno* (New York: Columbia University Press, 2008), 5.
36. Since this text is considered the culmination of Adorno's decades-long ruminations on aesthetics, and since drafts of the text began in the early 1960s, it would be difficult to determine chronologically whether his discussions of Kraus here came before what he wrote on Kraus in *Negative Dialectics*. For my purposes, however, chronology is less significant than understanding the function of the aphorism/poem within the larger (con)text.
37. *AS* 7, 104; Adorno, *Aesthetic Theory*, 66. Kraus is invoked three times in the section on "Natural Beauty," once with his contemporary Peter Altenberg. Adorno clearly wants to align Kraus's effort with what he calls the reorientation of aesthetics toward natural beauty. See *AS* 7, 99; Adorno, *Aesthetic Theory*, 63.
38. Pizer, "Concept of Origin," 15.
39. *AS* 7, 104; Adorno, *Aesthetic Theory*, 66.
40. Ibid.
41. Hullot-Kentor provides a more convincing reading of Adorno's citation of the aphorism in the context of his discussion of the relation between natural beauty and art beauty—a reading that anticipates how Adorno incorporates the aphorism in *Negative Dialectics*. He writes that this use of the aphorism "indicates an objective teleology of the new insofar as the new is the source from which origin evolves," and that with it Adorno introduced this form of memory as the "only alternative to barbarization." Hullot-Kentor, *Things beyond Resemblance*, 20.
42. Theodor W. Adorno, *Gesammelte Schriften, Band 5: Zur Metakritik der Erkenntnistheorie. Drei Studien zu Hegel* (Frankfurt am Main: Suhrkamp, 2003), 28; translated in Theodor W. Adorno, *Against Epistemology: A Metacritique. Studies in Husserl and the Phenomenological Antinomies*, trans. Willis Domingo (Oxford: Basil Blackwell, 1982), 20–21.
43. See J. M. Bernstein, *Adorno: Disenchantment and Ethics* (Cambridge: Cambridge University Press, 2001), 30.
44. See "Concept and Categories." *AS* 6, 139–207; *ND*, 135–207. Gillian Rose calls this chapter the central chapter of the entire text. Rose, *Melancholy Science*, 61.

45. This translation is primarily Ashton's, but I have made one alteration based on Hullot-Kentor's reading. What Adorno calls origin's static *Unwesen* was translated by Ashton as "mischief," whereas Hullot-Kentor's "hauntings" seems to capture more of what Adorno intends with this word, since the passage is about how this concept traditionally conceived can continue to haunt other possible usages of it. The point, however, is not to get rid of the concept of origin altogether, but to update its meaning, to dialecticize it. Hullot-Kentor, *Things beyond Resemblance*, 6. For more on the problems of translating Adorno in general—especially *Negative Dialectics*—see ibid., 234–35.

46. It is somewhat typical for Adorno to tease out the radical moment from within the conservative or even reactionary husk of an author's work; it operates, for example, in Adorno's essays on Eichendorff, George, and Goethe. See Adorno's published radio address, "On Lyric Poetry and Society." *AS* 11, 48–68; *NL* 1, 37–54.

47. John Pizer, *Toward a Theory of Radical Origin* (Lincoln: University of Nebraska Press, 1995), 82. For a thorough reading of Adorno's theory of the origin (in the larger context of other "radical" philosophies of the origin), see ibid., 71–110.

48. To be sure, Auschwitz haunts *Negative Dialectics* from its opening pages onward, and one of Adorno's central—and, to be sure, highly polemical—claims is that the procrustean framework of identity thinking manifested itself, mutatis mutandis, in totalitarianism and genocide.

49. Bernstein calls this line among the most important lines of the entire text insofar as it asserts that the contingent and fleeting need not be seen as opposed to reason (purified of instrumentality) but rather as integral to it and therefore accessible to another mode of experience. For more on this, see Bernstein, *Adorno*, 233 and 389.

50. Garloff makes the insightful argument that Adorno's essay on the essay form also speaks to the need for the exilic perspective as a counterpoint to the search for origins: "Against such a celebration of origins Adorno sets the transformative power of the essay, its tendency to develop further what exists rather than tracing back to origins." Garloff, "Essay, Exile, Efficacy," 82.

51. For a recent exposition of Adorno's reception of Heidegger and other existential ontologists, see Peter Gordon, *Adorno and Existence* (Cambridge, Mass.: Harvard University Press: 2016). Gordon's aim is to resuscitate Adorno's readings of these figures—specifically of Heidegger—whom Gordon argues to be more important for Adorno's thinking than is usually acknowledged.

52. As Hullot-Kentor has shown, Adorno's polemic(s) against Heidegger can be dated back to the 1930s, when Heidegger was ascending the philosophical throne. Adorno's prime target in "The Idea of Natural-History," for example, is Heidegger, in whom Adorno already identifies the conflation of myth and nature and the reduction of the Heideggerian concept of "historicity" (*Geschichtlichkeit*) to a static concept. "Heidegger's philosophy," Hullot-Kentor writes, was the "philosophical form of mythic terror taken by the disaster of the 1930s." Hullot-Kentor, *Things beyond Resemblance*, 236.

53. Rose, *Melancholy Science*, 91–93.

54. For a recent and much fairer assessment of the complex relationship between Adorno and Heidegger—that is, an assessment of where there may be

more affinities between these thinkers than Adorno would have cared to admit—see the set of essays collected in *Adorno and Heidegger: Philosophical Questions*, ed. Iain Macdonald and Krzysztof Ziarek (Palo Alto, Calif.: Stanford University Press, 2007).

55. My modified translation of Ashton's "That's it," which sounds too informal.

56. Emphasis added.

57. Without delving into a full-fledged discussion of how Adorno's reception of Benjamin's early theory of language informs his linguistic modernism, it should suffice to suggest that this is one place where the Benjaminian inheritance is at its most apparent, specifically the way Benjamin describes noncommunicative language in "On Language as Such and on the Language of Man," discussed in chapter 4. Given that Adorno's critique also pertains to questions of style, Rose offers a thorough account of what she calls Adorno's "search for style," which is intimately related to his notion of philosophical modernism. See Rose, *Melancholy Science*, 11–26.

58. Susan Buck-Morss argues that Adorno was convinced of the necessity of philosophy's modernism, anything short of which would be insufficient: "Convinced that social contradictions appeared within the material of philosophy in a mediated form, and that the philosopher, like the artist, had to be 'absolutely modern,' had to grasp these contradictions in their most current and (in an age of disintegration) their most antagonistic manifestation, Adorno took up the struggles bequeathed by the preceding generation of philosophers." Susan Buck-Morss, *The Origin of Negative Dialectics: Theodor W. Adorno, Walter Benjamin, and the Frankfurt Institute* (New York: Free Press, 1979), 66. From this we can infer that for Adorno, Heidegger's philosophical failure was a function of his insufficient modernism.

59. For a recent engagement with Heidegger's antisemitism—especially in light of the recent publication of the so-called *Black Notebooks*, see Peter Trawny, *Heidegger und der Mythos der jüdischen Weltverschwörung* (Frankfurt: Klostermann, 2015). For a recent philosophical vindication of Heidegger's invocations of the concept *Volk*, see James Phillips, *Heidegger's* Volk*: Between National Socialism and Poetry* (Palo Alto, Calif.: Stanford University Press, 2005).

60. Adorno may have in mind here Kraus's poem "Confession" ("Bekenntnis"), whose first stanza reads: "I am merely one of the epigones / who lives in the old house of language (*Ich bin nur einer von den Epigonen, / die in dem alten Haus der Sprache wohnen*)." *F* 443, 28, 1916; *G*, 93.

61. The passage, which follows a critique of the Kantian intelligible ego, references Kraus's poem "Lilacs": "There is a verse by Karl Kraus ('What has the world made of us') in which that [pure] will is pensively pondered; it is falsified by anyone who believes it to be in his possession. Negatively, it breaks through in the subject's painful perception that in their reality, in what became of them, all men are mutilated (*verstümmelt*). What would be different, the unperverted essence, is withheld from a language that bears the stigmata of existence (*des Seienden*)." *AS* 6, 292–93; *ND*, 297.

62. The reference to the "romantically liberal metaphoricist" is obscure. Adorno could be referring to the George Circle and the aura of mysticism it cultivated; he could also be referring to Heidegger. Though the use of "liberal" as a qualifier provides a challenge to both of these interpretations.

63. Jay, "Stigma of Inauthenticity," 23.

64. Max Beck and Nicholas Coomann locate the roots of Adorno's position in Weimar Germany, and specifically in Siegfried Kracauer's critical review of Martin Buber and Franz Rosenzweig's 1929 translation of the Bible. In this review, Kracauer charges Buber and Rosenzweig with being historically insensitive and is suspicious of their attempt to revitalize an ancient tongue (biblical Hebrew) and make foreign a modern one (German) because there is no critical impulse entailed in this process; they create a language that merely emits the aura of authority. Adorno was attuned to this review and praised Kracauer for being receptive to this kind of proto-jargon of authenticity. While Buber plays a very minor role in Adorno's late text, Beck and Coomann argue—by pointing to the first line of Adorno's text—that this accord between Adorno and Kracauer is not insignificant. Given that *Jargon* was published in 1964 and was written in part as a response to the perceived collusion between fascism and jargon, it is not surprising that the two German-Jewish author-translators recede into the text's background. For more on this discourse, see Max Beck and Nicholas Coomann, "Adorno, Kraucauer und die Ursprünge der Jargonkritik," in *Sprachkritik als Ideologiekritik: Studien zu Adornos "Jargon der Eigentlichkeit"* (Würzburg: Königshausen and Neumann, 2015), 7–27.

65. Following Eva Geulen, Jay makes the claim that Adorno, otherwise critical of Benjamin's "Artwork" essay, found a footnote in the essay on the "compromised nature of the claims to authenticity" helpful in formulating his own critique of the term. Benjamin claims that the work's authenticity (related to its "aura") is actually an aftereffect, a mode of beholding the work that can only be registered in the context of modern reproducibility. For Adorno, it is this belatedness of authenticity that he finds fruitful. See Jay, "Stigma of Authenticity," 18–20.

66. Gordon reappraises Adorno's critiques of the tradition of existential ontology (Kierkegaard, Heidegger, Jaspers, Buber, and others). His essential claim is that this aspect of Adorno's thought is more central to his larger critical project than has been hitherto considered. Adorno, for Gordon, is sympathetic to the philosophical *needs* addressed by these various existentialisms but is concerned with showing how such needs and the material conditions that inform them remain unfulfilled or ignored upon closer inspection. See Gordon, *Adorno and Existence*, 6–7.

67. Gordon writes: "With anatomical skill, Klemperer had dissected the barbarism of Nazi metaphor and style, taking special note of the regime's antipathy for reason and intellectual abstraction, its preference for concreteness, and its celebration of intuition (*Anschauung*) as a medium for 'essence' and 'soul'" (ibid., 89). To my knowledge, the most sustained comparative study of Kraus's and Klemperer's work is Peiter, *Komik und Gewalt*, 143–210.

68. Beck and Coomann, *Sprachkritik als Ideologiekritik*, 7.

69. The phrase "form of life" comes from Kraus's essay "Heine and the Consequences." *F* 329, 4, 1911; *UW*, 217; Franzen, *Kraus Project*, 285. In Adorno's short essay "Heine the Wound," he explicitly references Kraus's earlier polemic and refers to it as a binding "verdict" on the nineteenth-century German-Jewish poet. Adorno's claim about Heine, is, however, distinct from Kraus's and must be read in a postwar context. His essential claim is that Heine's "wound" is the wound of an unreconciled society, his poetry a symptom of this society, and his "guilt" the guilt of an entire nation. See *AS* 11, 95–100; *NL 2*, 80–85.

70. This would be antithetical to the type of nonsubjective recollection Adorno otherwise champions. This is also why he is suspicious of the very "category of authenticity" (*Eigentlichkeit*), which, he argues, was first introduced for descriptive purposes and addressed the question of "what is authentic in something," but which, through its cooptation by jargon, has become "a mythically imposed fate." See *AS* 6, 498; *JA*, 104.

71. Emphasis added.

72. For a compelling reading of how Adorno transitions from his (and Horkheimer's) use of the concept "instrumental reason" in *Dialectic of Enlightenment* to "identity thinking" in *Negative Dialectics*, see J. M. Bernstein, "Negative Dialectics as Fate," in *The Cambridge Companion to Adorno*, 19–50.

73. My modified translation of Tarnowski and Will's translation.

74. Müller, *Karl Kraus*, 273. For a thorough commentary on this piece and the set of similar pieces in Kraus's oeuvre that deal explicitly with the aural aspects of the journalistic medium, see ibid., 243–372. Arguing that Kraus anticipates media critiques that would only be systematically articulated over a half century later by figures such as Habermas, Müller writes that this essay "still reacts to the acoustic equivalent with idiosyncratic premonition, for in a strictly technical sense [this tone] has not yet had its breakthrough: that the tone will be heard is noticed in the interim by Kraus alone" (266).

75. Ibid., 269.

Coda

1. Broch, *Hugo von Hofmannsthal and His Time*, 81. For Broch, this phenomenon was best embodied in the sheen of Viennese *Gemütlichkeit* (a combination of warmth, coziness, and congeniality).

2. Franzen, *Kraus Project*, 13–14.

3. I learned this fact from a recent discussion with Lothar Müller, literary critic and editor of the Feuilleton section of the *Süddeutsche Zeitung*.

4. Harris, *Mediating Modernity*, 2.

5. Geert Lovink, *Networks without a Cause: A Critique of Social Media* (London: Polity, 2012), 2.

6. Ibid., 139.

7. It is worth pointing out, however, that Lovink actually draws from Elias Canetti's major work of social psychology, *Crowds and Power* (1960), at several junctures throughout his study. See Lovink, *Networks without a Cause*, 51, 160, and 166.

BIBLIOGRAPHY

Adorno, Theodor W. *Aesthetic Theory*. Translated by Robert Hullot-Kentor. Minneapolis: University of Minnesota Press, 1998.

———. *Against Epistemology: A Metacritique. Studies in Husserl and the Phenomenological Antinomies*. Translated by Willis Domingo. Oxford: Basil Blackwell, 1982.

———. *Critical Models: Inventions and Catchwords*. Translated by Henry W. Pickford. New York: Columbia University Press, 1998.

———. *Gesammelte Schriften, Band 5: Zur Metakritik der Erkenntnistheorie. Drei Studien zu Hegel*. Frankfurt am Main: Suhrkamp, 2003.

———. *Notes to Literature*. Vol. 1. Translated by Shierry Weber Nicholson. New York: Columbia University Press, 1991.

———. *Prisms*. Translated by Shierry Weber Nicholson and Samuel Weber. Cambridge, Mass.: MIT Press, 1983.

Agamben, Giorgio. *Remnants of Auschwitz: The Witness and the Archive*. Translated by Daniel Heller-Roazen. New York: Zone Books, 2002.

Anderson, William S. *Essays on Roman Satire*. Princeton, N.J.: Princeton University Press, 2014.

Anzenberger, Werner. *Absage an die Demokratie: Karl Kraus und der Bruch der österreichischen Verfassung 1933/34*. Graz: Leyker Verlag, 1997.

Arendt, Hannah. *The Origins of Totalitarianism*. New York: Harcourt, Brace, Jovanovich, 1973.

Aristophanes. *The Birds*. Translated by Jeffrey Henderson. Newburyport, Mass.: Focus, 1999.

———. *Die Vögel: Ein Lustspiel von Aristophanes*. Translated by Emil Schinck. Leipzig: Philipp Reclam, c. 1880.

Arntzen, Helmut. "Einige Dialogstrukturen in Karl Kraus' Drama 'Die letzten Tage der Menschheit.'" In *Sprachspiel und Bedeutung: Festschrift für Franz Hundsnurscher zum 65. Geburtstag*, edited by Franz Hundsnurscher, 427–38. Tübingen: Niemeyer, 2000.

———. *Karl Kraus und die Presse*. Munich: W. Fink, 1975.

———. *Literatur im Zeitalter der Information: Aufsätze, Essays, Glossen*. Frankfurt: Athenäum Verlag, 1971.

Balzac, Honoré de. *Lost Illusions*. Translated by Kathleen Raine. New York: Modern Library, 2001.

Baron, Frank, and Jon Blumb, eds. *Albert Bloch and the Blue Rider: The Munich Years*. Lawrence: Jayhawk Ink / University of Kansas, 2014.

Barthes, Roland. *Camera Lucida: Reflections on Photography*. Translated by Richard Howard. New York: Hill and Wang, 2010.

Beck, Max, and Nicholas Coomann, eds. *Sprachkritik als Ideologiekritik: Studien zu Adornos "Jargon der Eigentlichkeit."* Würzburg: Königshausen and Neumann, 2015.

Benjamin, Walter. *The Correspondence of Walter Benjamin, 1910–1940*. Edited by Gershom Scholem and Theodor W. Adorno, translated by Manfred R. Jacobson and Evelyn M. Jacobson. Chicago: University of Chicago Press, 2012.

———. *Gesammelte Briefe, Band II: 1919–1924*. Frankfurt am Main: Suhrkamp, 1996.

———. *The Origin of the German Tragic Drama*. Translated by John Osborne. New York: Verso, 2009.

———. *The Work of Art in the Age of Its Technological Reproducibility, and Other Writings on Media*. Edited by Michael W. Jennings, Brigid Doherty, and Thomas Y. Levin. Cambridge, Mass.: Harvard University Press, 2008.

Bergson, Henri. "Laughter." In *Comedy*, edited by Wylie Sypher, 61–190. Baltimore: Johns Hopkins University Press, 1956.

Bernstein, J. M. *Adorno: Disenchantment and Ethics*. Cambridge: Cambridge University Press, 2001.

———. "Negative Dialectics as Fate." In *The Cambridge Companion to Adorno*, edited by Tom Huhn, 19–50. Cambridge: Cambridge University Press, 2004.

Bloch, Albert. *Karl Kraus: Poems*. Boston: Four Seas, 1930.

Bloch, Ernst. *The Spirit of Utopia*. Translated by Anthony A. Nassar. Palo Alto, Calif.: Stanford University Press, 2000.

Bogel, Fredric V. *The Difference Satire Makes: Rhetoric and Reading from Jonson to Byron*. Ithaca, N.Y.: Cornell University Press, 2001.

Bowles, Daniel. *The Ends of Satire: The Legacies of Satire in Postwar German Writing*. Berlin: De Gruyter, 2015.

Brecht, Bertolt. *Collected Plays: Five*. Translated by John Willett. London: Methuen Drama, 2005.

———. *Die Gedichte in einem Band*. Frankfurt: Suhrkamp, 2007.

———. *Kriegsfibel*. Berlin: Eulenspiegel Verlag, 1994.

———. *War Primer*. Translated by John Willett. New York: Verso, 2017.

———. *Werke: Große kommentierte Berliner und Frankfurter Ausgabe*, edited by Werner Hecht et al., 30 vols. Berlin and Frankfurt am Main: Aufbau and Suhrkamp, 1988–2000.

Broch, Hermann. *Hofmannsthal und seine Zeit*. Frankfurt: Suhrkamp Verlag, 2001.

———. *Hugo von Hofmannsthal and His Time: The European Imagination, 1860–1920*. Translated by Michael P. Steinberg. Chicago: University of Chicago Press, 1984.

Buck-Morss, Susan. *The Dialectics of Seeing: Walter Benjamin and the Arcades Project*. Cambridge, Mass.: MIT Press, 1991.

———. *The Origin of Negative Dialectics: Theodor W. Adorno, Walter Benjamin, and the Frankfurt Institute*. New York: Free Press, 1979.

Calasso, Roberto. *The Forty-Nine Steps*. Translated by John Shepley. Minneapolis: University of Minnesota Press, 2001.

Canetti, Elias. *The Conscience of Words*. Translated by Joachim Neugroschel. New York: Farrar, Straus and Giroux, 1984.

———. *Die Fackel im Ohr: Lebensgeschichte 1921–1931*. Frankfurt: Fischer Verlag, 2005.

———. *Die Stimmen von Marrakesch: Aufzeichnungen nach einer Reise / Das Gewissen der Worte: Essays*. Munich: Carl Hanser Verlag, 1995.

———. *The Torch in My Ear*. Translated by Joachim Neugroschel. New York: Farrar, Straus and Giroux, 1982.

Dachselt, Reiner. *Pathos: Tradition und Aktualität einer vergessenen Kategorie der Poetik*. Heidelberg: Winter, 2003.

Dallago, Carl. *Ueber eine Schrift: Søren Kierkegaard und die Philosophie der Innerlichkeit*. Innsbruck: Brenner-Verlag, 1914.

Djassemy, Irina. *Der "Productivgehalt kritischer Zerstörerarbeit": Kulturkritik bei Karl Kraus und Theodor W. Adorno*. Würzburg: Königshausen and Neumann, 2002.

———. *Die Verfolgende Unschuld: Zur Geschichte des autoritären Charakters in der Darstellung von Karl Kraus*. Vienna: Böhlau, 2011.

Duttmann, Alexander García. *So ist es: Ein philosophischer Kommentar zu Adornos "Minima Moralia."* Frankfurt: Suhrkamp, 2004.

Eiland, Howard, and Michael Jennings. *Walter Benjamin: A Critical Life*. Cambridge, Mass.: Harvard University Press, 2014.

Esterhammer, Ruth. *Kraus über Heine: Mechanismen des literaturkritischen Diskurses im 19. und 20. Jahrhundert*. Würzburg: Königshausen and Neumann, 2005.

Evers, Kai. *Violent Modernists: The Aesthetics of Destruction in Twentieth-Century German Literature*. Evanston, Ill.: Northwestern University Press, 2013.

Fenves, Peter. *"Chatter": Language and History in Kierkegaard*. Palo Alto, Calif.: Stanford University Press, 1993.

Ferber, Ilit. *Philosophy and Melancholy: Benjamin's Early Reflections on Theater and Language*. Palo Alto, Calif.: Stanford University Press, 2013.

Ferris, David. *The Cambridge Introduction to Walter Benjamin*. Cambridge: Cambridge University Press, 2008.

Franzen, Jonathan. *The Kraus Project*. New York: Farrar, Straus and Giroux, 2013.

Freud, Sigmund. *Gesammelte Werke, Band X: Werke aus den Jahren 1913–1917*. Berlin: Fischer, 1969.

———. *The Standard Edition of the Complete Psychological Works of Sigmund Freud*. Vol. 14. Translated by James Strachey. London: Hogarth Press, 1981.

Ganahl, Simon. *Ich gegen Babylon: Karl Kraus und die Presse im Fin de Siècle*. Vienna: Picus, 2007.

———. "'Natur! Natur!' Die 'Zweite Revolution' in der 'Dritten Walpurgisnacht' von Karl Kraus." *Weimarer Beiträge: Zeitschrift für Literaturwissenschaft, Ästhetik und Kulturwissenschaften* 3 (2011): 325–44.

Garloff, Katja. "Essay, Exile, Efficacy: Adorno's Literary Criticism." *Monatshefte* 94, no. 1 (2002): 80–95.

Geller, Jay. *The Other Jewish Question: Identifying the Jew and Making Sense of Modernity*. New York: Fordham University Press, 2011.

Gilloch, Graeme. *Myth and Metropolis: Walter Benjamin and the City*. Cambridge: Polity, 1997.

———. *Walter Benjamin: Critical Constellations*. Cambridge: Polity, 2002.

Gilman, Sander. *Jewish Self-Hatred: Anti-Semitism and the Hidden Language of the Jews*. Baltimore: Johns Hopkins University Press, 1990.

Goltschnigg, Dietmar. *Die Fackel ins Wunde Herz: Kraus über Heine. Eine "Erledigung"?* Vienna: Passagen, 2000.

Gordon, Peter E. *Adorno and Existence*. Cambridge, Mass.: Harvard University Press: 2016.

Grage, Joachim. "Karl Kraus: 'The Miracle of Unison'—Criticism of the Press and Experiences of Isolation." In *Kierkegaard's Influence on Literature, Criticism, and Art, Tome 1: The Germanophone World*, edited by Jon Stewart, 157–67. Abingdon, U.K.: Routledge, 2013.

Greenberg, Jonathan. *Modernism, Satire, and the Novel*. Cambridge: Cambridge University Press, 2011.

Greiner, Bernhard. "*Polos* und *Polis*: Aristophanes's *Vögel* und deren Bearbeitung durch Goethe, Kraus und Peter Hacks." In *Ancient Comedy and Reception: Essays in Honor of Jeffrey Henderson*, edited by S. Douglas Olson, 629–726. Berlin: De Gruyter, 2013.

Habermas, Jürgen. *Strukturenwandel der Öffentlichkeit: Untersuchung zu einer Kategorie der bürgerlichen Gesellschaft*. Frankfurt: Suhrkamp, 1990.

———. *The Structural Transformations of the Bourgeois Public Sphere: An Inquiry into a Category of Bourgeois Society*, 6th ed. Translated by Thomas Burger. Cambridge, Mass.: MIT Press, 1991.

Haecker, Theodor. *Philosophie der Innerlichkeit*. Munich: Schreiber, 1913.

———. *Werke I: Essays*. Munich: Kösel, 1961.

———. *Werke III: Satire und Polemik: Der Geist des Menschen und die Wahrheit*. Munich: Kösel, 1961.

Hannay, Alastair. *Kierkegaard: A Biography*. Cambridge: Cambridge University Press, 2003.

Hansen, Miriam Bratu. *Cinema and Experience: Sigfried Kracauer, Walter Benjamin, and Theodor W. Adorno*. Berkeley: University of California Press, 2011.

Hanssen, Beatrice. *Walter Benjamin's Other History: Of Stones, Animals, Human Beings, and Angels*. Berkeley: University of California Press, 2000.

Harris, Stephanie. *Mediating Modernity: German Literature and the "New" Media, 1895–1930*. University Park: Penn State University Press, 2009.

Häusler, Maximilian. *Die Ethik des satirischen Schreibens: Karl Kraus, Hermann Broch und Robert Musil*. Heidelberg: Winter, 2015.

Hedges, Inez. *Framing Faust: Twentieth Century Cultural Struggles*. Carbondale: Southern Illinois University Press, 2009.

Hegel, G. W. F. *Vorlesungen über die Ästhetik I*. Vol. 14 of *Werke*. Frankfurt: Suhrkamp, 1986.

Heidegger, Martin. *Being and Time*. Translated by John Macquarrie and Edward Robinson. New York: Harper Perennial Modern Classics, 2008.

———. *Gesamtausgabe, Band 2: Sein und Zeit*. Frankfurt: Vittorio Klostermann Verlag, 2018.

Heller, Erich. *The Disinherited Mind: Essays in Modern German Literature and Thought*. New York: Barnes and Noble, 1971.

Hill, Carl. *The Soul of Wit: Joke Theory from Grimm to Freud*. Lincoln: University of Nebraska Press, 1993.

Hindemith, Wilhelm. *Die Tragödie des Nörglers: Studien zu Karl Kraus' moderner Tragödie "Die Letzten Tage der Menschheit."* Frankfurt: P. Lang, 1985.

Hollinger, David. "The Knower and the Artificer." *American Quarterly* 39, no. 1 (Spring 1987): 37–55.

Holzer, Anton. *Die letzten Tage der Menschheit: Der Erste Weltkrieg in Bildern. Mit Texten von Karl Kraus.* Darmstadt: Primus, 2014.

Houe, Paul, Gordon Marino, and Sven Hakon Rossel, eds. *Anthropology and Authority: Essays on Søren Kierkegaard.* Amsterdam: Brill Rodopi, 2000.

Huhn, Tom. "Introduction: Thoughts beside Themselves." In *The Cambridge Companion to Adorno*, edited by Tom Huhn, 1–18. Cambridge: Cambridge University Press, 2004.

Hullot-Kentor, Robert. *Things beyond Resemblance: Collected Essays on Theodor W. Adorno.* New York: Columbia University Press, 2008.

Iggers, Wilma. *Karl Kraus: A Viennese Critic of the Twentieth Century.* The Hague: Martinus Nijhoff, 1967.

Jameson, Fredric. *Late Marxism: Adorno or the Persistence of the Dialectic.* New York: Verso, 2007.

Jay, Martin. *Adorno.* Cambridge, Mass.: Harvard University Press, 1994.

———. "Taking on the Stigma of Inauthenticity: Adorno's Critique of Genuineness." *New German Critique* 33, no. 1 (97) (2006): 15–30.

Jonsson, Stefan. *Crowds and Democracy: The Idea and Image of the Masses from Revolution to Fascism.* New York: Columbia University Press, 2013.

Kant, Immanuel. "What Is Enlightenment." Translated by Lewis White Beck, Robert E. Anchor, and Emil L. Fackenheim. In *On History*, edited by Lewis White Beck, 3–11. Indianapolis: Library of Liberal Arts, 1981.

Kierkegaard, Søren. *The Book on Adler.* Edited by Howard V. Hong and Edna H. Hong. Princeton, N.J.: Princeton University Press, 2009.

———. *The Concept of Irony, with Continual Reference to Socrates / Notes of Schelling's Berlin Lectures.* Edited by Howard V. Hong and Edna H. Hong. Princeton, N.J.: Princeton University Press, 1992.

———. *Concluding Unscientific Postscript to Philosophical Fragments.* Vol. 1. Edited by Howard V. Hong and Edna H. Hong. Princeton, N.J.: Princeton University Press, 1992.

———. *The* Corsair *Affair and Articles Related to the Writings.* Edited by Howard V. Hong and Edna H. Hong. Princeton, N.J.: Princeton University Press, 2009.

———. *Kierkegaard's Journals and Notebooks.* Vol. 4. Edited by Niels Jørgen Cappelørn, Alastair Hannay, David Kangas, Bruce H. Kirmmse, George Pattison, Joel D. S. Rasmussen, Vanessa Rumble, and K. Brian Søderquist. Princeton, N.J.: Princeton University Press, 2011.

———. *The Present Age.* Translated by Alexander Dru. New York: Harper Perennial, 1962.

Knight, Charles. *The Literature of Satire.* Cambridge: Cambridge University Press, 2004.

Kraft, Werner. '"Es war einmal ein Mann . . .': Über die *Dritte Walpurgisnacht* von Karl Kraus." *Merkur: Deutsche Zeitschrift für europäisches Denken* 10, no. 22 (1968): 926–35.

Kraus, Karl. *Die Dritte Walpurgisnacht.* Munich: Kösel, 1952.

———. *Half-Truths and One-and-a-Half-Truths: Selected Aphorisms.* Translated by Harry Zohn. Chicago: University of Chicago Press, 1990.

———. *Qualtinger liest Karl Kraus*, performed by Helmut Qualtinger (Preiser, 1999), CD.

Kriebel, Sabine. *Revolutionary Beauty: The Radical Photomontages of John Heartfield.* Berkeley: University of California Press, 2014.

Krolop, Kurt. *Sprachsatire als Zeitsatire bei Karl Kraus: Neun Studien.* Berlin: Akademie- Verlag, 1987.

Lehman, Robert. *Modernism Impossible: T.S. Elliott, Walter Benjamin, and the Critique of Historical Reason.* Palo Alto, Calif.: Stanford University Press, 2016.

Lensing, Leo. "'Freud and the Child Woman' or 'The Kraus Affair?' A Textual 'Reconstruction' of Franz Wittels's Psychoanalytic Autobiography." *German Quarterly* 69, no. 3 (1996): 322–32.

———. "'Kinodramatisch': Cinema in Karl Kraus' *Die Fackel* and *Die letzten Tage der Menschheit.*" *German Quarterly* 55, no. 4 (1982): 480–98.

———. "Kraus the Mouse? Kafka's Late Reading of *Die Fackel* and the Vagaries of Literary History." In *Nexus: Essays in German Jewish Studies.* Vol. 3. Edited by William Collins Donahue and Martha B. Helfer, 71–95. Rochester, N.Y.: Camden House, 2017.

———. "'Photographischer Alpdruck' oder politische Photomontage? Karl Kraus, Kurt Tucholsky und die satirischen Möglichleiten der Photographie." In *Karl Kraus et son temps*, edited by Gilbert Krebs and Gerald Stieg, 173–88. Paris: Presses Sorbonne Nouvelle, 2018.

———. "War and the Press." In *A New History of German Literature*, edited by David Wellbery and Judith Ryan, 713–18. Cambridge, Mass.: Harvard University Press, 2005.

Le Rider, Jacques. *Modernity and Crises of Identity: Culture and Society in Fin-de-Siecle Vienna.* Translated by Rosemary Harris. New York: Continuum, 1993.

Lovink, Geert. *Networks without a Cause: A Critique of Social Media.* London: Polity, 2012.

Lukács, Georg. *Essays über Realismus.* Neuwied: Luchterhand, 1971.

Macdonald, Iain, and Krzysztof Ziarek, eds. *Adorno and Heidegger: Philosophical Questions.* Palo Alto, Calif.: Stanford University Press, 2007.

Mann, Michael. *Fascists.* Cambridge: Cambridge University Press, 2004.

Marcuse, Herbert. *One-Dimensional Man: Studies in the Ideology of Advanced Industrial Society*, 2nd ed. Boston: Beacon Press, 1991.

Mautner, Franz. "Über Karl Kraus' Komödie 'Wolkenkuckucksheim.'" In *Austriaca: Beiträge zur österreichischen Literatur: Festschrift für Heinz Politzer zum 65. Geburtstag*, edited by Winfried Kudszus and Hinrich Seeba, 315–28. Tübingen: Niemeyer, 1975.

McBride, Patrizia. *The Chatter of the Visible: Montage and Narrative in Weimar Germany.* Ann Arbor: University of Michigan Press, 2016.

Menke, Bettine. "Das Nach-Leben im Zitat. Benjamins Gedächtnis der Texte." In *Gedächtniskunst: Raum—Bild—Schrift Studien zur Mnemotechnik*, edited by Anselm Haverkamp and Renate Lachmann, 74–110. Frankfurt: Suhrkamp, 1991.

Merkel, Reinhard. *Strafrecht und Satire im Werk von Karl Kraus*. Frankfurt: Suhrkamp, 1998.
Mieszkowski, Jan. *Watching War*. Palo Alto, Calif.: Stanford University Press, 2012.
Mohr, Werner. *Albert Bloch: Caricaturist, Social Critic, and Translator of Karl Kraus*. Riverside, Calif.: Ariadne Press, 2003.
Müller, Burkhard. *Karl Kraus: Mimesis und Kritik des Mediums*. Stuttgart: Metzler, 1994.
Müller-Doohm, Stefan. *Adorno: A Biography*. Translated by Rodney Livingstone. London: Polity, 2009.
Nancy, Jean-Luc. *The Inoperative Community*. Translated by Peter Connor. Minneapolis: University of Minnesota Press, 1991.
Ng, Julia. "Each Thing a Thief: Walter Benjamin on the Agency of Objects." *Philosophy and Rhetoric* 44, no. 4 (2011): 382–402.
Niehoff, Reiner. *Die Herrschaft des Textes: Zitattechnik als Sprachkritik in Georg Büchners Drama* Dantons Tod *unter Berücksichtigung* Der Letzten Tage der Menschheit *von Karl Kraus*. Tübingen: Niemeyer, 1991.
Norberg, Jakob. "Anticapitalist Affect: George Lukács on Satire and Hate." *New German Critique* 45, no. 3 (135) (2018): 155–74.
———. "The Black Book: Karl Kraus's Etiquette." *Modern Austrian Literature* 40, no. 2 (2007): 45–64.
———. "Creative Destruction: Karl Kraus and the Paradox of Satire." *Seminar: A Journal of Germanic Studies* 49, no. 1 (2013): 38–51.
O'Brien, Mahon. *Heidegger and Authenticity: From Resoluteness to Releasement*. New York: Bloomsbury, 2013.
Peiter, Anne. *Komik und Gewalt: Zur literarischen Verarbeitung der Beiden Weltkriege und der Shoah*. Cologne: Böhlau, 2007.
Perloff, Marjorie. *Edge of Irony: Modernism in the Shadow of the Habsburg Empire*. Chicago: University of Chicago Press, 2016.
———. *Unoriginal Genius: Poetry by Other Means in the New Century*. Chicago: University of Chicago Press, 2010.
Peters, Paul. *Die Wunde Heine: Zur Geschichte des Heine-Bildes in Deutschland*. Bodenheim: Philo Verlagsgesellschaft, 1997.
Pfabigan, Alfred. *Karl Kraus und der Sozialismus: Eine politische Biographie*. Vienna: Europaverlag, 1976.
Pfäfflin, Friedrich, and Eva Dambacher, eds. *Marbacher Kataloge 52: Karl Kraus*. Marbach: Deutsche Schillergesellschaft, 1999.
Phillips, James. *Heidegger's* Volk*: Between National Socialism and Poetry*. Palo Alto, Calif.: Stanford University Press, 2005.
Pizer, John. *Toward a Theory of Radical Origin*. Lincoln: University of Nebraska Press, 1995.
———. "'Ursprung ist das Ziel': Karl Kraus's Concept of Origin." *Modern Austrian Literature* 27, no. 1 (1994): 1–21.
Plass, Ulrich. *Language and History in Theodor W. Adorno's* Notes to Literature. Abingdon, U.K.: Routledge, 2012.
Prager, Katharina. *Berthold Viertel: Eine Biographie der Wiener Moderne*. Vienna: Böhlau, 2018.
Pugh, David. "Heine's Aristophanes Complex and the Ambivalence of 'Deutschland: Ein Wintermärchen.'" *Modern Language Review* 99, no. 3 (2004): 665–80.

Rabinbach, Anson. *The Crisis of Austrian Socialism: From Red Vienna to Civil War, 1927–1934*. Chicago: University of Chicago Press, 1983.

———. *In the Shadow of Catastrophe: German Intellectuals between Apocalypse and Enlightenment*. Berkeley: University of California Press, 2001.

Reitter, Paul. *The Anti-Journalist: Karl Kraus and Jewish Self-Fashioning in Fin-de-Siècle Europe*. Chicago: University of Chicago Press, 2008.

———. "Edward Timms's '*Die letzten Tage der Menschheit* as a German-Jewish Tragicomedy and the Challenge to Translators': A Response." In *Nexus: Essays in German Jewish Studies*. Vol. 3. Edited by William Collins Donahue and Martha B. Helfer, 65–69. Rochester, N.Y.: Camden House, 2017.

Renner, Karl. *Das Selbstbestimmungsrecht der Nationen in besonderer Anwendung auf Oesterreich*. Leipzig: F. Deuticke, 1918.

Ribeiro, António. "Satirical Discourse and Intertextuality: The Dialogic Construction of Satirical Authority in *Die Fackel*." *Oxford German Studies* 45, no. 4 (2016): 444–58.

Riha, Karl. *Kritik, Satire, Parodie: Gesammelte Aufsätze zu den Dunkelmännerbriefen, zu Lesage, Lichtenberg, Klassiker-Parodie, Daumier, Herwegh, Kurnberger, Holz, Kraus, Heinrich Mann, Tucholsky, Hausmann, Brecht, Valentin, Schwitters, Hitler-Parodie und Henscheid*. Opladen: Westdeutscher Verlag, 1992.

Rose, Gillian. *The Melancholy Science: An Introduction to the Thought of Theodor W. Adorno*. New York: Verso, 2014.

Rubin, Jane and Hubert L. Dreyfus. "You Can't Get Something for Nothing: Kierkegaard and Heidegger on How Not to Overcome Nihilism." *Inquiry* 30, no. 1–2 (1987): 33–75.

Schiller, Friedrich. *On the Naive and Sentimental in Literature*. Translated by Helen Watanabe-O'Kelly. Manchester: Carcanet New Press, 1981.

———. *Sämtliche Werke, Band 5: Erzählungen, Theoretische Schriften*, 2nd ed. Munich: Carl Hanser Verlag, 2007.

Scholem, Gershom, ed. *The Correspondence of Walter Benjamin and Gershom Scholem, 1932–1940*. Translated by Gary Smith and Andre LeFevere. Cambridge, Mass.: Harvard University Press, 1992.

Schulte, Christian. *Ursprung ist das Ziel: Walter Benjamin über Karl Kraus*. Würzburg: Königshausen and Neumann, 2003.

Stephenson, R. H. "The Diachronic Solidity of Goethe's Faust." In *A Companion to Goethe's Faust: Parts I and II*, edited by Paul Bishop, 243–70. Rochester, N.Y.: Camden House, 2001.

Stieg, Gerald. *Der Brenner und Die Fackel: Ein Beitrag zur Wirkungsgeschichte von Karl Kraus*. Salzburg: O. Müller, 1976.

———. "Ein verfrühter Nachruf auf Karl Kraus und seine Folgen." In *Österreichische Satire (1933–2000): Exil—Remigration—Assimilation*, edited by Jeanne Benay, Alfred Pfabigan, and Anne Saint Sauveur, 3–12. Bern: Peter Lang, 2003.

Stocker, Brigitte. *Rhetorik eines Protagonisten gegen die Zeit: Karl Kraus als Redner in den Vorlesungen, 1919 bis 1932*. Vienna: Lit Verlag, 2013.

Stocker, Brigitte, and Peter Winslow, trans., "Two Runners," *a bit of pitch* (blog), n.d., http://www.abitofpitch.com/187-Two_runners#endnote_1.

Strauss, Leo. *Socrates and Aristophanes*. Chicago: University of Chicago Press, 1996.

Stremmel, Jochen. *'Dritte Walpurgisnacht': Über einen Text von Karl Kraus*. Bonn: Bouvier, 1982.

Stuhlmann, Andreas. *'Die Literatur—das sind wir und unsere Feinde': Literarische Polemik bei Heinrich Heine und Karl Kraus*. Würzburg: Königshausen and Neumann, 2008.

Szasz, Thomas. *Anti-Freud: Karl Kraus's Criticism of Psychoanalysis and Psychiatry*. Syracuse, N.Y.: Syracuse University Press, 1990.

Szondi, Peter. *Theory of the Modern Drama*. Translated by Michael Hays. Minneapolis: University of Minnesota Press, 1987.

Theobald, John. *The Paper Ghetto: Karl Kraus and Anti-Semitism*. Frankfurt: Peter Lang, 1996.

Thornhill, C. J. *Walter Benjamin and Karl Kraus: Problems of a Wahlverwandtschaft*. Stuttgart: H.-D. Heinz, 1996.

Timms, Edward. "*Die Letzten Tage der Menschheit* as a German-Jewish Tragicomedy, and the Challenge to Translators." In *Nexus: Essays in German Jewish Studies*. Vol. 3. Edited by William Collins Donahue and Martha B. Helfer, 53–64. Rochester, N.Y.: Camden House, 2017.

———. "From the Habsburg Empire to the Holocaust: *Die Fackel* (1899–1936) and *Der Brenner* (1910–54)." In *The Oxford Critical and Cultural History of Modernist Magazines*. Vol. 3, *Europe (1880–1940)*. Edited by Peter Brooker, Sascha Bru, Andrew Thacker, and Christian Weikop, 1014–19. Oxford: Oxford University Press, 2013.

———. "Karl Kraus and the Transformation of the Public Sphere." In *Changing Perceptions of the Public Sphere*, edited by Christian J. Emden and David Midgley, 164–82. New York: Berghahn Books, 2012.

———. Karl Kraus's Adaptations of Offenbach: The Quest for the Other Sphere." *Austrian Studies* 13 (2005): 91–108.

Tomko, Helena. "The Reluctant Satirist: Theodor Haecker and the Dizzying Swindle of Nazism." *Oxford German Studies* 46, no. 1 (2017): 42–57.

———. "Word Creatures: Theodor Haecker and Walter Benjamin between *Geschwätz* and Pure Language in the Late Weimar Republic." *New German Critique* 45, no. 1 (133) (2018): 23–47.

Tönnies, Ferdinand. *Ferdinand Tönnies on Public Opinion: Selections and Analyses*. Edited and translated by Hanno Hardt and Slavko Splichal. Lanham, Md.: Rowman and Littlefield, 2000.

Toulmin, Stephen, and Allan Janik. *Wittgenstein's Vienna*. Chicago: Ivan R. Dee, 1996.

Traverso, Enzo. "European Intellectuals and the First World War: Trauma and New Cleavages." In *Cataclysm 1914: World War I and the Making of Modern World Politics*, edited by Alex Anievas, 201–15. Leiden: Brill, 2015.

Trawny, Peter. *Heidegger und der Mythos der jüdischen Weltverschwörung*. Frankfurt: Klostermann, 2015.

Trüstedt, Katrin. "Fluch des Verfahrens: Karl Kraus und der 'Fall Kerr.'" *Modern Language Notes* 131, no. 3 (2016): 701–23.

Tucholsky, Kurt. *Gesamtausgabe, Band 14: Texte 1931*. Edited by Sabina Becker. Hamburg: Rowohlt, 1998.

Tunstall, Graydon. *Written in Blood: The Battles for Fortress Przemysl in WWI*. Bloomington: Indiana University Press, 2016.

Viertel, Berthold. *Karl Kraus: Ein Charakter und die Zeit*. Dresden: Rudolf Kaemmerer Verlag, 1921.

Voigt, Manfred. "'Die Mater der Gerechtigkeit.' Zur Kritik des Zitat-Begriffs bei Walter Benjamin." In *Antike und Moderne: Zu Walter Benjamins "Passagen,"* edited by Norbert Bolz and Richard Faber, 97–115. Würzburg: Königshausen and Neumann, 1986.

Wagner, Nike. *Geist und Geschlecht: Karl Kraus und die Erotik der Wiener Moderne*. Frankfurt am Main: Suhrkamp Verlag, 1982.

Wasserman, Janek. *Black Vienna: The Radical Right in the Red City, 1918–1938*. Ithaca, N.Y.: Cornell University Press, 2014.

Wawro, Geoffrey. *A Mad Catastrophe: The Outbreak of World War I and the Collapse of the Habsburg Empire*. New York: Basic Books, 2014.

Weber, Max. *The Vocation Lectures*. Translated by Rodney Livingstone. London: Hackett, 2004.

Weber, Samuel. *Benjamin's -abilities*. Cambridge, Mass.: Harvard University Press, 2010.

Weigel, Hans. *Karl Kraus oder die Macht der Ohnmacht: Versuch eines Motivenberichts zur Erhellung eines vielfachen Lebenswerks*. Vienna: F. Molden, 1968.

Weigel, Sigrid. *Walter Benjamin: Die Kreatur, das Heilige, die Bilder*. Berlin: Fischer Verlag, 2008.

Weitzmann, Erica. *Irony's Antics: Walser, Kafka, Roth and the German Comic Tradition*. Evanston, Ill.: Northwestern University Press, 2015.

Wennerscheid, Sophie. "The Passage of Negativity, or From Self-Renunciation to Revolution? Kierkegaard and Žižek on the Politics of the Impassioned Individual." In *Kierkegaard and Political Theory: Religion, Aesthetics, Politics and the Intervention of the Single Individual*, edited by Armen Avanessian and Sophie Wennerscheid, 141–66. Chicago: University of Chicago Press, 2015.

Wetters, Kirk. *The Opinion System: Impasses of the Public Sphere from Hobbes to Habermas*. New York: Fordham University Press, 2008.

Whittaker, John H. "Kierkegaard on the Concept of Authority." *International Journal for the Philosophy of Religion* 46 (1999): 83–101.

Youker, Timothy. "'The Sounds of Deeds': Karl Kraus and Acoustic Quotation." *Theatre Journal* 63, no. 1 (2011): 85–100.

Ziolkowski, Eric. *The Literary Kierkegaard*. Evanston, Ill.: Northwestern University Press, 2011.

Zupančič, Alenka. *The Odd One In: On Comedy*. Cambridge, Mass.: MIT Press, 2008.

INDEX